The Cambridge Introduction to
American Literary Realism

Between the Civil War and the First World War, realism was the most prominent form of American fiction. Realist writers of the period include some of America's greatest, such as Henry James, Edith Wharton, and Mark Twain, but also many lesser-known writers whose work still speaks to us today, for instance Charles Chesnutt, Zitkala-Ša, and Sarah Orne Jewett. Emphasizing realism's historical context, this introduction traces the genre's relationship with powerful, often violent social conflicts involving race, gender, class, and national origin. It also examines how the realist style was created; the necessarily ambiguous relationship between realism produced on the page and reality outside the book; and the different, often contradictory, forms "realism" took in literary works by different authors. The most accessible yet sophisticated account of American literary realism currently available, this volume will be of great value to students, teachers, and readers of the American novel.

Phillip J. Barrish is Associate Professor of English at the University of Texas, Austin.

The Cambridge Introduction to
American Literary Realism

PHILLIP J. BARRISH

CAMBRIDGE
UNIVERSITY PRESS

CAMBRIDGE
UNIVERSITY PRESS

University Printing House, Cambridge CB2 8BS, United Kingdom

Cambridge University Press is part of the University of Cambridge.

It furthers the University's mission by disseminating knowledge in the pursuit of
education, learning and research at the highest international levels of excellence.

www.cambridge.org
Information on this title: www.cambridge.org/9780521050104

© Cambridge University Press 2011

First published 2011

A catalogue record for this publication is available from the British Library

Library of Congress Cataloguing in Publication data
Barrish, Phillip.
  The Cambridge introduction to American literary realism / Phillip J. Barrish.
    p. cm. – (Cambridge introductions to literature)
  Includes bibliographical references and index.
  ISBN 978-0-521-89769-3 (hardback) – ISBN 978-0-521-05010-4 (paperback)
  1. American fiction–19th century–History and criticism. 2. American
fiction–20th century–History and criticism. 3. Literature and society–
United States–History–19th century. 4. Literature and society–United States–
History–20th century. 5. Realism in literature. 6. Popular literature–
United States–History and criticism. 7. National characteristics, American,
in literature. I. Title. II. Series.
  PS374.R32B37 2011
  810.9'1209034–dc23
  2011028104

ISBN 978-0-521-05010-4 Paperback

To my father Norman Barrish, whose broad insight, unfailing empathy, and lifelong commitment to honesty exemplify realism at its best.

Contents

x   *Contents*

Illustrations

Acknowledgments

I wish to thank the following colleagues for reading and commenting on portions of this book, as well as for helping to educate me in areas where my own knowledge was lacking: Evan Carton, James Cox, John Morán Gonzalez, Coleman Hutchinson, Martin Kevorkian, Julia H. Lee, and Gretchen Murphy. Sydney Bufkin and Ashley Miller were exemplary research assistants. I owe a debt to my editor Ray Ryan, not only for soliciting me to write the volume but also for his ability to exert pressure and show patience at just the right moments. I would also like to thank Peter Messent, a reader for Cambridge University Press, whose support and suggestions were equally invaluable. Elijah Barrish's astute questions kept me thinking throughout the writing process. Sabrina Barton, finally, is someone whom I can never thank enough. She read and improved, and then re-read and re-improved, every page of what follows.

Introduction: American literary realism

Heated debates about realism and art often take place outside of university classrooms. After watching a movie, for example, we may find ourselves questioning – perhaps even arguing over – how "realistic" the movie seemed. We praise certain films for how closely they appear to reflect actual, off-screen life, even if the "real life" they depict is quite distant from our own experiences. Other movies we reject for their implausible plot twists, over-the-top acting, contrived dialogue, or clumsy special effects. Sometimes we don't mind admitting that a movie isn't realistic and defend it on other grounds, perhaps for its beauty, romance, suspense, or humor. Regardless, evaluating a work's realism (or lack of realism) has become close to second nature for most movie viewers today, maybe because the only expertise it seems to require is something we all possess: the ability to observe the world around us.

Has it always been second nature for people to comment on how close to actual experience a work of narrative art seems? Aspects of realism as a literary mode, of course, can be traced at least as far back in Western literature as Homer's epic poem, *The Iliad*, where Olympian gods with supernatural powers coexist with graphic depictions of battlefield mayhem that still ring true. *The Iliad* also includes notably detailed accounts of rituals, weaponry, and some aspects of daily life among the Greek army. Similarly, many of Shakespeare's characterizations have long been praised for their likeness to life. *The Cambridge Introduction to American Literary Realism* focuses on the surprisingly recent moment in American literary history, however, when realism – as opposed, for example, to universal Truth – came to be regarded as a paramount value in fictional narratives: something to be striven for by fiction writers, celebrated or criticized by reviewers, and judged by readers. Over the course of this book we will explore the historical causes underlying literary realism's rise to prominence in the United States. We will also examine the different, and often contradictory, forms realism took in literary works by different authors; technical and stylistic questions involving how fiction writers actually go about creating what theorist Roland Barthes has called "the reality effect" (*Rustle of Language* 141); the philosophical issue of what relationship, if any, exists between realism produced on the

1

page and reality outside the book; and, finally, literary realism's relationship with powerful, often violent conflicts in late-nineteenth-century America involving race, gender, social class, national origin, and geographic region, among other factors. As we will see, American realism's intense engagement with its social and cultural context has always been integral to its power as literature.

Literary realism became a salient feature of the US literary scene in the decades following the Civil War (1861–65), a period scholar Stanley Corkin has identified with "the birth of the modern United States." Although the United States was born as a formal nation on July 4, 1776, what Corkin means is that a great many of the economic structures, cultural forms, and social and political conflicts, as well as modes of everyday life, that we think of as characteristic of contemporary America first took shape in the1870s, 1880s, and 1890s. America's Industrial Revolution was well under way by the middle of the nineteenth century, but its acceleration after the Civil War changed the United States from a rural country composed largely of distinct "island communities" (Wiebe, *Search for Order* xiii) to, by the start of the twentieth century, a primarily urban nation, one whose cities included extremes of wealth and poverty and featured large, densely populated slums. Ongoing technological advances – above all in transportation (the Transcontinental Railroad was completed in 1869) and in communications (the telegraph came into widespread use, followed by the telephone) – spurred the growth of a genuinely national economy in which large business monopolies and corporations played an increasingly significant role. The mass production of previously hard-to-come-by goods, along with new networks for national distribution, allowed for consumerism on an heretofore unmatched scale, constantly stimulated by mass advertising, which itself began to affect the texture of American experience. Many individuals' work lives changed as well, as new jobs and professions developed along with the new economy. For the first time even middle-class women worked outside the home in significant numbers, particularly in the bigger cities. A labor movement arose as workers strove to protect their wages and dignity at the same time that businesses sought to maximize profits.

Social conflicts also followed in the wake of unprecedented levels of immigration, particularly from areas of the world that hadn't previously sent many people to the United States, including eastern and southern Europe and Asia. Millions of new citizens dramatically expanded the nation's multicultural resources at the same time as they encountered xenophobia, hostility, and widespread anxiety about how to define American identity (foreshadowing today's contentious debates about immigration and its effects on the nation). In the Southwest, the forcible incorporation of portions of Mexico into the United States after the United States–Mexico War (1846–48), as well as continuing immigration from Mexico, brought into the nation tens of thousands of new Americans whose first language was Spanish and whose skin was brown. These Mexican Americans faced discrimination, economic exploitation, and often violence from white Americans hungry for land and resources. So did weakened but still powerfully determined Native American tribes, who fought violent removal from their lands in the often forgotten "Indian Wars" of the late nineteenth century. Also toward the end of the nineteenth century, the United States emerged as a notably larger player on the world's imperial stage, using military means to assert control over faraway areas from Hawaii to Puerto Rico to the Philippines (where local insurgents battled against a US military occupation from 1899 to 1902). Finally, the Civil War may have brought formal slavery to an end, but the nation's failure to follow through on Southern Reconstruction meant that racial injustices and conflicts would continue as a shaping – and often explosive – force in American life.

Originating in different parts of the country, but centering in the literary capitals of Boston and New York, a number of authors began attempting to write fiction more closely and more self-consciously responsive to the rapidly shifting world around them. Realist writers sought to understand and explain their changing society, as well as to resist it, celebrate it, influence it, and profit from it – but above all to depict it with what Henry James called "the air of reality." Fiction writers were not alone in their endeavor to get a handle on an increasingly complex – and, to many, seemingly unstable – social order. The post-Civil War decades saw the rise of a new class of "experts," including those who ambitiously expanded the purviews and sought to refine the methodologies of such emerging academic disciplines as anthropology and sociology. The latter, announcing itself as the "science" of society, developed models and laws explaining social change, as well as how societies regulate themselves while undergoing change. Sociologists studied race relations, the organization of urban life, and the question of how immigrants assimilate in new cultural contexts. Psychologists, meanwhile, sought to understand the differences among individuals as well as general principles underlying the workings of the human mind. Managers, engineers, and scientists constituted additional groups of experts with increasingly important roles in society. While scientists sought to understand underlying "laws" of the physical universe, and engineers worked on transportation systems, energy generation, and farm mechanization, managers developed systems for motivating and controlling employees and sought greater rationality and efficiency in the organization of large-scale enterprises, including the expanding federal government.

Literary realists claimed forms of expertise and professional authority that were in certain ways similar to these other figures on the late-nineteenth-century scene. Like scientists, literary realists prided themselves on their objectivity. Like ethnographers, anthropologists, and linguists, they saw themselves as students of those aspects of society soon to be referred to under the umbrella term "culture" – manners and customs, beliefs and values, family and kinship arrangements, varieties of speech. Like psychologists, literary realists probed the inner workings of individual minds and the human mind's relationship to the outside world. With sociologists, they looked for patterns in how American society changes and adjusts to change. Indeed, literary realism helped middle-class Americans in particular adjust to social change in the sense that realist works sought to make even wrenching changes legible, comprehensible, almost literally containable between two book covers. Some realists also shared an interest with sociologists in categorizing individuals into social "types" (the ruthless businessman, the "street tough," the newly self-confident "American girl"). To the extent that literary realism was invested in categorizing people, understanding their motivations, and charting their daily activities, it also overlapped with the new "scientific" managerial practices that were starting to become fashionable in the business world.

Like other late-nineteenth-century "experts" and professionals, most literary realist authors belonged primarily to the middle and upper-middle classes. However, as literary artists they also lay claim to their own distinct professional status – an ability to offer persuasively accurate, uniquely intimate delineations of what various social changes feel like from the inside. A realist text could use the device of shifting narrative perspectives to place us imaginatively within, for example, a conflicted capitalist, an unhappy wife, an ambitious doctor, and an angry laborer, potentially all in the course of a single book. If sociologists could call on the emerging science of statistics to study "the slum" (itself a newly defined concept), and professional engineers and architects could design structures utilizing newly mass-producible steel, literary realists honed their own techniques for approaching their material and creating the effects they desired. Among their tools was free-indirect discourse, a style that allows a text's narrative voice to maintain third-person objectivity while also, often in the same paragraph, speaking from the point of view and in the tone of a specific character. Free-indirect discourse encourages a reader to feel both inside of a character and, at the same time, distant enough to evaluate that character's emotions and thoughts. As we will see in the next chapter, the ability to enter into a character's feelings while also maintaining enough detachment not to be overly swayed by them was of critical importance in realism's attempt to differentiate itself from the most popular form of fiction writing in the period before the Civil War: literary sentimentalism.

Another technique important to literary realists was their very close attention to the surfaces of everyday life, which often led to incorporating into a text objects or small daily activities seemingly irrelevant to a story, but which added to the composite effect of actual reality. Here realists were also inspired by one of the nineteenth century's most exciting new technologies, photography, with its apparent ability to capture all the visible details of a city street, natural scene, or human face, and to do so with an aura of what William Dean Howells called "impartial fidelity" (quoted in Orvell, *The Real Thing* 124–25). Yet even as realists sought to produce that same effect of impartial fidelity in their writing, they insisted that their status as literary artists gave their work a significance beyond that of the "merely photographic" (Fluck, "Morality" 92). They would bring the disciplined imagination of professional artists to bear in re-creating the complexity and variety of individuals' inner experiences of a social world that was itself becoming more complex and various with every passing year.

Over the past few decades, literary scholarship has both expanded and diversified the group of writers we recognize as having played a meaningful part in realism's development during the period considered its heyday, roughly 1865–1914. Until very recently, such important writers as Sui Sin Far, Zitkala-Ša, and Pauline Hopkins would most likely not have been mentioned in an introductory volume such as this one. Only slightly longer ago, Kate Chopin and Charles Chesnutt, now widely recognized as major realist authors, would probably also have been ignored. The project of recovering from undeserved obscurity the many richly compelling works by white women and minority authors of both genders, works previously left out of the literary canon due to racial, ethnic, and gender biases, has been ongoing since the 1970s, and is still far from complete. Carried on by scholars, teachers, and editors, among others, the recovery process for a given work or author can involve three elements, including a work's rediscovery (for instance in old magazines and rare book archives), its reinterpretation under new critical frameworks, and its republication in new anthologies or other formats, so that the text becomes available to current readers, critics, and students. Such scholarly efforts have both enriched and productively complicated the entire field of American literary realism. At the same time as the canon has expanded, stimulating new readings developed from a variety of critical perspectives have supplemented previous interpretations of traditionally recognized realist authors such as Henry James, William Dean Howells, and Mark Twain.

The evolving richness of the field presents exciting opportunities for a book that aspires both to introduce new readers to American literary realism and, at the same time, to offer research and analysis that more advanced scholars will likely find of interest as well. Rather than attempting some sort of comprehensive "survey" of significant authors, which I feared might result in little more than a series of encyclopedia-style entries given the extent of the field and the space limitations of a single volume, *The Cambridge Introduction to American Literary Realism* is primarily organized around concepts, trends, and problems. For instance, one central problem the book explores, from different but related perspectives across several chapters, derives from the claim by William Dean Howells (an important practitioner and public promoter of American realism) that literary realism would help America more fully to achieve its democratic principles of equality, unity, and the toleration of difference. For Howells, American literary realism had the potential to represent "democracy in literature." "Men are more like than unlike one another," Howells proclaimed. The task of realism would be to "make them know one another better, that they may be all humbled and strengthened with a sense of their fraternity" (*Criticism and Fiction* 188).

American realist writers attempted to depict a wide range of Americans more accurately than prior literary modes had, including not only middle- and upper-class white citizens but also such politically disempowered and socially marginalized people as recent immigrants, Americans of color, and the urban and rural poor. What were the aesthetic, cultural, and political implications of these efforts, especially given that the preponderance of realism's reading audience was white and middle or upper class? Members of these classes often assumed themselves to be superior to lower-class and minority Americans. Did realist representations challenge or reinforce such assumptions of superiority? Might some works have done both at the same time? Constructions of gender identity in and by realist writing constitute another recurring theme, as does realist literature's exploration of different linguistic registers. Such questions reappear throughout the book, in different contexts and in relation to different authors and works.

As for its temporal scope, *The Cambridge Introduction to American Literary Realism* begins by discussing precursors to US realism in the decades prior to the Civil War and concludes with a brief consideration of the fate of realism at the time it was displaced, around the time of the First World War, by modernism as the type of literature that critics and readers considered at the forefront of innovation. Within these temporal boundaries, the sequence of chapters does not adhere to a strict chronological order. More than one individual chapter ranges from the 1870s to the first part of the twentieth century because doing so seemed most productive for exploring that chapter's guiding topic or topics. The book is designed to allow multiple entry points for those who wish to pursue a specific interest, whether it be a theme, issue, or particular author. In such cases, readers should use the index for guidance. When ideas or information mentioned in one chapter have been (or will be) more fully considered in another chapter, a parenthetic remark will let readers know, in case they wish to flip to that other chapter. Finally, I have tried in some cases to draw readers more deeply into the literature by inviting them to consider current critical controversies in which the arguments involved are especially stimulating to thought and debate.

Chapter 1

Literary precursors, literary contexts

As with so many other areas of American life, the publishing world underwent dramatic changes in the years following the US Civil War. These changes affected the ways in which authors understood their audiences and markets, their possibilities for generating income, and their own professional identities. Such wide-ranging shifts in authors' thinking could not help but have an impact on how and what they wrote. Publishing in the decades prior to the Civil War was still in the early stages of its development as a modern industry, at least in the United States; most books in America were either imported from Britain or else were pirated editions of books first published there. Most of those creating what we today think of as classic early American literature – from the Puritan poet Anne Bradstreet to Benjamin Franklin up through the American literary "Renaissance" (as it has become known) of the 1830s, 1840s, and 1850s – saw themselves not primarily as professional writers but as ministers, statesmen, reformers, lecturers, or simply citizens. Very few of these figures ever imagined supporting themselves by their writing.

It wasn't until the middle decades of the century that technological innovations – printing from metal plates, new processes for casting type and for manufacturing paper – allowed books to be produced quickly and cheaply enough, and in sufficient quantities, that they could begin to be purchased by consumers in large numbers, which allowed for the possibility of meaningful profits both to publishers and (at least in theory) to authors. The reading population was expanding at the same time as public education increased literacy. The producers of fiction who most immediately benefitted from these changes were those who published, and to a lesser extent those who wrote for, the period's cheap and immensely popular "story papers" (available for mere pennies) and "dime novels." Although most early dime novels targeted male readers with adventure tales (westerns, high seas, crime), growing numbers of women readers quickly boosted the sales of fiction focused on love and romance (whether in pioneer, urban working-class, or high-society settings). Written as escapist entertainment for the masses, this fiction was unapologetically formulaic and sensationalistic: it made no attempt to present itself either as art or, for that matter, as an accurate portrayal of Americans' real lives.

Authorship in nineteenth-century America

By the 1850s the marketplace for novels of more serious intent was dominated by women authors writing sentimental domestic fiction. Even these best-selling authors, however, tended not to think of themselves as fully professional literary artists in the modern sense. For example, in a burst of inspired outrage at Congress's passage of the Fugitive Slave Law, Harriet Beecher Stowe wrote the first American novel to sell one million copies, *Uncle Tom's Cabin, or, Life among the Lowly* (1852). Stowe refused to take any personal credit for her achievement, however, asserting that God had written the work through her. Susan Warner, who authored the also enormously popular novel *The Wide, Wide World* in 1850 and went on to publish dozens of books (some of them co-written with her sister Anna), claimed she wrote only in order to promote ideals of Christian piety and self-discipline and to help support her family. Stowe's and Warner's reluctance to identify themselves as professional writers was to some extent due to a cultural prohibition on women entering the male-reserved public sphere, particularly in order to express or develop themselves as individuals. Religious motivations or the need to help care for their families (which was seen as women's proper role) helped make *public*-ation seem more acceptable for mid-nineteenth-century female authors such as Stowe and Warner (see Kelley, *Private Woman*). None of this modesty, however, kept Nathaniel Hawthorne from his infamously misogynistic dismissal of such authors as a "damn'd mob of scribbling women," who should be "forbidden to write, on pain of having their faces deeply scarified with an oyster-shell" (quoted in Reynolds, *Historical Guide to Nathaniel Hawthorne* 33). Hawthorne believed that the "mob" of successful women authors was distracting potential readers (and purchasers) from his own more worthy works of fiction, works for which he was in the process of trying to carve a special niche in the literary marketplace.

Hawthorne, art, and literary romance

Nathaniel Hawthorne ultimately became the first American novelist to be widely identified not only as a creator of "high art," but also as a man who made the production of such art his profession. Working in concert with the visionary publisher and promoter James T. Fields, whose firm issued *The Scarlet Letter* in 1850, Hawthorne had come, by the time of his death in 1864, publicly to embody the fiction writer as professional artist (importantly, this does *not* mean that his works approached the sales or broad popularity of *Uncle Tom's Cabin* or *The Wide, Wide World*). Hawthorne's is an especially impressive achievement given that the novel, ever since its English-language emergence in the previous century, had been considered somewhat below other literary genres (poetry, drama) as a field for genuine art. Most readers thought that the novel might be good for the inspirational or sentimental uses to which writers such as Stowe and Warner put it. Or it might serve, as with books by writers such as Charles Dickens and James Fenimore Cooper, as respectable entertainment. Others worried that novels, with their frequent focus on exciting dramas of love and courtship, might put dangerous ideas into the heads of young women who read too many of them. Virtually nobody, however, thought of the novel as a genre that possessed even the potential to yield literary masterpieces that would last for centuries, as the drama of William Shakespeare and the epic poetry of John Milton had.

The story of how, against these odds, the publisher Fields promoted and marketed the indeed remarkable qualities of Hawthorne's writing to ensure that educated Americans would come to think of his novels as aesthetically comparable to great poems and plays is a fascinating one that we cannot pause over here (see Brodhead, *School* 17–47).The impressive cultural status achieved by Hawthorne's fiction, however, served as a model to be imitated and, if possible, surpassed by late-nineteenth-century literary realists such as Henry James, who dedicated his career to proving that the novel could be as "high" a form of art as any other, including painting and sculpture. Yet Hawthorne was also somewhat problematic as a model for James and other realist writers who rose to prominence in the generation following *The Scarlet Letter* because Hawthorne explicitly defined his own fiction in opposition to the kind of writing that would later be called realism. His famous preface to *The House of the Seven Gables* (1851) begins with the assertion that he prefers the label "Romance" rather than "Novel" for his work. "The latter form of composition," Hawthorne writes in reference to the Novel,

> is presumed to aim at a very minute fidelity, not merely to the possible, but to the probable and ordinary course of man's experience. The former [the romance] – while, as a work of art, it must rigidly subject itself to

laws, and while it sins unpardonably so far as it may swerve aside from the truth of the human heart – has fairly a right to present that truth under circumstances, to a great extent, of the writer's own choosing or creation.   (*Collected Novels* 351)

Profound insights into the inner truths of human nature, for Hawthorne, can be more effectively pursued if a writer does not constantly strive for a "minute fidelity" to the everyday experience of a specific time and place – the clothes people wear, their daily activities and social interactions, their physical sensations, but instead gives himself the liberty to create circumstances and characters, "fancy pictures," as he puts it on the next page, of his own choosing. To be sure, in less frequently quoted sentences from the same preface Hawthorne adds that "the fiction writer will be wise, no doubt … to mingle the marvellous rather as a slight, delicate, and evanescent flavor" of his work, instead of serving it as "the actual substance of the dish offered to the public." Yet even if the romance writer "disregard[s] this caution" and makes no effort at all to mingle the fantastical with the realistic, he does not "commit a literary crime" (351).

Other writers who produced what we now consider the literary classics of Hawthorne's age also did not consider a "minute fidelity" to commonplace experiences as their most important goal. Ralph Waldo Emerson, perhaps the era's most influential literary figure, claims in his early lecture "The American Scholar" (1837) to embrace the significance of "the feelings of the child, the philosophy of the street, the meaning of household life" (*Essays and Lectures* 68). He goes on to explain, however, that what is most important about "the meaning of" these everyday actualities is their "ultimate reason," which is "the sublime presence of the spiritual cause lurking" within them. Details of ordinary life are of value, in Emerson's thinking, not for their own interest but only insofar as they help to illustrate a transcendent "eternal law," the overarching "form and order" of the universe (69). For Emerson, as he puts it in "Nature" (1836), "every natural fact is a symbol of some spiritual fact" (20). Even Herman Melville's *Moby-Dick, or the Whale* (1851), so replete with copious and, for the most part, quite accurate details about the equipment and workings of nineteenth-century whaling ships, aims to "strike through the mask" (as Captain Ahab puts it) of everyday appearances in order to probe such philosophical mysteries as the nature of evil, man's place in the cosmos, and the meaning of obsession (178).[1]

As we will see, the realist writers who came along later in the century did not view the texture of everyday life as constituting a symbolic code for spiritual truths nor as merely a "mask" of surface appearances, needing to be broken through in order to reach what is truly meaningful and important.[2] Instead, the realists sought meaning and value precisely within the elements of daily existence as people were living it in their own modern America. As a result, realist writers faced harsh censure from critics who complained that it was the task of art to create beauty and inspire people toward the ideal, not to reproduce what these critics saw as the flat, tedious, and often depressing vulgarities of commonplace American life.[3]

Walt Whitman: Poetic Precursor

In 1855 Walt Whitman, a 36-year-old journalist and printer from Brooklyn, published a remarkable book of poems, *Leaves of Grass*, which he would subsequently add to, edit, and re-issue throughout his lifetime. Whitman's poems broke virtually all of nineteenth-century poetry's accepted rules. The poems dispensed with conventional regularities of rhyme, meter, and line-length in favor of a free verse whose more subtle music, Whitman insisted, grew organically from the "facts of the open air" he wished to voice (ix). Above all, Whitman aimed for his poetry – especially *Leaves of Grass*'s long central poem, later titled "Song of Myself" – to realize in a literal sense America's founding democratic ideals of freedom, tolerance, and equality. Lengthy poetic catalogues juxtaposed diverse men and women of widely varied regions, social classes, races, and occupations. The catalogues gave equal space and importance to, for example, a "tipsy and pimpled" prostitute, the President and his cabinet, and the hard-working crew of a "fish-smack" (22, 23). More so than any previous poet, Whitman emphasized the lives and activities of working people from urban street-pavers to teamsters and canal-workers; from farm laborers to sex workers; and from hunters and trappers supplying the fur trade to slaves working on Southern plantations. He attempted to convey the very *feel* of life in America's growing cities, through cataloguing not only sights but sounds: what he called "the blab of the pave" (18). Finally, *Leaves of Grass* also constituted an unprecedentedly frank celebration of sexuality and the human body: Whitman's poems praised copulation, homosexuality, masturbation, and sexual fantasy (for men and women). His poetic appreciation of the physical body extended even to the "aroma" of armpits (29).

In the first years after *Leaves of Grass* appeared many reviewers did not know what to make of it or of Whitman, including a young, pre-realist William Dean Howells who, in the very earliest book review he ever wrote (of the 1860 edition), could only conclude, "You cannot apply to him the tests by which you are accustomed to discriminate in poetry" (quoted in Cutler, "Literary Modernity" 134). In the decades following the Civil War, however, it became clear that the extraordinary range of American lives and places Whitman's poetry brought into literary representation; the multiple facets of rural, urban, and industrial existence he strove to convey to readers; the bodily desires and experiences to which he gave voice – all of these features anticipated and, in some cases, inspired realist fiction writers of the late nineteenth and early twentieth centuries.

During the 1880s, William Dean Howells, successful novelist, powerful editor, and prolific reviewer and columnist, became the nation's best-known explicator and defender of realism as a literary movement [see text box in Chapter 2]. Howells defined realism primarily in opposition to what he called "romance." The latter term was useful to him because it had more than one meaning in the literary discourse of the time. On the one hand, the concept of romance gave Howells a respectful way to allude to those writers whom, although he thought American literature should now develop in a different direction, he still considered his generation's most distinguished national predecessors, such as Nathaniel Hawthorne and Ralph Waldo Emerson. Hawthorne, as we have seen, had called his own novels "Romances," and Emerson's work was in close dialogue with the luminaries of German and British Romanticism. At the same time, Howells used the terms "romance novel" and "romanticistic" novel (a neologism he coined) in a derisive sense to refer to popular adventure narratives, historical romances of derring-do (what novelist Frank Norris dismissed as "the cut and thrust business"), and sentimental domestic literature written primarily by and for women. Speaking of "romanticistic" novels, Howells insisted, "If I do not find it is like life, then it does not exist for me as art; it is ugly, it is ludicrous, it is impossible" (*Selected Literary Criticism* III 216).

Sentimental fiction

Only in recent decades has literary scholarship, primarily thanks to research and insights by feminist literary critics, come to recognize the multi-dimensional importance of female-identified sentimental and domestic literature, whose popularity outstripped that of any other type of literature in pre-Civil War America. The best way to describe sentimental fiction is as novels and short stories that emphasize – and not only emphasize, but promote and celebrate – the power of strong feelings and emotions both to effect change within individuals and to connect individuals to one another. Nineteenth-century sentimental literature depicted intense feelings on the parts of its characters but, of equal importance, it also strove to provoke readerly identification with those feelings and thereby produce sympathetic tears, sympathetic fears, and sympathetic outrage.

Stowe's *Uncle Tom's Cabin* accomplished exactly that. The novel was not only immensely popular, but it also helped to turn many previously neutral or uninterested Americans against slavery. Abraham Lincoln is reported to have said to Harriet Stowe when he was introduced to her in 1862, as the Civil

War raged, "So you're the little woman whose book started this great war." Howells and James both expressed admiration for Stowe's novel, and there is no doubt that in meaningful ways *Uncle Tom's Cabin* anticipated and helped to spread realist techniques that became more prominent after the war, including such techniques as careful research, an emphasis on the essential factuality of what is portrayed, and gestures, at least, toward accurate depictions of dialect. But *Uncle Tom's Cabin* also epitomizes the use of what critic Jane Tompkins has called "sentimental power" (*Sensational Designs* 122). A passage from the novel demonstrates how literary sentimentalism mobilized readers' sympathies. Eliza, a house slave on a Kentucky plantation, has overheard a slave-dealer arranging to buy her beloved young son Harry and has determined to run away with him that very evening, despite the frost on the ground and the lack of time to make preparations for a journey. In describing Eliza's escape, Stowe addresses her readers directly:

> If it were your Harry, mother, or your Willie, that were going to be torn from you by a brutal trader, tomorrow morning, – if you had seen the man, and heard that the papers were signed and delivered, and you had only from twelve o'clock till morning to make good your escape, – how fast could you walk? How many miles could you make in those few brief hours, with the darling at your bosom, – the little sleepy head on your shoulder, – the small, soft arms trustingly holding on to your neck?   (67–68)

Presuming that most of her readers are women, and that many are mothers (or eager to imagine themselves mothers), Stowe asks her readers to enter almost physically into Eliza's sensations, to feel the endangered child's head on *their* shoulders, the child's soft arms holding onto *their* necks.

Stowe strove to evoke sentimental identification in *Uncle Tom's Cabin* with the aim of helping white middle-class women in the North experience through their sympathies at least some degree of the suffering that slave women in the South underwent, instead of merely grasping the fact of that suffering on an abstract or intellectual level. Stowe hoped that her novel would stimulate these women to act against the Fugitive Slave Law and against slavery itself, although such action would occur mostly through the women's appealing to their husbands, brothers, and sons, who unlike them were legally permitted to vote in elections and fight in the military. Stowe and other sentimental writers such as Susan Warner, Maria Cummins, and (in a slightly more sensationalist vein) E. D. E. N. Southworth employed similar strategies – that is, triggering strong sympathetic emotions in readers – as a way to lead their audiences toward a firmer embrace of Christian principles, devotion to the concept of the nuclear family as society's primary unit, and support for such reform movements as temperance.

Manliness and the realist critique of romance

William Dean Howells and other realists defined their own literary project in part by opposing it to "romance" genres – although, as we will see below, the relationship between realism and these genres was in fact more complex and ambiguous than most realists liked to admit. Viewing themselves as professionals with missions different from but related to those of scientists, sociologists, psychologists, and anthropologists, realist writers strove for an effect of objective, disinterested narration. This did not mean that most literary realists did not also want their writing to have an impact on individual readers or on society at large. Howells, for instance, profoundly hoped that realism would produce greater understanding and solidarity across America's deepening divisions of social class. But he believed that the best way to achieve such goals was to cleave as closely as possible to reality as most people experienced it. The facts of daily American life, as lived in different regions and by people occupying different social stations, would speak for themselves if they were presented more fully and openly than previous literature had cared to attempt. Sentimental fiction's manipulation of readers' feelings by depicting so many scenes of intense emotionality, Howells believed, caused more harm than good insofar as it interfered with readers viewing the world rationally and in proper perspective.

An important subplot in Howells's best-known novel, *The Rise of Silas Lapham* (1885), directly challenges what Howells saw as the pernicious effects of sentimental fiction, in this case its glorification of self-sacrifice in the name of a romantic principle. In *Silas Lapham*'s subplot, two sisters, Irene and Penelope, as well as their parents, believe that Tom Corey visits their house to court Irene, the more conventionally pretty girl who, largely because she believes Tom loves her, falls in love with him. When it turns out that all along Tom has wished to marry Penelope, who has herself secretly come to love him too, Irene is heart-broken and humiliated. Penelope, blaming herself for Irene's suffering, determines to sacrifice her own desires and never see Tom again, although this will not solve Irene's problem and will leave both Tom and herself bereft. Penelope comes to this resolution after having read a book that many of the ladies in the novel enjoy, *Tears, Idle Tears*, whose title Howells concocted as an allusion to sentimental literature. A female character describes the book as "perfectly heart-breaking, as you'll imagine from the name; but there's such a dear old-fashioned hero and heroine in it, who keep dying for each other all the way through, and making the most wildly satisfactory and unnecessary sacrifices … You feel as if you'd done them yourself" (174).

It is just this sort of "old-fashioned" literature that Howells has the thoughtful Reverend Sewell, who tries to advise the family through its crisis, decry as "perverted," even "monstrous" in its effects on readers (212, 175). If it were not for the popularity of such novels devoted to "the shallowest sentimentality," Sewell asserts, the usually perceptive Penelope would not have been drawn to "a false ideal of self-sacrifice" (212). She would have seen that it makes most sense that "one suffer instead of three, if none is to blame ... That's sense, and that's justice" (212). Sewell, who can be taken here as speaking for Howells himself, makes an implicit plea for literary realism: "The novelists might be the greatest possible help to us if they painted life as it is, and human feelings in their true proportion and relation, but for the most part they have been and are altogether noxious" (175).

Realist writing by men certainly contained highly emotional, even tear-jerking moments. Such moments sometimes served, for instance, to facilitate the bonding between two male characters, as when, in Mark Twain's *Adventures of Huckleberry Finn* (1885), Jim tearfully confesses to Huck an incident in which he beat his young daughter for not listening to him, without realizing that she was deaf (Camfield, *Sentimental Twain* 11). In the same novel, however, Twain parodies feminine emotionalism in his characterization of Emmeline Grangerford, a teenaged girl famous in town for her series of paintings showing tearful women, who mourn with equally great intensity for dead lovers and for dead canaries. Grangerford's paintings have titles such as, "Shall I Never See Thee More Alas," "And Art Thou Gone Yes Thou Art Gone Alas," and, for the painting of a woman with a dead canary, "I Shall Never Hear Thy Sweet Chirrup More Alas." The repetitive, clichéd, archaic language that Grangerford chooses for her titles signifies to us that the paintings' emotional content is equally contrived.

A more explicit criticism of literary sentimentality came from a young Henry James, who had not yet managed to publish any fiction of his own. In the course of reviewing Rebecca Harding Davis's *Life in the Iron Mills* (1861) – often regarded today as a direct predecessor of American literary realism and naturalism (as we will see in the next chapter) – James acknowledged Davis's originality in treating industrial factory workers as fit material for fiction. But he simultaneously accused her of "drench[ing] the whole field beforehand with a flood of lachrymose sentimentalism" (*Essays* 221). "Nothing is more trivial," James continued, "than that intellectual temper which, for ever dissolved in the melting mood, goes dripping and trickling over the face of humanity, and washing its honest lineaments out of all recognition" (222).

Whether by illustration of a made-up sentimental novel's insidious effects, as in Howells's *The Rise of Silas Lapham*, by mockery, as in *Huckleberry Finn*, or by direct criticism, as in the young Henry James's comments about Rebecca Harding Davis, male realists continued to scorn what they saw as the typically forced and artificial emotionality of women's cultural productions. Although some mid-nineteenth-century fiction writers who made heavy use of domestic sentimentality's imagery and textual strategies were men (e.g., Timothy Shay Arthur, author of *Ten Nights in a Bar-Room, and What I Saw There*), recent scholars have convincingly argued that male realists insisted on portraying the sentimentalism they despised as essentially feminine at least in part out of anxiety about their own masculine status (Bell, *Problem of American Literary Realism*; Derrick, *Monumental*). Nineteenth-century American men were supposed to prove their manliness by success in what was conventionally regarded as the cutthroat world of business or on the field of battle, or both. Key male realist writers who became prominent in the late 1870s and the 1880s, including Howells, James, and Twain, had not fought in the Civil War, although they were of the appropriate age to have done so.[4] By casting the literary effects achieved by successful women writers as cheaply manipulative, shallow, and dangerously out of control, male realists tried to separate themselves from whatever seemed "feminine" about being an author in their society. The realists thus carved out their own professional identities as serious, disciplined, and responsible artists who, rather than wantonly tugging at their readers' heartstrings, sought to present "life as it is, and human feelings in their true proportion and relation" (Howells, *Silas* 175). Realist writing might reach readers' hearts, but that would not be realism's primary goal or *raison d'être*. If readers were emotionally moved, it should be by a "simple, natural, and honest" portrayal of life itself (Howells, "Editor's Study," 1887 [76.451], 155).

Although it was female-identified sentimental and domestic writing from which realists sought most energetically to differentiate their work, other types of "romanticistic" fiction (in Howells's phrase) written during their own era, much of it by men, also constituted a crime against the standard of showing "life as it is, and human feelings in their true proportion and relation." Realist writers expressed their disgust at the popularity of romantically written historical novels, a popularity that grew to new heights during the 1890s. Using what critics regarded as sloppy historical research and overblown, clichéd prose, historical romances characteristically depicted red-blooded men proving their bravery, strength, and nobility in settings that ranged from the Ancient Roman Empire to Tudor England to Revolutionary-era America.[5] William Dean Howells was not alone at the time in speculating about a connection between what he called "the horrid tumult of the swashbuckler swashing on his buckler" in American fiction and the United States' apparently growing hunger to project military force on the global stage (Howells, "New Historical Romances" 936, quoted in Kaplan, "Romancing the Empire" 659–60).

Realist critics of romantic historical novels traced the baleful genre back to Sir Walter Scott, the Scottish author who essentially invented it and whose work served as a model for James Fenimore Cooper's popular *Leatherstocking Tales*, written between the 1820s and 1840s and set during the eighteenth century in America's Northern woods. Such novels of Scott's as *Rob Roy* (1817), *Ivanhoe* (1819), and *Redgauntlet* (1824) were widely admired in the United States and were frequently reprinted and circulated well into the realists' own era, especially in the Southern states. Mark Twain took Scott's historical fiction as a particular target of acrimony and ridicule, contending that the entire American South had been perverted by the author. In Twain's eyes, Scott's novels about chivalric medieval knights and warriors glorified battle and glamorized such practices as fighting deadly duels over perceived insults to "honor," a concept whose use within romantic discourse Twain found silly and juvenile.[6] Scott's writing also glamorized death, especially in the service of historically lost causes, such as the ongoing right of the Scottish-descended Stuart dynasty to rule Britain long after they had been overthrown and replaced. For Twain, it was the "Sir Walter disease" that had made the white South so sensitive to the slightest infringement by the national government on the traditional "rights" of slaveholders and slave-holding states, and so ready to fight in defense of Southern honor. "Sir Walter had so large a hand in making Southern character, as it existed before the war," Twain wrote in 1882, "that he is in great measure responsible for the war" (*Mississippi Writings* 501). After the war, it was still the "Sir Walter disease" that led the defeated South to resist social progress by making a cult of what was referred to as the noble "Lost Cause" of the Confederacy. The very name of the Ku Klux Klan was intended to connote a warlike tribe or "clan" of Scottish Highlanders similar to those celebrated in Scott's fiction.

Twain's critique of Scott also casts aspersions on the version of male identity Scott and his writing represented, and thereby suggests through implicit contrast the form of manly professionalism that literary realists wished to embody. Twain's calling Scott's style "flowery," and his finding at the heart of Scott's writing "the jejune romanticism of an absurd past that is dead, and out of charity ought to be buried," implies that Scott's version of masculine identity is, at best, immature and out of date and also, perhaps, somewhat effeminate (*Mississippi Writings* 500). If it were not for the "enchantments" cast by Sir Walter, which have set the Southern "world in love with dreams and phantoms; with decayed and swinish forms," what would prevail there instead would be "practical, common-sense, progressive ideas, and progressive works," like those performed by the professional engineers and inventors Twain always admired (one of whom he made the hero of *A Connecticut Yankee in King Arthur's Court*) (*Mississippi*

Writings 500). By contrast to Scott's "medieval chivalry-silliness," Twain and other realists sought to align their own version of manliness with rationality, truth-telling, and progressive thinking. If, in realist author Hamlin Garland's dismissive words, romanticist writers found castles more interesting than railway stations, the realists claimed for themselves a male identity suited to the complex challenges and opportunities facing modern America (Garland, "Productive Conditions" 155).

Realism's debts to romance

American literary realists defined their manly professional identities – and the nature of their own writing – in opposition to literary "romance," by which they meant not only domestic sentimentality but also the sort of romantic historical novels initiated by Scott. The realists owed more to these denigrated modes of fiction than they acknowledged, however. For instance, in depicting the daily lives of women in their homes, mid-nineteenth-century sentimentalist novelists devoted closer attention to the quotidian details of everyday existence – clothes, food, those trivial spats among family members that everyone has experienced – than previous American fiction ever had. In doing so, women writers of domestic literature anticipated and helped lay groundwork for the "solidity of specification," the "truth of detail" in fiction that late-nineteenth-century realists would celebrate as a "supreme virtue" for novels and strive to achieve in their own work (James, *Essays* 53).

The Southwestern Humorists

In addition to the other precursors discussed in this chapter, another significant influence on post-Civil War American realism was exercised by a group of writers, today little-known, whom scholars refer to as the "Southwestern Humorists," who began publishing in the 1830s. Writing at a time when the category of "professional author" did not yet exist in America, Augustus Baldwin Longstreet, George Washington Harris, Jim Thorpe, and William Gilmore Simms, among others, spent most of their time working in gentlemanly professions such as the law, medicine, and the military. The literature they originated, however, was unique for its period. Set in states and territories bordering the Mississippi, which were then regarded as the nation's "frontier," their fiction characteristically centered on a backwoodsman with a comical name telling tall tales to a more sophisticated narrator figure, who would subtly invite readers to laugh at, not with, the backwoodsman. (In fact, the Southwestern Humorists can be said to have invented the stereotypical male figure mocked in later phases of US culture as a hillbilly, a redneck, or "white trash.") Despite the genre's focus on humorous characters and obviously exaggerated tall tales, Southwestern Humor included several elements that would later be of crucial significance to the realist project. The genre features, for instance, many of the earliest examples of dialect writing in American literature, which Longstreet apologetically (but with tongue in cheek) described as "coarse, inelegant, and sometimes ungrammatical language." Longstreet further noted for readers – again, despite the importance of humor and exaggeration in the genre – that the writing of himself and his peers was constituted by "fanciful combinations of real incidents and characters." In his own work, he added, "some of the scenes are as literally true as the frailties of memory would allow them to be."

The particular brand of humor that the Southwestern writers brought to literature rendered them especially meaningful to Samuel Clemens as he shaped the pseudonymous persona of "Mark Twain." Many other realist writers would later dismiss their writing as vulgar and trivial, but in several significant areas the Southwestern Humorists got there first.

For example, Louisa May Alcott's *Little Women* (1868), a still-popular classic of domestic fiction (although it was written slightly after the genre's heyday), includes many passages of heavy sentimentality, as well as didactic moral lessons with Christian overtones and a memorable example of sentimental domesticity's many idealized mothers. In the first chapter, Marmee makes use of the well-known Christian allegory, *The Pilgrim's Progress*, to instruct her four daughters, who are nothing but grateful for the moral inspiration: "Our burdens are here, our road is before us, and the longing for goodness and happiness is the guide that leads us through many troubles and mistakes to the peace which is a true Celestial City" (18). The teenaged Beth's death from a disease she contracted while charitably assisting an impoverished widow and her six children has made generations of readers shed sympathetic tears. Yet along with its sentimental and moralistic elements, *Little Women* also contains detailed and realistic descriptions, for instance of some props and costumes the girls make for a play they perform at home, which occurs in the same chapter as Marmee's didactic speech:

> Very clever were some of their productions … antique lamps made of old-fashioned butter-boats, covered with silver paper, gorgeous robes of old cotton, glittering with tin spangles from a pickle factory, and armor covered with the same useful diamond-shaped bits, left in sheets when the lids of tin preserve-pots were cut out.   (22)

The concrete details *Little Women*'s narrator gives regarding the homemade costumes and props render the objects almost materially present to a reader, who can virtually *see* the everyday butter dishes wrapped in silvery paper. Note, in particular, the information we are given about the "spangles" the girls use to decorate their robes and create their "armor": they are scraps of tin left over from the canning process at a pickle factory. That particular detail is one that even an experienced reader of sentimental fiction (a reader easily able to fore-see, for instance, that the angelic and physically weak Beth will die before the book ends) could not have anticipated. It is a detail so banal, yet at the same time unpredictable, that it evokes precisely what James would call "the air of reality" (*Essays* 53; see Chapter 3, below). In addition, the casual allusion here to a factory, presumably located near the girls' home, where a machine cuts lids for tin cans from sheets of metal, points to just the sorts of historical changes – in this case, the shift of formerly home-based production processes (pickling and canning) to an industrial factory – that the literary realists would make it their project to incorporate into American literature.

Slave Narratives and Literary Realism

Truth-based accounts written by African-American slaves who had escaped their bondage, which scholars today refer to as slave narratives, played a significant role in the abolitionist movement's growth and eventual success. In providing first-hand accounts of the horrors of slavery, works such as *Narrative of the Life of Frederic Douglass, an American Slave, Written by Himself* (1845) brought powerfully home to their mostly white readers the full humanity of those who suffered under, and resisted, Southern slavery. This writing was revolutionary in that it embodied the achievement of a public voice, as well as literacy, for those whom slavery had tried to rob of both. Slave narratives expanded the purview of American literature to include both people and subject matter that had previously been unrepresented or misrepresented, which later became a primary goal of the realist literary project. As realism would later do, slave narratives also often included concrete and specific details involving living and labor arrangements on plantations, as well as slaves' clothing and food. Finally, slave narratives helped to break a path for literary realism in their frankness about the human body and sexuality. Narratives did not shy away from reporting the most brutal physical aspects of slavery, including bloody whippings and rapes, as well as the harsh physical effects of overwork, insufficient nourishment, and other abuses. That the human bodies described in slave narratives were often victimized and in pain made their actual physicality seem still more vivid in mid-nineteenth-century America, where "respectable" public discourse tended to represent bodily experiences in euphemistic and abstract terms, if at all.

As with sentimental domestic novels, the tradition of historical fiction associ-ated with Sir Walter Scott was also more relevant to late-nineteenth-century realist writers than might appear from their frequently harsh criticisms of it. Even with Scott's romantic idealization of characters and his glorification of chivalric codes, his work played a vital role in demonstrating the potential for fictional narrative to engage with a changing historical world rife with social conflicts and cultural differences. Scott's introduction of historical fiction advanced the then-young novel genre in two related ways that would later prove crucial to late-nineteenth-century American writers, including Twain, his severest judge. First, historical fiction is by definition structured around the passage of historical time. The pleasure a reader derives from it at least partly depends on the continual recognition of how his or her own time both differs and descends from the past the novel depicts. Further, Scott was drawn to portraying characters, as well as cultures and societies, who find they must react in the face of some political or historical change. American literary realists writing in the decades after the US Civil War set most of their fiction during their own present time, but they viewed their time as defined by change more than by anything else. The realists were deeply interested in the effects, on individuals and on American society at large, of the immense alterations they saw occurring all around them – changes in technology, in the economy, in political and legal institutions, in the very make-up of the US population – even if the characters in realist fiction rarely respond to such changes with swordplay, as Scott's characters might. Critic Harry Shaw has remarked that much of what is "important about realism stems from its attempt to come to grips with the fact that we live in a historical world," by which Shaw means a world that changes over time (*Narrating Reality* 6). Scott may have used a romanticizing lens, but his focus on a past – usually that of his own British Isles – in which the seeds of the present are at least intermittently visible made him the first major novelist to put "the fact that we live in a historical world" at the center of his work.

Second, Scott's portrayal of Scottish Highlanders, and Scotland in general, as having a culture – customs, values, modes of speech, clothes, weapons – related to but also distinct from that of England meaningfully advanced the use of regional and cultural differences as a thematic background for narrative fiction. As we will see in later chapters, such differences, especially as manifested between a dominant culture and a relatively disempowered or minority culture, were of fundamental importance in the development of American literary realism. Regionalist or "local-color" realist writers, for example, tended to depict American rural and village life as a mode of existence quickly moving into the past, which their works at least implicitly contrasted with modern urban living. Ironically, given his vituperative criticism of Scott, Mark Twain's own portrayal of the American South as a stubbornly "backward" region – albeit a region whose cultural forms, thought-systems, and, especially, speech patterns he was devoted to capturing in his fiction – can be said at least loosely to follow the model first laid out in Sir Walter's portrayal of the Scots. And of course, as we will return to in later chapters, the narrative representation of cultural difference lay at the heart of American realism's treatment of race, ethnicity, and social class.

American and European realisms

American literary realism is frequently presented as if it emerged within a literary context that included only US writers. American realism did develop in its own way and at its own pace, and some of the social conditions it responded to were specific to the late-nineteenth-century United States. These specifically American conditions included the powerful impact of the Civil War and its long-unresolved aftermath (above all the nation's ongoing treatment of African Americans, over 12 percent of the population, as second-class citizens), as well as a massive post-War influx of immigrants representing an unprecedentedly wide range of national and ethnic backgrounds (see Chapters 9 and 10). All of these developments occurred, moreover, within the context of a nation whose official founding principles of democracy and equality could be called upon to support literary realism's commitment to focusing on common everyday people. In addition, there is also no question that much of the writing that US realists defined themselves *against* (even as it also influenced their work) was by American authors. But leading American realists cited European realists as *positive* influences on their writing much more frequently than they cited American authors. As a self-conscious aesthetic movement, modern realism began in Europe.

The first consistent use of realism as an aesthetic term occurred in France during the early 1850s, initially in reference to the paintings of Gustave Courbet. Courbet rejected the formalities and idealizations of the classical art tradition, as well as the exotic subject matter of romantic art. Instead, he painted pictures of working- and lower-middle-class people performing everyday tasks, including manual labor. Courbet also painted intensely lifelike, nonidealized nudes, including a scandalous close-up of an adult woman's genitalia labeled "L'Origine du Monde" ("The Origin of the World"). When his paintings were rejected for 1855's official French Universal Exhibition, Courbet set up his own Pavillion du Réalisme near the official exhibition site.

French literary reviewers adopted the term "realism" from art criticism almost immediately to describe the work of some of Courbet's literary contemporaries, particularly Gustave Flaubert, whose 1857 novel *Madame Bovary* depicted the life and death of an alienated, lower-middle-class housewife in the French provinces. Flaubert set as his task to represent in literature "commonplace situations and trivial dialogue. To write the *mediocre* well and to see that it maintains at the same time its appearance, its rhythm, its words" (quoted in Fluck, "Morality" 87). The term realism was also used retroactively by critics to describe the massive achievement of Honoré de Balzac, whom American realist Henry James would later describe as the "founder" of literary realism (*French Writers* 49). Balzac took as his lifelong project the writing of a series he called *La Comédie Humaine* (*The Human Comedy*), which ultimately included almost ninety volumes (1829–48). Balzac attempted in the series to give fictional life to every division and sub-division of French society of his time. He offered detailed pictures of the worlds of Parisian actresses, high-ranking church officials, provincial tradesmen, journalists, the nobility, midwives, and army officers, among others. For James, although Balzac wrote before the term "realism" was in use, he was the writer who first "saw the real as clamouring to be rendered" and who "rendered it with unequalled authority" (*French Writers* 97, 99).

In fact, well before the mid-nineteenth-century French advent of the term "realism," eighteenth-century English writers such as Daniel Defoe and Henry Fielding began incorporating into their work central elements of what would later be called realist fiction. Key figures in creating the genre of the novel as such, these authors characteristically focused more on the middle and lower classes than on the aristocracy, took a deflationary attitude toward the conventions of chivalric romance, and paid careful attention to the accoutrements of daily life (even on Robinson Crusoe's island). Writing in 1897 about the history of literary realism, Howells insisted that contemporary realism "is a fresh impulse of a kind in English fiction that has always existed. We haven't anything more realistic in the work of today than Defoe's novels" (*Selected Literary Criticism II* 287). Both Howells and James also wrote extensively about such later British literary realists as Jane Austen, George Eliot, William Makepeace Thackeray, Anthony Trollope, George Moore, Thomas Hardy, and others, although Howells remarked in 1887 that "A true arrangement of the literatures in which realism has attained the ascendancy over romance would place the Russians first; the French, by virtue of Zola's strength, second; the Spanish next; the Norwegians fourth; the Italians fifth; the English last" (quoted in Becker, "Modern Realism" 133).

As Howells's ranked list indicates, the writers who developed realism in the United States after the Civil War wrote in response to their own local and national circumstances, but they were quite aware of participating in an international literary movement. Indeed, Howells took as one of his most important tasks when he served as editor at the prestigious magazines the *Atlantic*

Monthly and then *Harper's Monthly* to help his American readers become better acquainted with (or, in many cases, learn about for the first time) European realist writers from Scandinavia to Spain, including the realist whom Howells came most to admire, the Russian Leo Tolstoy. When asked by *Munsey's Magazine* at the age of sixty to name his "favorite novelist," Howells insisted that he had many favorites and that the list changed almost daily, growing in length the longer he lived. Announcing that he would purposefully "leave out romantic fiction" in favor of "the realistic," he proceeded to name novelists representing at least twelve countries, adding that he had lately "got hold of a novel by a Polish novelist, Sinkiewicz, which instantly became my favorite ... I imagine [it] pictures very faithfully the society of Poland at this moment" (*Selected Literary Criticism II* 286).

In other words, what we now designate as American literary realism did not emerge in a literary vacuum. Its borders cannot be marked as cleanly as the organization of literature anthologies, the listings in college course catalogues, or the titles of books such as this one might seem to suggest. Realists born in the United States, including Howells, James, Wharton, and others, saw themselves as part of an international group of writers with roughly similar approaches and aims. Within the US literary context, modes of writing that some literature anthologies and scholars present as "pre-" or even "anti"-realist (transcendentalism, sentimentalism, other varieties of "romance") had significant overlaps, both chronologically and in methods and themes, with literary realism. Characteristics that we now consider central to literary realism, such as close attention to the surface details of everyday life, can be found in American fiction written well before the Civil War, while post-Civil War "realist" texts not infrequently include within them key features even of the "romanticistic" writing the realists denigrated, such as moments of high sentimentality.

Toward the end of his career in 1907, Henry James conceded that "it is as difficult ... to trace the dividing line between the real and the romantic as to plant a milestone between north and south" (*Essays* 1067). In the following chapter we will consider three US works of the 1860s and 1870s that played key roles in mediating between literature that utilizes certain "realist" techniques, including the attention to quotidian details we find in mid-nineteenth-century works of sentimental domesticity and slave narratives' vivid depictions of wounded bodies, and, on the other hand, later nineteenth-century fiction that self-consciously aims at "realism as a basic literary goal and concept" (Becker, "Modern Realism" 4).

Chapter 2

The "look of agony" and everyday middle-class life: three transitional works

In 1861, the same year that the Civil War (1861–65) began, the reclusive poet Emily Dickinson wrote,

> I like a look of agony,
> Because I know it's true;
> Men do not sham convulsion,
> Nor simulate a throe.

Dickinson's poem asserts that the "look" or appearance of agony – sharp, intense pain – carries with it a conviction of reality.

In seeming accord with Dickinson's view, the earliest texts that scholars generally recognize as heralding the advent of literary realism in the United States are Rebecca Harding Davis's "Life in the Iron Mills" (1861), which depicts physically and mentally deforming labor in a factory town, and John W. De Forest's *Miss Ravenel's Conversion from Secession to Loyalty* (1867), which was especially noted for its grueling Civil War battle scenes. What, we must ask, is the relationship between realism and the depiction of intensely painful experience? Is there a tension here with realism's other well-known emphasis on commonplace, everyday experience?

Both Davis's "Life in the Iron Mills" and De Forest's *Miss Ravenel's Conversion from Secession to Loyalty* reveal a strong and continuing influence from modes of fiction prevalent during the first half of the nineteenth century. For example, not only does "Life in the Iron Mills" contain obviously symbolic and allegorical elements that the realists would later associate with literary romance, it also includes a preachy narrator who often addresses the reader directly, as well as an explicit Christian framework and a humbly self-sacrificing female character named Deborah – all characteristics of domestic sentimental fiction. *Miss Ravenel's Conversion from Secession to Loyalty* idealizes the "family homestead" which, after misunderstandings and separations, lovers Lillie Ravenel and Captain Colburne finally achieve (465). These works further share with sentimental literature tragic scenes of drawn-out suffering and death.

But the specific depictions of pain and suffering for which readers tend to remember Davis's and De Forest's texts are mostly unaccompanied by those "tears, idle tears" (in Howells's mocking phrase) that so often mark sentimental literature. Additionally, the suffering these works portray occurs in notably new and modern contexts. Davis's depiction of a smoky, noise-filled factory town, where immigrant workers are battered by unending labor and harsh living conditions, and De Forest's depiction of Civil War battlefields, where corpses are produced on an industrial scale, opened two key fields to literary representation. We will begin this chapter by discussing "Life in the Iron Mills" and *Miss Ravenel's Conversion from Secession to Loyalty* as important transitional works in American literature's movement toward realism. We will then turn to a third transitional work, William Dean Howells's first novel, *Their Wedding Journey* (1871), whose focus on familiar, even banal aspects of middle-class experience signified the rise to prominence of a mode of realist fiction that diverges from Davis's and De Forest's emphasis on the "look of agony."

Writing the factory: "Life in the Iron Mills"

Rebecca Harding Davis was a young writer unpublished outside the pages of her local newspaper in Wheeling, West Virginia when, in December of 1860, she submitted her first major piece of fiction to the *Atlantic Monthly*, at the time the nation's most prestigious magazine (see text box below). Davis, who could trace her American ancestry back to before the Revolution against Britain, came from a privileged family. She had more in common with the well-educated, mostly financially comfortable readers in the *Atlantic*'s audience than she had with the immigrant laborers whom "Life in the Iron Mills" introduced both to those readers and to American literature. Wheeling, however, was an industrial town. Almost one-third of its population of 16,000 people were first-generation immigrants working in the town's iron, glass, and textile plants (Williams, *West Virginia* 50). As a young woman Davis spent hours walking in and around Wheeling. She observed the industrial plants, those who worked in them, and the workers' living conditions more closely than many people of her class, especially women, ever had the opportunity (or chose) to do (Tichi, "Introduction" 6). Davis made use of her personal observations when she became the first American author to attempt a serious portrayal of the nation's new industrial realities and their effects on the laborers who kept factories running both day and night.

Realism and Magazines

In the latter part of the nineteenth century, magazines played a uniquely significant role in the nation's literary culture. Original American novels almost always appeared as monthly magazine serials – in some cases running for a year or more – before being published as discrete books. The *Atlantic Monthly* was founded in 1857 by upper-class Bostonians and had links to such well-known literary figures as Ralph Waldo Emerson, Henry Wadsworth Longfellow, and Harriet Beecher Stowe. Designating itself "A Magazine of Literature, Art, and Politics," the *Atlantic* (as those in the know referred to it) aimed at a well-educated, middle- to upper-class readership. The magazine quickly established a reputation of standing for high literary standards, strong cultural and political nationalism, and liberal (but rarely radical) thought. Almost from the beginning, the merits of literary realism were debated within its pages and, under the editorial reign of William Dean Howells, which began in 1871, the magazine would become the nation's most prominent publisher and promoter of realist fiction. Periodicals that both resembled and competed with the *Atlantic*, and which published many of the same realist authors, included *Harper's Monthly*, *Scribner's Magazine*, and the *Century*. Beginning in the 1890s, however, magazines such as the *Century* and the *Atlantic Monthly* began to find themselves sharing their eminence in US literary culture with a new breed of mass-circulation magazines that recruited many of the same "brand-name" realist authors – including Howells, James, Sarah Orne Jewett (see Chapter 5) and others – whose careers and status had originally developed in the context of the older periodicals (Glazener, *Reading for Realism* 236). Charging 10–15 cents instead of the 35 cents per issue charged by *Century* and the *Atlantic*, new monthlies such *McClure's*, *Munsey's*, and *Cosmopolitan* (launched in 1886 but revamped in 1890) took advantage of cheaper half-tone printing processes to include more illustrations, as well as photos. They included livelier discussions of current events than the older "quality" magazines had, and preferred illustrated features on famous writers' personalities and daily lives (homes, work-spaces, habits) over lengthy essays evaluating writers' actual work or their place in literary history. Writers such as Henry James complained about the vulgarization of culture that a focus on writers' "personalities" in lieu of their literary contributions connoted for him, but neither James nor other so-called "high realists" (see Chapter 4) hesitated to take advantage of the new market for their work.

"Life in the Iron Mills" relates the story of a Welsh immigrant laboring in a factory or "mill" where iron is produced. Hugh Wolfe lives a life "like those of [his] class: incessant labor, sleeping in kennel-like rooms, eating rank pork and molasses, drinking – God and the distillers only know what; with an occasional night in jail, to atone for some drunken excess" (42). But Hugh has an artist's love of beauty. In his few spare moments every day, he sculpts crude but powerful figures from "korl," a scrap substance left over from the iron-making process. Hugh is loved by Deborah, a partially disabled factory girl, "almost a hunchback," whom he is kind to but does not love.

One day some wealthy visitors to the iron mill stumble upon a striking korl figure Hugh has formed, a woman whose look of ravenous hunger symbolizes to Hugh his own starvation for "summat" beyond his daily struggle for the barest necessities of life. The visitors praise the artistry of the statue and tell Hugh that he has the potential to be "a great sculptor, a great man" (56). Beyond verbal encouragement, however, they make no gesture to help him to achieve the artistic potential they have identified in him and soon move on. But Deb, who has been listening from the side, manages to pick the pocket of one of the visitors, Mr. Mitchell, before he leaves and later gives Hugh a wallet full of money. Hugh gradually convinces himself that he has the right to use the money to change his life. But he and Deb are both soon arrested for the theft. The despondent Hugh kills himself before his nineteen-year sentence can begin. Deb, who as a women received a lesser three-year prison sentence, is subsequently adopted by a Quaker woman and brought to live with her in the hills. In a quick final paragraph that many readers have found facile, and that Davis may have added in order to end her dark story with at least some ray of hope, we are told that after years of "slow, patient Christ-love," the Quaker succeeds in making "healthy and hopeful" Deborah's once "impure body and soul" (73).

The bulk of Davis's story is devoted to what its title suggests. From the beginning of "Life in the Iron Mills," the narrator adopts the position of a guide who wishes to show her well-off readers how lives are lived beneath the smoke and soot of industrial cities such as Wheeling. "This is what I want you to do," the narrator announces. "I want you to hide your disgust, take no heed to your clean clothes, and come right down with me, – here, into the thickest of the fog and mud and foul effluvia. I want you to hear this story" (41). The narrator has already marked herself as economically and socially privileged by details ranging from the fact that she writes while sitting in her personal library to her sophisticated use of occasional French phrases. Yet even as she indicates that she shares her presumed readers' privileged social class, the narrator challenges them for what she suspects is their lack of interest in or insight into America's new industrial poor, on whom her tale will focus. The narrator accuses readers of the *Atlantic Monthly* of being "amateur," "lazy" "*dilettante*[s]," who cling to abstract, fancy-named theories of life and its meaning, rather than looking seriously and carefully at America's painful new realities (40–41).

The narrator's criticism of her presumed readers implicitly differentiates her own approach to the nitty-gritty realities of industrial America from theirs. If the readers' attitudes are lazy, amateur, and dilettantish, then the narrator's approach to the industrial poor must be committed, knowledgeable, and professional. For instance, asserting that "not many even of the inhabitants of a manufacturing town know the vast machinery of the system by which the bodies of workmen are governed," the narrator describes for her readers the alternation of twelve-hour day and night shifts, which allows the new factories to run "unceasingly" throughout the year (45). Supplying additional behind-the-scenes information, she adds that the factories' appearance of observing the Sabbath day is, in actuality, only a "half-courtesy to public censure." The factories may temporarily "veil" their fires on Sunday, "but as soon as the clock strikes midnight, the great furnaces break forth with renewed fury" (45).

In addition to conveying information that demonstrates her own extensive knowledge of the factories' inner workings, the narrator shows her empathy by trying to communicate to her audience that basic human emotions, such as pain, jealousy, and loneliness, are felt just as much in the "foul" world of the iron workers as in the readers' own homes: "You laugh at it? Are pain and jealousy less savage realities down here in this place I am taking you to than in your own house or your own heart – your heart, which they clutch at sometimes? The note is the same, I fancy, be the octave high or low" (47). It may at first appear as if the narrator is suggesting to her readers that the inner emotions, the "note," they and the laborers hold in common could become the basis for bonds of sympathy across the gulf of class ("be the octave high or low"). Such a suggestion would seem in precise accord with the discourse of sentimentality already prevalent in nineteenth-century American culture: recall the identification based on shared maternal feelings that Stowe works to establish between white Northern women and the fleeing slave Eliza in *Uncle Tom's Cabin*, published less than a decade prior to "Life in the Iron Mills" (see Chapter 1).

But where Stowe tells readers that first and foremost they should be sure that "*they feel right*" about slavery, and urges the power of prayer to help other "Christian men and women of the North" to "feel right" (Stowe, *Uncle Tom's Cabin* 515), the narrator of "Life in the Iron Mills" appears more skeptical of the possibility that her readers will be able or even wish to identify with the mill workers on the basis of shared human feelings. The feelings that Davis specifies as shared are themselves isolating ones, as when she describes the "apathy and vacancy" that often pervades Deborah, and then continues: "One sees that dead, vacant look steal sometimes over the rarest, finest of women's faces … and then one can guess at the secret of intolerable solitude that lies hid beneath the delicate laces and brilliant smile" (47). Even if found among both rich and poor women, "dead" feelings of solitude and apathy, like "pain and jealousy," are significantly more difficult to imagine than shared maternal love as the basis for building meaningful emotional identification across social class lines. As if further distinguishing her text from the sentimental tradition, Davis has the incisive Mr. Mitchell insist that "reform is born of need, not pity" (57). Deborah's eventual healing may result from years of "Christ-love" directed at her by the Quaker woman who lives among the hills, but it does nothing to change conditions in the iron mills.

At several points, the language the narrator of "Life in the Iron Mills" uses to describe the mill workers itself acts as an obstacle to middle- and upper-class readers identifying with them or imagining themselves in the workers' place, as Stowe urges her readers to do with Eliza. At the beginning of the story, the narrator refers to the mass of workers who stream past her library window as "dull, besotted" men, "stooping all night over boiling cauldrons of metal, laired by day in dens of drunkenness and infamy" (40). The men live "massed, vile, slimy lives, like those of the torpid lizards in yonder stagnant water-butt" (41). Here and elsewhere, the narrator reveals, whether intentionally or not, that she shares some of the "disgust" she asks her readers to "hide" (not the same, it should be noted, as ridding oneself of it). Davis thus establishes a para-doxical position for her narrator, at once solidly of the same social class and background as her presumed readers and sharing some of their own visceral responses, but also with a unique commitment to understanding America's new realities, however disturbing or painful they might be. It is a position that subsequent realist writers and texts would continue both to occupy and to explore.

The narrative stance of "Life in the Iron Mills" helps frame a question that would also be of pressing importance for other realist writers, including William Dean Howells, Charles Chesnutt, and Sui Sin Far. To what extent could realist writing help to bridge the ever-more obvious differences dividing American society, including differences of social class, race, ethnicity, religion, and geographic region? With only a few exceptions, literary realism remained a genre written primarily by and for middle- and upper-middle-class Americans. Works of literary realism were only very rarely, if ever, addressed to or read by the disempowered people frequently represented in those texts. As we saw in Chapter 1, realist writers criticized sentimental literature's mode of evoking emotions and fostering emotional identifications as forced and arti-ficial. If sentimentality's reliance (in the realists' view) on emotional manipu-lation made it an unstable basis for improving society, could the unbiased observations and clear-eyed depictions that the realists strove to achieve in their own fiction serve more successfully to promote mutual comprehension and solidarity across the nation's inarguably real divides?

When a group of men that includes Kirby (whose father owns the mill), the well-off physician Dr. May, and the man-about-town Mr. Mitchell tours the iron mill in Davis's story, they are struck by the harsh, degrading conditions. When Hugh Wolfe directly asks Dr. May to help him change his life, however, May becomes flustered and turns away. Instead of helping, the doctor goes home and prays "that power might be given to these degraded souls to rise." After making his prayer, the doctor "glowed at heart, recognizing an accomplished duty" (58). As a proto-literary realist, Davis is clearly ironic toward the doctor's sentimental feeling that he has "accomplished" anything with his prayer, other than to make himself feel virtuous. Yet the resolutely non-sentimental Mr. Mitchell, who is the only upper-class character within the story able to understand and articulate the meanings Hugh tries to express in his sculpture of a working-class woman, also sees no way in which he might be able to help Hugh or effectively alter the system that keeps Hugh struggling at a barely subsistence level: "It would be of no use. I am not one of them" (57). Davis and subsequent realist writers recognized and worried about the possibility that the experience of reading a text such as "Life in the Iron Mills," even if it helped middle-class readers to arrive at more realistic understandings of impoverished Americans, might ultimately produce as little actual change or action as either Dr. May's sentimental prayer or Mr. Mitchell's incisive grasp of the situation does. We will return to this question of realist literature and its potential social effects throughout *The Cambridge Introduction to American Literary Realism*.

Writing the Civil War: *Miss Ravenel's Conversion from Secession to Loyalty*

The Civil War is the single most traumatic event the United States has ever experienced, including the attacks of September 11, 2001. During the four years that it was fought, more American soldiers died than perished in the combined totals of all US wars from the Revolution of 1776 to the Korean War of the 1950s, a period that includes both world wars (Faust, *This Republic* xi). In addition, unlike other military conflicts both before and after it, the Civil War was fought almost entirely on the United States' own territory. When it began in 1861 nobody predicted that the war would last more than a year, if that; but when Lee surrendered to Grant at Appomattox in 1865, the 620,000 dead soldiers represented 2 percent of the American population at the time.

A similar ratio today would mean six million Americans dead, all having died in a war against other Americans, and this is not to count the civilians who died due to the Civil War (Faust, *This Republic* xi). The Civil War, moreover, was fought in an unusually brutal fashion, combining intimate trench warfare with new, high-powered military technology that allowed killing to occur on an industrial scale. In *The Red Badge of Courage* (1895), the most famous novel about the American Civil War, realist Stephen Crane would compare its battlefields to "the grinding of an immense and terrible machine," one whose "grim processes ... produce corpses" (38).

The effect of this "immense and terrible machine" on survivors, military and civilian, North and South, was devastating. Every dead soldier left behind family and friends who now became widows, orphans, mourners. Wounded and traumatized veterans, many of them amputees, returned to nearly every city, town, and village in the nation. The Civil War was also the world's first extensively photographed conflict. Photographic images of soldiers, of camp life, and, most striking of all, of the "harvest of death" on battlefields were displayed and sold in galleries, as well as through mail-order catalogues, and were widely discussed (Zeller, *Blue and Gray* 107, 3). A *New York Times* reporter viewing an 1862 exhibit called "The Dead of Antietam" at the studio of well-known photographer Matthew T. Brady wrote, "Mr. Brady has done something to bring home to us the terrible reality and earnestness of war. If he has not brought bodies and laid them in our dooryards and along the streets, he has done something very like it" (quoted in Zeller, *Blue and Gray* xi).

By contrast to the new medium of photography, popular literary genres of the pre-War period, which often favored domestic subjects and which tended to use idealized characters to illustrate familiar moral lessons, were ill prepared to deal with the unprecedented carnage and trauma of the war. In an 1867 review in the *Atlantic Monthly*, a young William Dean Howells asserted that the Civil War had not only left upon the US treasury "the burden of a tremendous national debt" (it reached $2.7 billion by the end of the war), but had also "laid upon our literature a charge under which it has hitherto staggered very lamely" ("Review" 121). Howells was not yet the major public spokesperson for American literary realism – at the time, no such movement had formed. Yet he complained that the only fiction being published about the Civil War was overly romantic: "The heroes of young-lady writers in the magazines have been everywhere fighting the late campaigns over again, as young ladies would have fought them" ("Review" 121). Note once again how a realist writer defines realism by opposing it to the writing of "ladies" (see Chapter 1 for additional discussion of this issue).

Howells's review singled out one new novel for praise, however. *Miss Ravenel's Conversion from Secession to Loyalty* was the first work of fiction "to treat the war really and artistically," down to the "hard swearing" that characterized some soldiers' speech ("Review" 121). The novel's author, Captain John W. De Forest, was a 41-year-old Civil War veteran who had participated in several battles and campaigns. While in the field, he had kept a journal and also written several unusually descriptive letters to his wife, which he drew on in composing the book. The bulk of the plot is a love story about a young Southern woman, Lillie Ravenel, whose father is a Union sympathizer. Although Lillie begins by favoring the Confederacy, the harsh treatment her father receives from his fellow Southerners, as well as two attractive Union soldiers who vie for her affections, successfully convert her from "secession to loyalty." After some romantic mistakes and the death of the first of the soldiers she had married, Lillie ends the novel with a blushing acceptance of Captain Colburne's marriage offer and a plan to make a home with him in New England.

More striking to Howells and other early reviewers than the love story or its symbolic reunification of North and South was De Forest's realistic portrayal of army life in and out of battle. A reviewer for *Harper's Weekly* praised the book's "air of reality," while the *New York Citizen* went so far as to call it "the best war novel ever written" (both reviews quoted in Scharnhorst, "Introduction" xxi). The *Boston Evening Transcript* said that the battle scenes "give the impression of being drawn from life" (quoted in Scharnhorst, "Introduction" xxi). What are the features that led reviewers to find the depiction of war in De Forest's novel so realistic? For one, the novel offered an unusual number of specific details, as in this description of a makeshift field hospital:

> In the centre of this mass of suffering stood several operating tables, each burdened by a grievously wounded man and surrounded by surgeons and their assistants. Underneath were great pools of clotted blood, amidst which lay amputated fingers, hands, arms, feet and legs, only a little more ghastly in color than the faces of those who waited their turn on the table ... A smell of blood drenched the stifling air, overpowering even the pungent odor of chloroform. (260)

In addition to striking visual images (the piling up of amputated body parts), this passage provides other reality-evoking sensory details, such as the conflicting smells of blood and chloroform (chloroform was a widely used anesthetic at the time). De Forest also described noises for his readers, such as the "stupendous clamour" of exploding munitions, and tells, too, of the munitions' effect on nature: "Magnolias, oaks and beeches eighteen inches or two feet in diameter were cut asunder with a deafening scream of shot and of splitting fibers" (251, 250). De Forest captured the sense of panicked confusion during battle to which many soldiers later testified, as well as the "fierce excitement," even "intoxication," that some also admitted to having felt (254, 255). Moreover, even the "hero" of De Forest's book, Captain Colburne, avoids popular clichés of military heroism. He refuses to break his ranks and attempt the rescue of a wounded soldier from the midst of battle because "Army Regulations" forbid such attempts until after the battle has been decided (254).

Just as much as the adrenalin-heightened experience of battle, De Forest portrays the days and weeks of boredom, insects, mud, bad rations, and fatigue, as well as both loneliness and camaraderie, that pervaded soldiers' experiences. De Forest's soldiers not only swear, as Howells noted, but they drink, sometimes heavily. American war novelists of the twentieth century, from Ernest Hemingway to Tim O'Brien, have followed De Forest's lead in emphasizing the often mundane realities of time spent out of battle as much as the experience of fighting itself. Like De Forest, when these novelists do portray battle it is not from above, as a top general or subsequent historian of military strategy might see it, but from the ground, where the overriding sensation is often one of chaos. Looking back at De Forest's 1867 novel almost thirty years later, Howells judged that it "was of an advanced realism before realism was known by that name" (*Passions* 223).

Writing the ordinary: *Their Wedding Journey*

When he began work on his first novel, however, Howells laid out a terrain for his own realism very different from the chaotic scenes of combat, injury, and death so notable in De Forest's text. In a letter to his father at the time he began *Their Wedding Journey*, Howells announced "I see clear before me a path in literature which I believe no one else has tried, and which I believe I can make most distinctly and entirely my own" (quoted in Reeves, "Introduction" 13). He meant the "path" of portraying humdrum aspects of contemporary middle-class existence. Based in part on a trip he and his wife Elinor had taken, Howells's novel describes the honeymoon trip of fictional characters Basil and Isabel March from Boston to Niagara Falls, traveling through New York City. If "the look of agony" (in Emily Dickinson's phrase) helped give the stamp of reality both to De Forest's portrayal of Civil War battlefields and to Davis's portrayal of nineteenth-century industrial laborers, Howells strives for the veracity of the "ordinary." He sets the tone of *Their Wedding Journey* early on by announcing that readers should not expect to encounter anything unusually thrilling or shocking. In telling us about Basil and Isabel's honeymoon, he as narrator will "have nothing to do but to talk of some ordinary traits of American life as these appeared to them, to speak a little of well-known and easily accessible places, to present now a bit of landscape and now a sketch of character" (3).

William Dean Howells: Realism's Dean

William Dean Howells – prolific writer, powerful editor and reviewer, and enthusiastic intellectual combatant – served as American literary realism's most visible representative during the latter decades of the nineteenth century. Originally from a small town on the Ohio frontier, and without much formal education, Howells (1837–1920) wrote more than one hundred books. From his influential positions as editor of the *Atlantic Monthly* from 1871–81 and, later, columnist for *Harper's Monthly* and *Harper's Weekly* magazines, Howells promoted the careers of (and personally mentored) many of the realist writers we will discuss in later chapters, including Mark Twain, Sarah Orne Jewett, Stephen Crane, Charles Chesnutt, and Abraham Cahan. Howells was the preeminent figure in what became known as American literature's "realism wars." Fought mostly in magazines and newspapers from the mid 1880s through the mid 1890s, the battle consisted of miscellaneous reviewers printing often biting critiques of realism as vulgar, ugly, and flat, when not obscene, and counter-attacks by Howells and others on romantic fiction as simultaneously juvenile and superannuated. Howells added that those who rejected realism in favor of romanticism embodied a self-righteous "petrifaction of taste" that would surely die out ("Editor's Study," 1887 [76.451] 155). Ironically, as we will discuss in Chapter 7, in the first and second decades of the twentieth century a younger generation of American realists would reject Howells himself for being too bound to genteel conventions. Writing to his close friend Henry James in 1915 (a year before James's death), Howells mourned, "I am comparatively a dead cult with my statues cast down and the grass growing over them in the pale moonlight" (Anesko, *Letters* 460).

Some pages later, Howells explains that he will push his emphasis on "ordinary ... American life" still further than first indicated: "As in literature the true artist will shun the use even of real events if they are of an improbable character, so the sincere observer of man will not desire to look upon his heroic or occasional phases, but will seek him in his habitual moods of vacancy and tiresomeness" (55). Throughout the book, and in much of his later fiction, Howells purposefully flirts with the danger of boring his readers by featuring more of the typical, familiar, even vacant and tiresome episodes of life than he does of those other moments, in reality far fewer, in which we experience sudden danger or transcendent passion. Most famously, in his 1890 realist masterpiece *A Hazard of New Fortunes* (discussed more fully in Chapter 6, below), Howells devotes almost one hundred pages to the Marches' search for a suitable apartment in New York City. In the apartment-hunting episode, Basil and Isabel (*Their Wedding Journey*'s protagonists reappear in this later novel, now well into middle age) make such everyday discoveries as that classified advertisements sometimes exaggerate how bright and airy an apartment is or what counts as a separate room. Rents turn out to be higher than the Marches had hoped (another familiar experience, alas, to anybody who has ever looked for an apartment in a major city), so Basil and Isabel must lower their expectations. Irritating each other along the way as they bicker about neighborhoods, what they can and can't afford, and possible furnishings, they ultimately circle back to an apartment they had earlier rejected as too small and too full of decorative bric-a-brac. The very fact that the entire apartment-hunting episode has nothing extraordinary about it is, for Howells, precisely what provides it with the convincing flavor of real life. Similarly, during their first appearance twenty years earlier in *Their Wedding Journey*, the Marches travel hundreds of miles, encounter boat delays, bad (and occasionally good) train-station food, and see the sights. But nothing more dangerous occurs than that Isabel refuses to re-cross a rickety bridge over part of Niagara Falls, which makes Basil briefly panic about how they will ever get back to the mainland. Ultimately, Isabel sees that another small group of tourists is about to go around her to get to the bridge, which embarrasses her into walking across the bridge first. (Critic James Cox aptly praises Howells as the first American writer to recognize "that embarrassment is a central emotion of middle-class social existence" ["Rise of Silas Lapham" 123]).

Indeed, one might argue that the overriding theme of *Their Wedding Journey* is the difference between real American middle-class existence and "heroic," romantic, or exciting portrayals of life. From the start, the book breaks from literary convention by concentrating on the period after a marriage occurs, instead of focusing, as marriage novels from Jane Austen onward typically have, on the exciting months of courtship, obstacles, and blossoming love that finally culminate in a wedding. In addition, rather than the adolescent or late-adolescent protagonists of the typical marriage story, Basil and Isabel are well into adulthood when they marry. By contrast to most stories about marriage, we receive relatively little information, and certainly no vivid details, regarding how Basil and Isabel first met, the moment in which each realized he or she loved the other, the manner in which Basil proposed, their first kiss, and so forth. Instead, Howells strives to convey the couple's everyday experience of marriage, which after all constitutes a much greater proportion of most spouses' total time together than does the usually briefer, if more intense, period of courtship.

From the start, Basil and Isabel share Howells's distaste for romantic clichés and artificially produced excitement. On the way to a well-known Niagara landmark, a carriage driver playing tour guide retells some overly familiar legends about Indian burial grounds on Goat Island. Rather than the driver's tales adding an extra thrill to Basil and Isabel's enjoyment of the expedition, "under the influence of his romances our travelers began to find the whole scene hackneyed" (194). Throughout their journey the Marches take a certain pride in their ability to spot the commonplace or cheaply commercial beneath the supposedly exotic. At Niagara they notice a "news-man's booth" selling moccasins supposedly made by local Indians but actually manufactured, they deduce, by local Irish immigrants, whom they refer to ironically as "the Irish aborigines." So too, they recognize the booth's "cups and vases of Niagara spar" (a crystalline mineral native to the area) as in fact cheap imports from Devonshire, England (196).

Notice that the realist sensibility exhibited here is significantly more complex than might be expected by a reader familiar only with Howells's frequently quoted recommendation that American writers focus on the "simple, natural, and honest" aspects of life. The Marches know that what appears to be simple, natural, and honest, such as the fake "Niagara spar," often isn't. The souvenir stand tries to use tourists' interest in local authenticity as a marketing tool. When the Marches recognize that the "Niagara spar" is imported from England, and that the moccasins on sale have been produced not by the area's actual "aborigines," who would of course be Native Americans, but by immigrant workers from Ireland, they show their sophisticated grasp of the modern world in which they live. The post-Civil War modernization of American industry and of the economy has not only produced the convenient railroads and steamships that enable the Marches to cover so much territory during their wedding journey; technological and economic modernization has also had a wide-ranging impact on American culture itself. Anticipating developments that would accelerate throughout the twentieth century and into the twenty-first, the Marches realize (even if they do not explain it in so many words) that local industries have been undercut by the increasing globalization of capitalism. "Authenticity" has become a commodity and can no longer be taken for granted. Buying snacks from local vendors at a train-stop in Canada, the Marches wonder, with a sigh, "what thing characteristic of the local life will they sell us in Maine when we get there? … Pop-corn in its native tissue-paper, and advertising the new Dollar store in Portland?" (177).

Howells gives the Marches a sophisticated sense of America's changing realities. Rather than being merely caught up in the process of modernization, the protagonists of *Their Wedding Journey* observe and analyze that process, even as they also participate in it. By contrast, thinking back to Rebecca Harding Davis's "Life in the Iron Mills," the stunted, blighted lives of Hugh and Deb reveal modernity's dark underside to readers, but Davis does not grant the characters themselves the ability to think analytically about the changing world in which they live and suffer. Davis does indicate that Hugh Wolfe's brain is "full of thwarted energy and unused powers" (62), which changed life circumstances might have allowed him to unlock. But when asked what the working-class woman he has sculpted seems to hunger for so desperately, Hugh can only reply, "I dunno" (54). As for Deb, she spends much of the story in a "stupor," at times seeming almost to become one with the pile of ashes on which she rests "like a limp, dirty rag" (46).

We are left with a stark contrast between, on the one hand, the pervasive signs of difference and distance that separate the narrator of "Life in the Iron Mills" from the story's main characters and, on the other hand, the sense of identification that connects the narrative voice of *Their Wedding Journey* with Basil and Isabel March. Of course the Marches belong to the same social grouping – urban, middle-class professionals – as Howells himself, while the immigrant laborers Davis portrays in "Life in the Iron Mills" share neither her own comfortable middle-class position, her education and articulateness, nor her family's distinguished American heritage. In addition, beyond the specific tragedy that gives her story its plot, Davis indicts Hugh and his father's life of material deprivation and perpetual labor as itself an ongoing crisis and tragedy, only slightly less extreme in its harsh effects than Deb's ill-considered theft of the wallet. The differences between the Marches and the Wolfes as literary subjects, and the contrast in the types of relationship their respective narrators establish with them, anticipate what would later become an important tension in realist writing. Some realists of the 1880s and 1890s would define their task as bringing into focus the quotidian dimensions of middle-class experience in works featuring relatively sophisticated protagonists who bear some degree of conscious control over their lives. Other writers would be drawn toward depicting humans suffering in extreme situations, often in contexts far removed from average middle-class existence, because they believed these experiences of extremity came closest to touching the bedrock of reality, what writer Frank Norris would describe in 1903 as "the red, living heart of things" (*Literary Criticism* 75). We will return to this tension in

Chapter 7, when we discuss the term "naturalism," which some critics have found appropriate to designate the mode of realistic writing Norris represents. Our next chapter, however, explores some of the key literary techniques by which realist writers gave what Henry James called the "odour" of reality to their fictional creations.

Chapter 3

Creating the "odour" of the real: techniques of realism

Like other writing, realist literature consists at its most basic level of words on pages. The pages are usually bound into magazines or books (or, these days, reproduced on screens). When we read novels or stories, we generally do so sitting down or reclining in a physical space – a living room or bedroom, a café, an airplane – that bears little resemblance to the scene portrayed in the text we are reading. No matter whether we are reading in a bus full of noisy people or alone in bed, however, we will be unable fully to enter into the fictional narrative unless we can shut out the world around us, at least temporarily. In a more complex process, we also must simultaneously keep looking at but, in another sense, stop "seeing" what is literally in front of our eyes – the gray or black ink, the quality of the paper, our own thumbs as they hold the book open – in order to "see" instead the fictional world (the place, the people, the objects) the author uses those physical materials to evoke.

Among the differences that distinguish the fictional modes of literary realism, literary sentimentalism, and literary sensationalism from one another are the techniques that each employs to help the reader enter imaginatively into the worlds they create. Sensationalist works use, among other devices, a quick succession of dramatic, even shocking events with the aim of creating such bodily responses in the reader as shortened breath and a pounding pulse. Chapters frequently end on suspenseful notes to encourage the reader to quickly turn the next page. Sentimental literature strives to prompt strong emotional responses, often manifested in physical tears, as readers sympathize with characters' suffering. Realist writers certainly included both sentimental and sensational elements in their work, and they were by no means averse to provoking strong responses in readers. At the same time, however, realist authors such as William Dean Howells, Henry James, and Edith Wharton publicly defined their writing against these (in Howells's derisive term) "romanticistic" genres (see Chapter 1). If romanticistic fiction can appeal to readers' desires temporarily to escape their own quotidian existences for fantasized lives of passion, danger, and excitement, where good and evil are easily identifiable (and good usually prevails), realism has the burden of inviting readers into a world whose governing claim to their interest is to be as plausible, as actual, as the readers' own world.

The "air of reality"

How do realist works make readers feel as if they are gaining access to a "real" social and natural world, one that could exist within their own contemporary United States? How do writers cause what Henry James called "the odour" of the real to rise from their pages (*Essays* 52)? As literary realism's most sophisticated theorist, James understood very well that realism, like other representational forms, did not and could not provide readers with direct, unmediated entry into a tangible reality other than their own; words on a page do not literally open a window for readers to peer through or, for that matter, climb through into somebody else's house or life. Instead, as James insists in his famous essay "The Art of Fiction," literary realism's task is to give readers the "impression" of gaining such access, even as the readers in fact remain seated staring at a physical book (*Essays* 50). Writers should strive to evoke the "illusion of life" (*Essays* 53), the "atmosphere of authenticity" (149): the "air," the "sense," the "strange, irregular rhythm" of reality itself (53, 52, 58). In short, James recognized that literary realism was an art like any other. As such, it depended on the artist's imagination and, just as importantly, on artistic choices involving form, style, and technique. Realism differed from many other forms of art, however, in having as a central aim that readers should, at least for a time, forget a work's status as artifice, and feel themselves to be perceiving reality itself. As author Frank Norris put it in 1897, realist fiction "is what seems real, not what is real" (*Literary Criticism* 51). The rest of this chapter will explore different techniques that realist writers employed to achieve what James called "the sense of reality" (*Essays* 52). How is fiction that is inscribed on a written page made, in Norris's phrase, to *seem real*?

Henry James and Psychological Realism

Author Henry James shared with his older brother William a fascination with human consciousness and its complex modes of interacting with the world. William James became the United States' first professor of psychology (at Harvard), as well as a founding figure in the most influential school of American philosophy: Pragmatism. While William used science and methodical philosophic inquiry in his attempt to understand the mind's multiple ways of processing experience and reported his findings in scholarly and other non-fiction writing, Henry explored the workings of consciousness by writing creative fiction. His novels and short stories were produced over a long career stretching from the final year of the Civil War through the early years of the First World War, during which time he lived in the United States, France, and, ultimately, England. As his career went on, James's increasing commitment to depicting nuances of thought, perception, emotion, and meaning not only as experienced by a single person but also in the dynamics among two or more people led him to develop a unique writing style, which some readers love and others find off-putting. "Jamesian" style is marked by complex sentences that accumulate phrase upon phrase in an attempt to capture usually unspoken layers of thought and intuition. In the following example from *What Maisie Knew* (1897), a precocious young girl tries to connect with her awkwardly estranged father as he holds her on his lap: "If he had an idea at the back of his head she had also one in a recess as deep, and for a time, while they sat together, there was an extraordinary mute passage between her vision of this vision of his, his vision of her vision, and her vision of his vision of her vision" (525).

James's intense self-consciousness about his own creative process, as well as his unprecedented (at the time) insistence that novel writing should be recognized as an Art with a capital A, led him to produce a remarkable body of critical and theoretical writing about fictional forms and techniques. James expressed his theories about literary narrative, several of which are addressed in the current chapter, in widely circulated essays such as "The Art of Fiction" (1884), in twenty-three critical prefaces he wrote for the New York edition of his own collected works (1907–1909), and in innumerable reviews of other authors. His ideas still actively influence writers and critics, as well as the scholarly field of "narratology," which studies the structural elements of story-telling.

Solidity of specification

In "The Art of Fiction," Henry James names "solidity of specification" as "the supreme virtue of the novel – the merit on which all its other merits ... depend" (*Essays* 53). Concrete specifics, "truth of detail," help create a novel's air of reality (53). Such details might concern, among many other possibilities, the visual elements that contribute to a scene's setting; the physical objects that may or may not play a part in the action; the precise words characters speak to one another; and/or a given character's thoughts, emotions, or sensations, even if inchoate or contradictory. A realist writer's capacity for close observation is thus of cardinal importance. James urges that a would-be writer, as she moves through life, should "try to be one of the people on whom nothing is lost" (53). At the same time, however, an artist needs always to make choice about which details to include and which to exclude, as well as how details should be arranged and presented. Even a photograph must always be taken from a particular angle and focused in a specific manner, with some material included and some left out of its frame. The details involved in an apparently simple action, such as a woman crossing her room to open the door after hearing a knock, are theoretically infinite, as are the angles from which the action might be described in a literary text (including the point of view, for instance, of somebody listening from an apartment one story down). Even a so-called "slice of life," James emphasized in a later essay, cannot be conceived outside the artist's "question of where and how to cut it" (*Essays* 145, 144–45). For William Dean Howells, as well, the art of "realism becomes false to itself, when it heaps up facts merely" ("Editor's Study," 1886 973). Howells correctly points out that certain choices of inclusion, exclusion, and presentation are made "instinctively" by the artist. Regardless, such choices are unavoidable (973).

A well-known passage from Mark Twain's *Adventures of Huckleberry Finn* exemplifies how "solidity of specification" works to confer "the sense of reality" on a text. Huck, a young teenager, describes for readers the beginning of day viewed from a Mississippi River bank:

> The first thing to see, looking away over the water, was a kind of dull line – that was the woods on t'other side; you couldn't make nothing else out; then a pale place in the sky; then more paleness spreading around; then the river softened up away off, and warn't black any more, but gray; you could see little dark spots drifting along ever so far away – trading scows, and such things; and long black streaks – rafts; sometimes you could hear a sweep screaking … Then the nice breeze springs up, and comes fanning you from over there, so cool and fresh and sweet to smell on account of the woods and the flowers; but sometimes not that way, because they've left dead fish laying around, gars and such, and they do get pretty rank; and next you've got the full day.   (135–36)

It is the precisely observed "truth of detail" here that makes us feel as if Huck is genuinely looking at the scene he describes: the pale place in the sky that gradually spreads, the changing color and texture of the river as the light brightens, the "little dark spots" that Huck knows are rafts or trading scows, the precise sound the long oars make as they move, which Huck (in an act of onomatopoeia) invents the word "screaking" to try to capture. We can also recognize Twain's artistry in the selection and presentation of the details Huck notices. The passage includes such traditional literary devices as alliteration ("pale place"), assonance ("sweep screaking"), and anaphora ("then a ... then more ... then the ..."). The placement in the passage of the dead fish and their "rank" smell, however, is essential to the passage's realism. Just at the moment when Huck's description of the sunrise seems as if it might veer into familiar platitudes about fresh air and sweet flowers (and hence start to evoke literary conventions rather than unmediated reality), Twain has Huck introduce the jarring sensory detail of the smelly fish, further specified as "gars" (a bony freshwater species). The dead fish in this passage render vividly literal what Henry James meant by the "odour" of the real.

Certain realist writers further sought to achieve the air of reality by extending their use of "solidity of specification" to include real street addresses, names of actual local businesses and other landmarks, and casual references to real-life celebrities, politicians, or other well-known individuals. When Carrie Meeber of Theodore Dreiser's novel *Sister Carrie* (1900) sets out to look for a job, she enters a neighborhood full of factories, businesses, and street intersections that actually existed in 1880s Chicago, in which Dreiser had worked as a newspaper reporter. She looks longingly at shoes and jackets in The Fair, one of Chicago's first department stores, and eats lunch with the traveling salesman Drouet at the restaurant of the real Windsor Hotel, located at the corner of Washington and Dearborn streets. Dreiser goes so far as to provide dollars-and-cents prices on the menu Carrie looks at: "Half broiled spring chicken – seventy-five. Sirloin steak with mushrooms – one twenty-five" (42).

If one thinks further about precisely how a certain category of detail contributes to a text's achieving the aura of real life, what becomes interesting about the menu prices in *Sister Carrie* is that the actual numbers, in themselves, have no narrative function. It is not the case, for instance, that Drouet has less than two dollars to spend on his and Carrie's lunch, so that, when confronted with these specific prices, he is forced to order the chicken for them both even though she might prefer the steak – which could be a potentially meaningful moment for the tenor of their developing relationship. That Carrie habitually notes prices does tell us something about her character (as well as her need to watch pennies at this early point in her career). And of course the steak and chicken prices must remain within a certain range of historical plausibility. Still for the purposes of the plot, for conveying character, or even for suggesting the sort of restaurant the Windsor was in 1889 (the year in which Dreiser tells us the book is set), it would not matter if the chicken cost sixty-five cents, eighty-five cents, or even ninety cents. In other words, the precise content of the detail, the number itself, is less significant than the sheer fact that Dreiser provides it. The very presence of such specific prices in *Sister Carrie* connotes actuality, regardless of whether or not these prices are truly identical with those on the Windsor's 1889 menu. In and of itself, the dollars-and-cents price signifies concrete reality to the reader.

Influential narrative theorist Roland Barthes has pointed to the use of a similar sort of detail in the novels of such realists as the French writer Honoré de Balzac: details, that is, with no identifiable function in relation to the work's plot, its development of characters, or its use of narrative mechanisms such as foreshadowing. These details also appear to have no symbolic meanings or resonances in the larger context of the work (Barthes, *Rustle of Language* 141–48). Jonathan Culler has referred to such details as "descriptive residue" (Culler, *Structuralist Poetics* 193). Details whose *content* is more or less meaningless, Barthes argues, in fact play an important role in how Balzac achieves "l'effet de réel" in his novels – the effect of reality, often translated as "the reality effect." Reality itself is full of details that have no discernible meaning or significance for us; they simply exist in the background of our awareness. If nothing else, such details help us to feel grounded in a solid world with a full, independent existence outside of our own minds.

Realist stories, realist discourse

Narrative theorists distinguish between the events, objects, settings, and personages of a narrative, and the means by which this information is conveyed or "told" to a reader. A variety of different terms have been used for these two facets of narrative, but a useful pair of words when discussing realist fiction is *story* (*what* happens? *who* does it happen to?) and *discourse* (*how* is the reader made aware of the story?). The next section of this chapter will discuss discourse in realist fiction, but we begin here with story, the question of what sorts of plots and characters realists tended to choose for their works so as best to correlate with "our general sense of 'the way things happen'" (James, *French Writers* 1065).

Complaining in an 1890 *Harper's* "Editor's Study" column about the popularity of British fantasy and adventure writers H. Rider Haggard and Rudyard Kipling, Howells praised by contrast the plotting of a now-forgotten novel that, at the time, he considered a good example of realism, *Miss Brooks*, by Eliza Orne White: "Nothing happens; that is, nobody murders or debauches anybody else; there is no arson or pillage of any sort; there is not a ghost, or a ravening beast, or a hair-breadth escape, or a shipwreck, or a monster of self-sacrifice, or a lady five thousand years old in the whole course of the story" ("Editor's Study," 1890 804). Howells's use of the word "nothing" is purposefully ironic here. Although it would not be accurate to say that realist writers, including Howells, never incorporated into their fiction murders, mysteries, wrecks, narrow escapes, and so forth, American literary realism had as a key goal to uncover the interest, the suspense, the drama in moments that others might think of as uneventful or boring – those times when it only *appears* to those looking for obviously spectacular events that "nothing happens."[1]

Henry James, for instance, judged as "obviously the best thing" in his 1881 novel *The Portrait of a Lady* his portrayal of a night during which protagonist Isabel stays up late pursuing a complex train of thought (*French Writers* 1084). Her late-night meditation has been provoked by an only momentary glimpse she had earlier in the day of her husband Gilbert Osmond lounging casually in a chair and gazing steadily but silently at their mutual friend Madame Merle, who looked back at him from her standing position several feet away. As she ponders the glimpse hours later, Isabel is not approached by another person, nor does she stir from her chair – and in fact she reaches no definitive conclusions; this is merely her first clue that her husband shares a deep and private bond with Madame Merle. Still, in re-reading his book many years later, James believes that he has succeeded in making Isabel's act of "motionlessly *seeing*" as "'interesting' as the surprise of a caravan or the identification of a pirate" would be to readers of an adventure book (1084). Even a story such as Stephen Crane's "The Open Boat" (1897) about four men trying to survive a shipwreck on the open sea – a potentially sensationalistic event that most readers had not experienced in their own lives – focuses mostly on the repetitive conversations and tense but monotonous routines the men fall into as they try to stay afloat. The close of the story, in which the boat falls apart, one man drowns, and the other three manage to swim ashore through rough surf, is portrayed only very briefly and in the same matter-of-fact tone that characterizes the rest of the story.[2]

As is usually true for episodes in real life, in most cases the endings of realist fictions avoid the dramatic closure common to other fictional genres. Realist Hamlin Garland mocked romantic novels in which, "The brave youth always succeeds; the pure girl secures the approbation of heaven; the immoral are miraculously changed by the power of some good woman. The drunkard keeps his pledge; the villain dies endowing an orphan asylum." Such endings, Garland insists, are "contrary to life as a matter of common observation" ("Productive Conditions" 156). Opposing false idealizations of life, the realist story does not always, as Garland puts it, "round out" right (156). James's *The Portrait of a Lady* closes with Isabel on a train returning from England to Rome, but it is unclear what she will or can do about her unhappy marriage once she arrives there. Charles Chesnutt's *The Marrow of Tradition* (1901) leaves open whether an African-American doctor who survives a brutal race riot in a North Carolina town will be able to save the dying son of a leading white supremacist and, if the doctor does manage to save the boy (he is on his way up the stairs when the book stops), whether that will change anything either in the segregated town or in his own life. Even when something that would seem like closure does occur at the end of a realist novel – such as the deaths of the main characters in novels by Edith Wharton and Kate Chopin of a drug overdose and drowning (respectively) – the meaning and implications of the seemingly decisive event are left ambiguous. In both Wharton's *The House of Mirth* (1905) and Chopin's *The Awakening* (1899) it remains uncertain whether we should understand the protagonist's death as an accident or as a suicide.

The ambiguity surrounding the deaths of Wharton's Lily Bart and of Chopin's Edna Pontellier also points to the attribute most critical to literary realism's portrayal of character: realist characters should possess what Howells called "the God-given complexity of motive which we find in all the human beings we know" ("Editor's Study," 1886 972). For Howells, the styles of characterization found in "romance" genres of fiction – including domestic sentimentality, sensationalism, and historical romance – derived from the tradition of allegory, in which figures are personifications of abstract qualities such as "charity," "faith," or "sin," and are often named accordingly. Characters in romance novels "are apt to be ... limited to the expression of one principle, simple, elemental" ("Editor's Study," 1886 972). Equally as important as the creation of complex characters, characters whose motives are often mixed and whose actions and reactions are not always predictable, realist writers should leave the evaluation of their characters, as well as the interpretation of larger meanings in a work, as much as possible to readers themselves. As a realist writer, one's task is to disappear behind the elements that compose one's story. "The facts, the characters, and conditions" of a realist story should not be visibly "operated" by the author (Howells, "Editor's Study," 1890 801). It should seem, Howells asserted, as if all of these have been "let appear, not made appear" by the writer (801). "The business of the novelist," Howells added in a later essay, "is to put certain characters before you, and keep them before you, with as little of the author apparent as possible" (*Selected Literary Criticism II* 283). Writer Frank Norris agreed: "The more remote his [the author's] isolation, the more real will appear the things and people of which he treats, the more will his story seem to have a life of its own" (*Literary Criticism* 55). Yet, as Howells, Norris, and other realists also understood (though not always as consciously and consistently as

Henry James did), conveying an effect of objectivity, neutrality, transparency is no simple thing in the practical presentation of a fictional story, all of whose elements, after all, are actually chosen by the writer.

If Howells insists that "it is no part of the author's business to be other than the colorless medium through which the reader clearly sees," that "colorless medium" must still be created by words on a page – in other words, by discourse ("Editor's Study," 1890 804). How to present the story so that it arrives to the reader *as if* coming through a colorless medium remains very much "the author's business" ("Editor's Study," 1890 804).

Direct quotation: letting characters speak for themselves

Realists made extensive use of what James called the "scenic method," in which information, events, and characters' personalities are conveyed primarily through dialogue, allowing a novel's authorial or narrative voice to rest quietly in the background. Although realist novels and short stories are not as strongly devoted to dialogue as dramatic scripts, realist fiction includes a noticeably higher proportion of characters' speech, on average, than did earlier fiction by American writers such as Hawthorne and Melville. It is not a coincidence that many leading realists also wrote for the theater. Conversation in realist fiction, rather than serving as a medium for the exchange of abstract ideas (as in the ancient tradition of philosophical dialogues, for instance), reveals and develops character. Above all, speech becomes a form of action: insinuations are planted, gossip is circulated, intimacies are developed, conflicts are pursued (explicitly or implicitly), feelings and positions are felt out, lies are told, secrets are revealed, threats are conveyed, proposals and promises are made, decisions are not only reached but implemented. Some of the most violent moments in realist fiction occur through dialogue, as in Wharton's *The House of Mirth* (1905), when the socially powerful Bertha Dorset says in parting conversation with other guests after a dinner party, "Miss Bart is not going back to the yacht" (227). Though it might seem an unadorned statement of information, in context this nine-word sentence conveys Bertha's accusation, in front of the assembled guests, that Lily Bart is trying to steal her wealthy husband. Bertha herself knows the accusation is false, but the comment, which she delivers in a "voice of singular distinctness" (227), functions nonetheless as a dramatic action: a ruthless move by which Bertha, scapegoating Lily, seeks to retain her own secure economic and social status. The seemingly innocuous piece of dialogue carries a direct and painful blow: it ensures Lily's social ostracism and her disinheritance by her aunt, events which culminate in her death.

Linguists and narrative theorists use the term "direct discourse" for the technique of displaying speech to a reader via direct quotation (instead of using, for instance, summary or paraphrase). Generally appearing within quotation marks, direct discourse allows readers to feel as if they are themselves overhearing a conversation, rather than having characters' words pre-sifted or paraphrased for them. Indeed, for many realist writers it was important that readers not only "hear" the words their characters say, but also receive at least some sense of what the characters *sound* like. In the extended quotation from *Huckleberry Finn* above, the vernacular language that Twain puts in Huck's mouth contributes strongly to the passage's achieving what Henry James referred to as the "very note" of real life (*Essays* 58). Huck says "warn't" for "wasn't" and "laying around" instead of the technically correct "lying around." He uses a double negative, "couldn't make nothing else out," which standard English frowns on but which is entirely plausible for a young Southern boy with little formal education. As Chapter 5's discussion of dialect in literary regionalism (also called local color) will explore in more depth, portraying with an aura of authenticity the wide variety of syntax, pronunciation, idioms, and diction characteristic of diverse Americans' actual speech was an important priority for writers associated with realism. But even works not primarily identified with regionalism employed devices ranging from non-standard spelling in direct discourse (for example, "ah'm" for "I am" and "mawning" for "morning" in the mouth of one of Howells's Southern characters) to descriptions of a voice's aural qualities: a character in *The Rise of Silas Lapham* "had a slow, quaint way of talking, that seemed a pleasant personal modification of some ancestral Yankee drawl, and her voice was low and cozy, and so far from being nasal that it was a little hoarse" (Howells, *Hazard* 113, *Silas* 37).

Omniscient vs. point-of-view narration

Mark Twain used his character Huck as the first-person narrator of *Adventures of Huckleberry Finn*, which today is the most widely read of all late-nineteenth- and early-twentieth-century works of American literary realism. A first-person narrator such as Huck, who is also a character in the story, represents one effective technique by which an author can attempt to vanish behind the "reality" he sets out to present to the reader: the entirety of *Huckleberry Finn*'s story is not only told in Huck's voice, but also filtered through his vision. We never see directly any scenes or events other than those Huck personally witnesses. Nor does the reader learn thoughts, from the inside, of any character besides Huck.

Although many realist writers experimented with first-person narration in the decades after the Civil War, most ultimately opted against it as too limiting (as Twain himself decided for several others of his fictional works). In a realist text, first-person form restricts a work's narration to the vocabulary and sentence structures that the fictional character serving as narrator would plausibly use. Moreover, no visual or other details can be relayed to the reader that the character herself does not attend to, even when such details might fall within the character's line of vision. For example, a first-person narrator who, as a character, has little interest in how others dress presents a significant challenge to an author who wants readers to possess such information. Wishing to avoid these limitations, realist writers flexibly combine various modes of narration in their works, including the "direct discourse" of quoted dialogue and different varieties of third-person narration.

Realist writers often shift back and forth between several varieties of third-person narration within a single chapter, or sometimes even a single paragraph. In realist fiction, the most characteristic version of third-person narration is "limited" narration, followed closely by "omniscient" narration. Omniscient means "all-knowing." An omniscient narrator has the ability to know things that no single character does. Such a narrator knows from the start how the story will turn out. She can know about "off-stage" occurrences, outside of a character's own knowledge, that may be significant for that character. She has the option of describing a scene from a position above it, or from any other angle, and thus including details in her description that characters themselves might miss. To the omniscient narrator, all characters' thoughts, motives, and feelings are accessible – which doesn't mean she will choose immediately (or for that matter ever) to share such information with readers. Given such a narrator's ability to move effortlessly through space, time, and the individual boundaries of characters, third-person omniscient narration can serve as an effective strategy for achieving that effect of objectivity, of a story and its characters seeming to reach readers through a "colorless" medium, for which Howells urged American realists to strive.

As an example of omniscient narration, the following passage from Wharton's *The House of Mirth* begins by conveying Lily Bart's thoughtless and somewhat arrogant opinions about two of her female cousins, and then comments on the degree to which Lily's opinions match (or in this case fail to match) reality:

> [Lily] knew that Gerty Farish admired her blindly, and therefore supposed that she inspired the same sentiments in Grace Stepney, whom

> she classified as a Gerty Farish without the saving traits of youth and enthusiasm. In reality, the two differed from each other as much as they differed from the object of their mutual contemplation. Miss Farish's heart was a fountain of tender illusions, Miss Stepney's a precise register of facts as manifested in their relation to herself. She had sensibilities which, to Lily, would have seemed comic in a person with a freckled nose and red eyelids ... But poor Grace's limitations gave [her sensibilities] a more concentrated inner life, as poor soil starves certain plants into intenser efflorescence. She had in truth no abstract propensity to malice: she did not dislike Lily because the latter was brilliant and predominant, but because she thought that Lily disliked her. It is less mortifying to believe one's self unpopular than insignificant, and vanity prefers to assume that indifference is a latent form of unfriendliness.   (128)

Immediately after sharing Lily's inner perspective with us – Lily's false assumption that Grace Stepney admires her blindly, her misguided lumping of her two cousins together in her mind – the narrator states the "reality" Lily fails to grasp. The narrator's omniscience allows her to penetrate the "heart[s]" not only of Lily, but also of both cousins. Gerty, the narrator informs us, is full of tender illusions about Lily, while by contrast Grace quietly stores up "facts" that bear on herself. To convey the intensity of the feelings Grace develops along with her perception that Lily dislikes her, the narrator supplies an elaborate botanical simile unavailable to the characters. But we the readers learn immediately that even the precision of Grace's "facts" does not go as deep as the "truth" accessible to the narrator: Lily does not pay enough attention to Grace even to dislike her. The narrator then concludes the passage with a pithy and rather abstract insight about human nature.

Wharton's text provides readers with no reason to doubt either the accuracy or the neutrality of the narrator's assessments here. The dispassionate tone of the passage, as well as that none of the three characters appears to possess the narrator's full respect or sympathy, heightens the impression of objectivity. Yet if the high degree of omniscience – this narrative voice comes across as completely "all-knowing" – allows us to feel that we are accessing actual truths about the inner selves of these three women, it also creates a sense of distance. We may be gaining a portion of the characters' inner reality, which even they do not fully recognize, but access to this "truth" comes at the expense of any feeling of intimacy with Lily or with either of the other women. The omniscient narrative illuminates for us at least some of what all three cousins think and feel in regard to each other, and the reader no doubt accepts the information as valid, but we are not placed in a position really to inhabit either Lily's, Gerty's, or Grace's perceptions and mental processes – to experience the texture, as it were, of the character's consciousness by seeing through her eyes.

Most works of literary realism include stretches both of third-person omniscience and of dialogue in quotation marks. But realism's most characteristic style of "telling" readers *what* happens, and *who* is involved, in a given story is third-person limited narration, also called point-of-view or character-focalized narration. As with first-person narration, readers view a scene as it is filtered through one character's eyes and are privy to that character's inner responses. By contrast with first-person narration, however, the author retains the option of expressing whatever that character sees and thinks in language (vocabulary, syntax, figurative comparisons) the character himself might not employ. In other words, the *voice* conveying perceptions from the focalizing character's point of view is not restricted to the character's own linguistic habits. For instance, in Chopin's *The Awakening*, protagonist Edna Pontellier first enters the reader's horizon from the point of view of Mr. Pontellier, Edna's husband:

> Mr. Pontellier finally lit a cigar and began to smoke, letting the paper drag idly from his hand. He fixed his gaze upon a white sunshade that was advancing at a snail's pace from the beach. He could see it plainly between the gaunt trunks of the water-oaks and across the stretch of yellow camomile. The gulf looked far away, melting hazily into the blue of the horizon. The sunshade continued to approach slowly. Beneath its pink-lined shelter were his wife, Mrs. Pontellier, and young Robert Lebrun. (4)

With Mr. Pontellier, we view the approach of the sunshade as it moves slowly toward him from the beach, across a field of yellow flowers, finally reaching the veranda on which he is sitting. Not until the sunshade gets close enough for him to recognize the figures walking under it do those figures come into focus for us. At the same time, Mr. Pontellier may or may not consciously notice that the advancing sunshade is "pink-lined"; regardless, the narrator points it out to us. Similarly, the adjective "gaunt," the adverbs "idly" and "hazily," the participle "melting" – these specific words probably do not enter Mr. Pontellier's own mind at the moment, but they help the narrator effectively to paint for readers what Mr. Pontellier sees, as well as convey something of his mellow mood.

Free-indirect discourse

Perhaps the most nuanced mode of narration available to realist writers is a variant of point-of-view that narrative theorists call "free-indirect discourse."

Jane Austen did most to develop free-indirect discourse for English-language fiction early in the nineteenth century, and the French writer Gustave Flaubert advanced the mode still further in the middle of the century. Not coincidentally, both Austen and Flaubert were deeply admired by late-nineteenth-century American realist writers. Free-indirect discourse hovers between the first and third persons as it conveys characters' thoughts and feelings. It employs third-person syntax (e.g., "he" and "she," instead of the first-person "I"), as well as the past tense, but it articulates thoughts with the present-tense first person's immediacy, directness, and diction. In Stephen Crane's *The Red Badge of Courage*, private Henry Fleming feels anxiety as he marches toward his first battle:

> The swift thought came to him that the generals did not know what they were about. It was all a trap. Suddenly those close forests would bristle with rifle barrels. Ironlike brigades would appear in the rear. They were all going to be sacrificed. The generals were stupids. The enemy would presently swallow the whole command. He glared about him, expecting to see the stealthy approach of his death.   (19)

Free-indirect discourse kicks in with the excerpt's second short sentence. Except for the past tense of "was," the sentence could easily have formed itself inside Henry's mind ("It's all a trap"). Free-indirect discourse blurs the third-person narrator's perspective with that of Henry. In the short sentence, "The generals were stupids," even the narrator's diction is infiltrated by Henry's own colloquial wording: "stupids" as a plural noun comes not from the narrator's vocabulary but from Henry's own inner verbalization of his thoughts. It is as if the character's moment-by-moment thoughts temporarily assume partial control of the narrator's voice, which remains visible only in the continued use of the past tense ("the generals *were* stupids").

Note that the first and last sentences of the quoted excerpt employ a more standard form of third-person limited (point-of-view) narration, in which the narrator tells us what is going on inside of Henry's head, rather than allowing Henry's thoughts to speak, as it were, for themselves. Such fluid shifts among narrative modes are common in realist fiction, although in most cases the reader, by design, does not consciously notice the shifts as they occur. Realist writers move among omniscient narration, standard third-person limited narration, free-indirect discourse, and directly quoted dialogue in much the same way as, in a standard Hollywood drama, the camera fluidly changes its position, angle, and distance. Both the camera's movement and the subsequent editing of such a film aim to provide viewers with all of the story-related information that the director wishes, but without ever calling attention to the camera's presence and thus breaking the illusion of reality. Similarly, the flexibility of narrative mode in American realist fiction works to create the effect of a free-standing reality that seems to be, in Howells's words, "let appear, not made appear."

Narrator as imperfect historian

In a famous passage, Henry James complains that the British novelist Anthony Trollope "took a suicidal satisfaction in reminding the reader that the story he was telling was only, after all, a make-believe" (*Essays* 1343). Trollope, James explains elsewhere, has a habit of admitting, "in a digression, a parenthesis or an aside" – within his fictional works themselves – that "the events he narrates have not really happened, and that he can give his narrative any turn the reader may like best" (*Essays* 46). For James, Trollope's "terrible crime" betrays an essential tenet of literary realism: fictional events should always be presented to readers as if they have indeed "really happened." (46). The point is not literally to perpetuate a hoax on readers, to deceive them into taking a fictional work about fictional people as belonging to a non-fiction genre, such as journalism, history, or biography. The external scaffolding – what narrative theorists call the "paratext" – of a late-nineteenth- or early-twentieth-century novel routinely identifies its status as a work of fiction: a title or blurb that uses the word "novel"; a list of the author's previous fictional works; an introduction or preface in which an author (or somebody else) discusses the intentions, ingredients, or creative process involved in the work's production. In more recent works, of course, we find a legal notice on the copyright page assuring all and sundry that the characters in the work are imaginary. But it is part of literary realism's meaning as a genre that a story's actual status as "a make-believe" should not be admitted within the space of the story's narration. As we have already seen in this chapter, American realist writers go to great lengths to try to ensure that the characters and events they write about will be experienced, by readers while reading, as having an autonomous reality, separate from the act of story-telling.

The narrative techniques we have been discussing aim to achieve Howells's "colorless medium," in which the narrator – for that matter the very fact that a story is being told (rather than directly witnessed) – is made as unobtrusive as possible for readers. In free-indirect discourse, the narrative voice virtually disappears as it is taken over by a character's feelings, thoughts, and sometimes language. During direct dialogue, the narrator does disappear, visible only perhaps in the quotation marks and paragraphing conventions she adds to the characters' words. Omniscient narration, for its part, gives the narrator such an elevated and penetrating perspective that readers tend not to conceptualize the narrator as a person telling a story. At times, however, a third-person narrator will step out of the shadows in order to underline specific features of the event or characters that help to confirm their status as real. A common gesture in realist fiction, for example, is explicitly to call the reader's attention to how a turn of events or a character's behavior deviate from what literary conventions may have led readers to expect or perhaps even desire.

For instance, in John W. De Forest's 1867 novel *Miss Ravenel's Conversion from Secession to Loyalty* (frequently considered a transitional work of American literary realism; see Chapter 2), the third-person omniscient narrator makes the following remark upon an encounter between two characters who, three hundred pages later, will fall in love and marry:

> Of course it would be agreeable to have a scene here between Colburne and Miss Ravenel; some burning words to tell, some thrilling looks to describe … [But] they met like a young lady and gentleman who were on excellent terms and had not seen each other for a month or two. This is not the way that heroes and heroines meet on the boards [i.e., the theater] or in some romances; but in actual human society they frequently balk our expectations in just this manner. Melodramatically considered, real life is frequently a failure.   (133)

De Forest's narrator strategically blames the balking of readers' expectations on real life itself. He would have liked to provide us with a more dramatic or even melodramatic scene, but in a realist text even an omniscient narrator is not all-powerful because "actual human society" will frequently fail to seem thrilling in the old conventional ways. In calling explicit attention to how his characters *fail* to behave in the more exciting manner fictional characters are supposed to behave, a realist writer can give his fictional characters an increased dimension of authenticity.

Paradoxically, a narrator who calls explicit attention to gaps in his own omniscience can add still more to the effect of reality a work achieves for its fictional events and characters. For James, a fiction writer should never let down the presumption that the events he relates are as factual as (if often more intimate than) anything a non-fiction writer might conceivably record for the public. He praised Balzac as a vastly imaginative fiction writer who managed never to surrender the stance, within his novels, of an historian of the actual, a reporter who informs his audience about an ostensibly free-standing world with its own independent reality: "The situation, the person, the place, the motive exposed, the speech reported – these things were in his view history, with the absoluteness and the dignity of history" (*French Writers* 110). In his own fiction, James employed several tactics for sustaining the bluff, for not allowing "the tone of the historian" to "give itself away, as they say in California" as a fictitious effect, a card trick (*Essays* 46). One of these tactics was to emphasize the gaps and absences in his own knowledge of the events that he as historian was ostensibly relating.

James expressed frequently his preference for using, in his own work, character-focalized narration, where the reader's experience is filtered through the intricacies of a character's consciousness. Critics have correctly observed that James uses this device in part to help conceal, or at least make as unobtrusive as possible, the narrator's presence as a story-telling entity. (Another advantage for a psychological realist such as James is that filtering events through a character's consciousness can illuminate the underlying psychological dynamics shaping that particular character's processes of perception.) Often overlooked, however, is that at moments James's third-person narrators will step forward and speak directly to the reader. When the largely third-person narrator of *The Portrait of a Lady* (1881) uncharacteristically employs the first person to inform us directly, "I know not whether it was on this occasion or on some other" that a particular discussion between Madame Merle and Isabel Archer occurred, or when that narrator states apologetically that "no report has remained" of what exactly Isabel said to her sister to prompt a particular remark by the sister to the sister's husband, the narrator's conscientious foregrounding of his own areas of ignorance, no matter how inconsequential they may seem, serves a distinct purpose (221, 389). By bringing periodically to our attention the difference between what his characters actually did and said and his own not-quite complete, not-quite omniscient, knowledge of those actions and statements, the ostensible "historian" confirms the independent reality of the people and events to which he, like all historians of reality, can only ever have imperfect access. As with the other techniques of realism this chapter has surveyed, well-placed narrative admissions of failure play their part in a writer's achieving "the air of reality" for his or her creation made of words.

Chapter 4

Conflicting manners: high realism and social competition

Speaking at an influential and portentously named "Conference on the Heritage of the English-speaking Peoples and Their Responsibility," hosted by Kenyon College in 1947, literary critic Lionel Trilling tried to explain a term that he believed was "nearly indefinable" but nonetheless fundamental to any attempt at articulating the identity of a nation or people. "Manners," Trilling asserted, should not be understood as synonymous with the rules of politeness, which can be written down and mastered. Nor are manners equivalent to easily identifiable customs or any other "highly formulated departments of culture," such as morals ("Manners, Morals, and the Novel" 11–12). Rather, the term manners refers to "what never gets fully stated" but instead constitutes "a culture's hum and buzz of implication." Manners are the "evanescent context of [a culture's] explicit statements." Insofar as manners consist of "that part of a culture which is made up of half-uttered or unuttered or unutterable expressions of value," they reveal truths about the inner workings of a culture that are inaccessible if one reads only official documents or standard histories. Manners, Trilling continued, are indicated by "small actions," such as the posture and bearing of a waiter while he is putting down a plate on a customer's table. They include such subtleties as "the tone of greetings and the tone of quarrels" in a given culture, as well as "slang and humor," "the arts of dress or decoration," and even "the way children play" and "the nature of the very food we prefer" (12).

   As no doubt seemed appropriate for a conference held at a moment just after one war had ended (the Second World War) and another was beginning (the Cold War), Trilling's speech initially asserted that manners "are the things that for good or bad draw the people of a culture together and that separate them from the people of another culture." Trilling's wording here may have appeared to suggest a jingoistic vision of "English-speaking" culture as homogeneous, unique, and in some sense opposed to non-English-speaking cultures (the Germans? the Russians?). But he immediately went on to complicate things by adding, "in any complex culture there is not a single system of manners but a conflicting variety of manners." He continued, "what we mean by a culture is the adjustment of this conflict." Turning to literature, whose relation to "manners" he had in fact been invited to address, Trilling went on to argue that both "conflict" and attempted "adjustment" between differing sets of socio-cultural manners have been a key focus for the novel, ever since its founding as a literary form.

In support of Trilling's argument, literary historians have long identified the rise of the novel in eighteenth- and nineteenth-century Europe with challenges posed by the rising middle classes to the social, economic, and political domination by the hereditary aristocracy (e.g., Watt, *Rise of the Novel* 48–49). Yet, true as Trilling's claim about conflicting manners may be as regards the general history of the novel, the claim has special relevance to the United States, and especially to American literary realism. As we have already seen in previous chapters and will continue to explore throughout this book, the United States underwent massive changes with unprecedented rapidity in the decades after the Civil War. These changes occurred along a wide variety of fronts: industrial and economic, social and cultural, demographic, and even geographic as borders expanded and the nation acquired its first overseas territories. The nation was altering so rapidly that to many it seemed to have lost whatever sense of coherent identity it might once have had.

Manners, in the sense Trilling uses the term, have always constituted a remarkably sensitive register of social developments and conflicts, not only as manners shift with changing times but also when, as is often the case, some people cling to traditional manners as a point of stability in an evolving (or, as it may seem to them, a dissolving) world. People's contestations of and negotiations over social change are frequently experienced at the most profound personal level as conflicts and tensions regarding what counts as "proper," or even acceptable manners at a given time and place. American literary realism took as its mission to represent the *texture* of the sometimes barely comprehensible and often deeply disruptive changes the nation was undergoing during the period. Realist writers generally eschewed violent physical clashes and shocking plot twists as more proper to cheap sensationalist writing. Instead, their favored technique for conveying the texture of change – and the feelings of friction change brings – was to focus on manners in conflict.

As future chapters will demonstrate, a wide variety of American realist writing depicted conflicts about manners – in the broad meaning of the term manners that Trilling develops – as a means of representing social and economic tensions between the leisure classes and working classes, between city dwellers and rural inhabitants, between men and women, and between immigrant and "native-born" Americans. In addition, works of literary realism explored conflicting manners not only between but also *within* social groupings, and even within discrete individuals. In Jewish-American writer Abraham Cahan's *The Rise of David Levinsky* (1917), for example, immigrant protagonist and first-person narrator David finds work as a traveling salesman in the swiftly modernizing garment industry. He sells mass-produced versions of women's clothing "copied" from "high-class designer[s]" – in other words, what we would today call fashion knock-offs (443). David remains painfully conscious of the "Talmud gesticulations" he has brought with him from the old country, especially when he is speaking with buyers for large American stores (327). Typifying what Trilling means by "manners," these vigorous hand motions, along with the swaying, bobbing motion traditionally used when reading the Jewish Talmud, became second nature to David during his intensive early training to become a religious scholar. They conflict, however, with the more reserved style that he finds among American businessmen. David tells us (narrating from a time many years later) that whenever he engaged in energetic business conversations during his first years on the road his gesticulations were "a habit that worried me like a physical defect. It was so distressingly un-American. I struggled hard against it. I had made efforts to speak with my hands in my pockets; I had devised other means ... All of no avail" (327). As a realist author, Cahan stresses David's inner experience of manners in conflict because it so viscerally captures not only the immigrant character's personal struggles as he moves from a non-English-speaking pre-modern community to the capitalist United States, but also America's own changing population, its shifting business models, and its increasingly complex cultural identity.

Manners and cultural prestige

As with *The Rise of David Levinsky*, virtually all works of American realist fiction might, strictly speaking, be viewed as novels (or short stories) of manners in conflict. Scholars tend to use the term "novel of manners" most frequently, however, in reference to works whose stories focus on the same social groupings that constituted realism's primary reading audience: that is, the predominantly Anglo middle, upper-middle and upper classes. A related term used by scholars, "high realism," further connotes novels whose authors were perceived by their late-nineteenth- and early-twentieth-century audiences as sophisticated cosmopolitans, with personal knowledge not only of US but of Western European cultures and traditions (particularly French, Italian, and English). High realism's leading practitioners, who included William Dean Howells, Henry James, and Edith Wharton, spent substantial time living in Europe, and each published non-fiction books about the people, culture, art, and architecture they encountered there, as well as incorporating European settings and references into their fiction. These "high realists" strove to produce realist fiction that was Art with a capital A. They self-consciously focused their artistic efforts not only on the characters and social terrain whose reality they were trying to evoke, but also on matters of literary form, style, and language.

High realists' public image as serious Artists with cosmopolitan sophistication was produced not only by their actual writing (which would often casually display, for example, their authors' fluent knowledge of French or Italian), but also by the elite magazines in which their fiction was usually published before being released in book form. Periodicals such as the *Atlantic Monthly* and the *Century* claimed an elevated cultural position, one that their publishers implicitly (and sometimes explicitly) paralleled with other prestigious cultural institutions, such as the symphony halls, opera houses, and fine art museums that became increasingly prominent in large American cities after the Civil War (Glazener, *Reading for Realism* 22–36). The founders of these impressive institutions intended them, at least in part, to help reinforce a division between "high" cultural forms, embraced by the educated upper classes, and supposedly "lower" forms of cultural expression popular among the "masses," including vaudeville theaters, popular music generated in New York's "Tin Pan Alley," and mass-produced chromolithographs. Widely available, indeed sometimes given away in advertising promotions, "chromos" were color reproductions of natural and other scenes; they were frequently used as home decorations among people who could not afford original oil paintings and who, according to many upper-class observers, would not have appreciated the difference anyway.

Drawing a firm line between "higher" and "lower" cultural forms was more than a neutral gesture of aesthetic evaluation. It also allowed members of the economically comfortable classes to claim intrinsic superiority of judgment, which helped them to justify not only their wealth but also their ongoing social authority in the hanging nation. For the most part Henry James and Edith Wharton, who were raised among the nation's East Coast elite, supported the social and cultural authority of established white upper-class Americans over the nation's working classes and people of color – which isn't to say that James's and Wharton's fiction does not sometimes raise questions about or even undercut that authority. By contrast, William Dean Howells grew up in an Ohio family that struggled economically. His political philosophy, especially during the middle portion of his career, verged on socialism. Both in his temperament and in his everyday practices, however, Howells tended to accept class, racial, and ethnic hierarchies, as well as the privileges of upper-middle-class existence. (Howells himself was keenly aware of the contradictions between his political beliefs and his own daily choices; see Chapter 6.) Even leaving aside these authors' individual political beliefs, their devotion to prestigious publishing institutions as well as their writerly choices involving vocabulary, prose style, and the use of cultural allusions, aligned their version of realism far more with the cultural orientation of well-educated members of the middle and upper classes than with the working classes and the poor.

As we will return to in subsequent chapters, labor strife, public demonstrations by the unemployed, and other manifestations of inter-class conflict were frequent occurrences in the latter decades of the nineteenth century and caused anxiety and concern, even fear, among the middle and upper classes. However, "high" realist works tend to keep the lower classes, as well as tensions between them and other classes, outside of their literary purview. Works by Howells, James, and Wharton include only a very small proportion of characters whose socioeconomic position falls below the middle class. Although there are exceptions, when cross-class interaction does occur in these texts, such as that between employers and their workers or servants, it tends to happen in the background or else entirely out of the reader's sight.[1] High realist fiction, it is fair to say, implies the social and cultural preeminence of the economically comfortable classes and, by the same token, the relative unimportance of the working classes and the poor, in large part by pushing the latter to the edge of (or off) the page. At the same time, of course, working people's labor remains essential to the comforts of the classes above them in the social hierarchy – a truth these works do sometimes render manifest if one reads them carefully enough. Even so, open tension between members of the nation's economically comfortable classes and those Americans whom Jacob Riis referred to as "the other half" hardly ever appears in high realist fiction.

Instead, tension frequently emerges among new and old members of the upper classes. Regardless of the sometimes quite different stories, characters, and thematic concerns highlighted by individual texts, novels by high realist writers often exhibit one feature in common: they depict *intra-class* competitions over prestige and social status among the economically comfortable. In numerous works by Wharton, James, Howells, and other authors writing in the high-realist mode, Americans of the established upper classes strive to protect the exclusivity of their elevated positions in society from characters who represent the "new rich" – the latter, in many cases, having accumulated even more money than is possessed by characters whose wealth is of older standing. Despite (and in many ways because of) the new rich's rapidly increasing economic power, members of the longer-established upper classes endeavor in these works to maintain their own monopoly on the power to decide which forms of cultural expression, as well as what kinds of "manners," will be broadly regarded as most proper and authoritative, even by lower-class Americans who do not themselves adopt them.

Historically speaking, during the late nineteenth century the number of millionaires in the United States increased from only a few hundred in 1860 to 4,500 by 1900 (Phillips, *Wealth and Democracy* 37). This increase played a major role in the growing gap between the nation's upper and its lower classes. Emphasizing the increased public visibility of millionaires (and would-be millionaires), historians often refer to the period as the Gilded Age, a phrase borrowed from the title of a satiric novel co-written by Mark Twain and Charles Dudley Warner in 1873. While the wealth of the established rich was often lodged in real estate (sometimes including slum tenements) and other investments, the Gilded Age's new rich derived their money from such booming sectors of the modern economy as energy, transportation, and the mass production of consumer goods, and they often hailed from the Midwest and other locations outside of the Eastern seaboard cities of Boston, New York, and Philadelphia. America's established upper classes found they had no choice but to share their traditional economic predominance with others who had been able to take advantage of the swiftly changing US economy to achieve material success – in some cases, enormous success. In this context manners, those subtle, often unspoken codes of behavior and value, became critically important to the old rich's attempts to maintain their cultural authority and exclusive social status. In Henry James's first popular success, "Daisy Miller" (1878), Mrs. Costello, "a person of much distinction" among old-money inhabitants of New York City, attempts to teach the art of drawing such distinctions to her nephew Mr. Winterbourne, who has lived in Europe for most of his life (250). She tells him that the very fact Daisy Miller – a pretty and well-dressed American girl he has met in the garden of the expensive Swiss hotel where they are all guests – was so friendly to him without a formal introduction proves first and foremost that she and her family are "the sort of Americans that one does one's duty by not – not accepting," despite the millions Daisy's father has made in the upstate industrial town of Schenectady. When pressed by Winterbourne to allow him to introduce Daisy to her, Mrs. Costello insists that her "duty" to maintain the standards of elite American society prevents her from consenting: "I can't, my dear Frederick. I would if I could, but I can't" (250). Firmly drawing such lines, Mrs. Costello believes, is yet more important when Americans are traveling abroad, so that "observant Europeans" are reminded of the "great truth" that *some* Americans wealthy enough to take extended overseas vacations are socially superior to *other* Americans with the same or even greater material resources (287).

Unlike European nations, the United States has never possessed a hereditary nobility, in which formal aristocratic titles are passed down within families and carry significant public status in themselves, in addition to whatever wealth or property might accompany them. During America's Gilded Age, the lack of an official aristocratic hierarchy with ranked titles and positions often had the ironic effect of exacerbating social anxieties among both the new and the old rich. Such anxieties were played out on the ground of "manners." As a form of literature defined by its careful, focused attention to the everyday details of modern American life, as well as to individuals' inner experiences of their daily lives, realist fiction was uniquely well situated to probe the often very subtle dynamics involved in questions of social status among contemporary Americans. In Howells's *The Rise of Silas Lapham* (1885), for example, Persis, wife of the uneducated former farmer but now millionaire Silas Lapham – Silas is publicly known as the "mineral paint man" for the mass-marketed product that has made him wealthy (23) – agonizes over the proper form to use in responding to a written dinner invitation from the snobbish Mrs. Corey. The Corey family has long been established in the socially elite Boston society into which Persis and Silas hope their own two daughters will ultimately be accepted. Persis's painful confusion derives from her awareness that while the Laphams may have "twice their money" (163), the Coreys' long-standing social elevation gives them an important form of what theorists have called "social capital": that is, the power to confer (or withhold) admittance for her daughters into an elite circle of upper-class Bostonians (Bourdieu, "Forms of Capital" 102–105). Such admittance, or the lack of it, will help, in turn, to determine the potential marriage partners to which Irene and Penelope Lapham are exposed. For these reasons Persis "did not find it so simple a matter to accept the invitation. Mrs. Corey had said 'dear Mrs. Lapham,' but Mrs. Lapham had her doubts whether it would not be a servile imitation to say 'Dear Mrs. Corey' in return; and she was tormented as to the proper phrasing throughout and the precise temperature which she should impart to her politeness" (179). Persis is not wrong to be anxious about such seemingly trivial details as how to address her letter of acceptance, as Mrs. Corey – herself conflicted about her son Tom's apparent romantic interest in one of the Lapham daughters – is prepared to judge the Lapham family's manners severely. In her view it is bad enough that Tom has in effect become one of Silas's employees by accepting an executive position in his paint company.

One marker that Persis Lapham has not yet internalized the manners approved by would-be enforcers of old-money superiority such as Mrs. Corey is Persis's boastful mention of the fact – even though it occurs in a private discussion with her husband – that the Laphams have "twice the money" of the Coreys. As we will see in later sections of this chapter, although material resources lay at the root both of social power and of social prestige in late-nineteenth-century America, an array of important strategies employed by the old rich to differentiate themselves from the new rich – and hence to attempt to hold onto their position of social superiority – involved the old rich displaying superior discretion about their wealth. The display of discretion, which appeared in areas ranging from conversational styles to seemingly unrelated questions of taste in décor and food, allowed the established rich to claim that they possessed more "class" even than people of the same wealthy class as themselves. First, however, we will consider practices of display most often associated with the new rich in the literature of the period, above all what economic sociologist Thorstein Veblen dubbed "conspicuous consumption."

How to display wealth

Observers of American society have noted since early in the nation's history that, in a relatively new capitalist democracy with no formal aristocracy, money necessarily plays a major role in determining social status. "When the prestige attached to what is old has vanished," wrote Frenchman Alexis de Tocqueville in his monumental *Democracy in America* (1840), there is "hardly anything left but money which makes very clear distinctions between men or can raise some of them above the common level" (615). Wealth, however, cannot help to raise one's public prestige "above the common level" if it is not made known to the public in question. Making their money visible to others was of particular importance to the Gilded Age's new rich, who did not possess the already-established status of those whose families had been affluent for generations. In a still-influential book called *The Theory of the Leisure Class*, first published in 1899, Thorstein Veblen explored the precise mechanisms by which material wealth could be displayed to others and thereby translated into social prestige. Veblen coined the term "conspicuous consumption" to describe the practice of displaying one's wealth by purchasing excessive amounts of visibly expensive commodities: jewelry, clothes, rare culinary delicacies, yachts, mansions – the more elaborate and, Veblen argued, the more wasteful the better. (He sometimes refers to conspicuous consumption as "conspicuous waste.") Veblen explained that a related practice, "conspicuous leisure," publicly demonstrated a wealthy individual's complete freedom from any need to engage in materially productive labor. Veblen did not claim that every time an affluent person invited friends to lounge with him on his new yacht his only motivation for doing so was a competitive display of wealth, but he insisted that such motives, whether conscious or not, played a role in both the design and the purchasing of luxury goods, as well as in many everyday commodities and practices common among all those with disposable income (a telling phrase in itself).

Veblen also noted an intriguing gender dynamic at work in both conspicuous consumption and conspicuous leisure. In households of sufficient prosperity, women were implicitly given the job of displaying the household's wealth through wasteful spending and a complete abstention from materially productive labor. Veblen referred to wealthy women's conspicuous consumption as "vicarious" because, he argued, it served before all else to show off their fathers' or husbands' "ability to pay," regardless of whatever public complaints a man might make about his wife's extravagant habits (43, 119). In Edith Wharton's *The House of Mirth* (1905), millionaire Gus Trenor waves "his whip in the direction of the Bellomont acres," a country estate on whose "opulent" acres his wife throws lavish weekend parties. Trenor grumbles to a sympathetic guest, "Judy has no idea of what she spends," but in the same breath he hastens to add, "not that there isn't plenty to keep the thing going" (84). Wives such as Judy Trenor exhibited their husbands' wealth not only by ostentatious spending but also by themselves embodying valuable commodities. At a dinner party Judy Trenor's "glaring good looks" suggest "a jeweller's window lit by electricity" (57). Because law and custom in nineteenth-century America meant that married women rarely retained money or property in their own names, their conspicuous consumption served almost by definition to display a particular man's "ability to pay," in Veblen's phrase.

Veblen, whom Wharton, Howells, and other realist authors read and admired, focused *The Theory of the Leisure Class* primarily on the function of both conspicuous leisure and conspicuous consumption as a means by which the affluent made their wealth visible to others. He devoted only a small amount of space, however, to considering how subtle differences in matters such as *style* of consumption, including above all taste preferences, might play a role in intra-class conflicts over cultural authority among the well-to-do. Taste is a category of manners. For those who live in a consumer-oriented society and whose income exceeds the bare modicum necessary for physical survival, questions of taste are woven deeply into the texture of everyday life.

As the French sociologist Pierre Bourdieu has noted, in most social contexts individual judgments of taste not only classify the objects at which they are directed (food, fashion, décor, art), they also classify the individuals making those judgments (*Distinction* 5–6). In the late nineteenth and early twentieth centuries, the realist novel of manners achieved a more probing and nuanced exploration of the complex and dynamic relationship among money, manners, and status within the American leisure classes than the still-developing social sciences could, including the incisive work of Thorstein Veblen. It did so in part by closely investigating the role of taste in establishing and maintaining social hierarchies.

Money, gender, and taste in Edith Wharton's *The House of Mirth*

In the upper-class New York world that Edith Wharton depicts in *The House of Mirth*, people from established old-money families regard public discussions of money or business as "vulgar" (205). Nevertheless, the world *The House of Mirth* depicts is also one in which business logic and capitalistic modes of dealing have permeated people's consciousnesses to such an extent that they shape casual interactions of daily life, as well as those intimate relationships, including marriage and friendship, that we usually prefer to think of as separate from crass calculations of profit and loss.[2] As a character from another high realist text, Henry James's *The Wings of the Dove* (1902), explains in a comment that could just as well apply to the world of *The House of Mirth*, "every one who had anything to give ... made the sharpest possible bargain for it, got at least its value in return" (333).

Lily Bart, the protagonist of Wharton's novel, was born into old New York society, but her father went bankrupt just before he died, leaving her with rich friends and highly refined personal tastes but very little money of her own. Lily's mother – also dead when the novel begins – has taught Lily to regard her unusual beauty as a value, and Lily decides that she will be "very expensive" for any man who seeks her in marriage (10). Having been brought up among New Yorkers with established wealth, the "atmosphere of luxury" is, Lily feels, "the only climate she could breath in." Hence, while waiting for a potential husband with sufficient "capital" (12), Lily tacitly arranges non-monetary exchanges with her wealthy friends in order to keep enjoying the luxury in which "her whole being dilated" (27). These exchanges, though mutually understood, must remain unspoken to avoid the tinge of vulgarity the refined upper classes always attach to any open concern with the business world or with money as such – despite the fact that their own lifestyle depends on having plenty of it (27).

Lily's best friend Judy Trenor, for example, includes Lily in the luxurious weekend parties she throws at Bellomont despite knowing that Lily does not have the means to reciprocate by inviting Judy to similar events. Instead, in an unspoken but mutually understood bargain, Lily must "pay" for inclusion in her friend's parties by employing her well-honed social skills to make sure that the elaborate events go smoothly and that each of the wealthy guests has a good time (41, 28). Lily also accepts that part of her job on such weekends is to wake up early (despite her own preference to sleep late) and act as a sort of social secretary for Judy, writing thank-you notes, invitations, and so forth. In addition to including Lily in the festivities, Judy further compensates her for such services by occasionally helping "replenish" Lily's "insufficient wardrobe" with gowns and jewels she herself no longer wants (28). The importance of keeping the business-like nature of such exchanges unspoken, however, is indicated by how Judy looks "askance" at Lily on an occasion when Lily delicately hints "her preference for a cheque" (83).

Tellingly, the character Simon Rosedale, a "new" multimillionaire who also possesses the social disadvantage of being Jewish in a social circle colored by anti-Semitism, becomes a racial scapegoat for other characters (and to an extent Wharton's narrator) because he makes too obvious the business-type calculations that underlie virtually all of the book's personal relationships. Lily resents the "plump rosy man of the blond Jewish type" for what she thinks of as his Jewish habit of "appraising people as if they were bric-a-brac," and specifically for his overly open appearance of calculating the value to him of being seen with the beautiful but unmarried Lily in public (14). Lily and all of her old-money friends continuously appraise people for their social value and calculate the social costs and benefits to themselves of potential social actions, but they know better than to do it in Rosedale's "shoppy manner" (85). By blaming Rosedale's "air of appraising people" on his Jewishness, which they equate with vulgarity, the old-money characters again help themselves to feel superior.

Edith Wharton and Old New York

From what she would later describe as her "first conscious moments," Edith Newbold Jones loved to "make up" stories (*A Backword Glance* 33). Even before she could read, she insisted on holding a book in her hands for "inspiration" as she devised her tales – preferably a book densely printed in "thick black type" (34). The old-money New York family into which Edith was born (in 1862) valued propriety above all and was generally suspicious of artists. Her parents and their social circle regarded novel writing, in particular, "as something between a black art and a form of manual labor," and the idea that a young girl of their own class might aspire to be a writer seemed especially scandalous (*Backword Glance* 69). From when she was a young woman Wharton not only devoured all of the literature she could find but also read widely in the sciences, social sciences, philosophy, and art history. Her first published book, *The Decoration of Houses* (1897), was co-written with an architect and focused on principles of interior design. An intensely visual person, Wharton would be passionate throughout her life about home and garden design. The title of her first novel, *The House of Mirth* (1905) – a bestseller that almost immediately made Wharton a literary celebrity – alludes to a passage from Ecclesiastes, but the title also anticipates the extent to which carefully delineated homes, gardens, household furnishings, and clothing permeate her fiction.

An indefatigable traveler, for many years Wharton maintained residences both in the United States and in France, where she believed women were taken more seriously as adults with minds than in America. She had settled permanently in the latter nation by the time the First World War broke out. Always highly energetic and well organized (she famously spent three hours writing in bed every morning before commencing the rest of her day), she worked feverishly to establish and fundraise for a network of charities, orphanages, and convalescent homes devoted to caring for the rush of often-traumatized refugees that flooded into Paris during the war. The French government recognized Wharton's humanitarian efforts by naming her a Chevalier of the National Legion of Honor in 1916, making the American civilian a signal exception to its wartime policy of reserving such high-ranking honors for French military personnel only (Lee, *Edith Wharton* 503). Wharton received an equally notable award in 1921 when *The Age of Innocence* (1920) won the first Pulitzer Prize ever awarded to a woman novelist. She remained a highly productive writer until her death in 1936.

"Superior distinction"

It is vital both to the story Wharton tells and to the social structure depicted in *The House of Mirth* that Lily's craving for luxuries is far from indiscriminate. Waking up in a guest room at the Trenor's Bellomont estate, Lily happily breathes in the "charm" of the room's décor, including the "curved sides of an old marquetry desk" and the "harmonious porcelain and silver" of her breakfast tray, which also contains "a handful of violets in a slender glass" (41). "Mere display," the narrator tells us, "left her with a sense of superior distinction; but she felt an affinity to all the subtler manifestations of wealth" (41). Lily's preference for a room containing a few "harmonious" objects of understated elegance – instead of the profusion of ostentatiously expensive items evoked by the phrase "mere display" – might initially seem a rejection both of conspicuous consumption and of the competition over status that, according to Veblen, underlies it. In fact, however, Lily's personal "affinity" for "tokens of a studied luxury" reflects a phenomenon to which Veblen does not pay sufficiently nuanced attention: a group-wide practice by which the old rich try to hold on to their privileged cultural position, felt by Lily as "the sense of superior distinction" she experiences when in the presence of expensive ostentation (41).

Although Lily differentiates the delicate antique desk, the harmonious breakfast tray, the discreetly arranged flowers from "mere display," she recognizes these objects as "subtler *manifestations* of wealth" (my emphasis). That is, these tasteful objects render wealth manifest, or visible, just as a display of gaudily expensive items would, but they achieve this task by subtler means. After all, somebody – no doubt an early-rising servant – spent time and care arranging the "porcelain and silver" on Lily's breakfast tray in order to produce the "harmonious" effect she so enjoys. Having such a skillful and well-trained servant in one's household signifies the possession of wealth over a longer period of time than would be required simply for the purchase of showy objects. "Subtler manifestations of wealth" require more skill, experience, and time to achieve than "mere display" does. They also convey a relatively relaxed, confident attitude toward the display of wealth, one not so marked by the anxious sense of over-eagerness that obvious ostentation can suggest. In a later scene, one of Lily's old-money cousins mocks the overly elaborate front of a mansion constructed on Fifth Avenue by a new millionaire: "The man who built it came from a *milieu* where all the dishes are put on the table at once. His façade is a complete architectural meal; if he had omitted a style his friends might have thought the money had given out" (168). As William Dean Howells astutely phrased it in *Criticism and Fiction* (1891), in late-nineteenth-century America, in the absence of a formal aristocracy, "pride of caste" manifested itself as "pride of taste" (187).

A tour-de-force scene set among wealthy Americans visiting the French Riviera allows Wharton to demonstrate the potential for even a very brief passage of realist fiction to capture nuances in the dynamic American relationship between money and social status missed by other forms of discourse at the time, including Veblen's sociology. Lily is one of several characters in *The House of Mirth* who possess ample pride both of caste and of taste, but who do have sufficient money at their disposal to maintain what they view as an appropriate lifestyle. A unique form of exchange occurs between such characters and members of the new rich who are eager to acquire membership in the innermost circles of elite society. In effect, financially needy people with backgrounds similar to Lily's are able to exchange their social and cultural capital (that is, their networks of family and social connections and their embodied knowledge of old-money manners and taste) for financial capital, or money. As the scene in question opens, we find several old-money Americans gathered on the steps of the Casino Hotel in Monte Carlo, trying to decide where to have lunch. The only member of the new rich among them is Louisa Bry, wife of "Welly" Bry, who has recently made a killing on the stock market. Mrs. Bry has in effect hired the socially smooth and well-connected – but financially impecunious – Carry Fisher to help her and her husband cross over into the exclusive social circle of the established rich by introducing her friends and, at the same time, discreetly tutoring Mrs. Bry on how to behave (196).

Showing off what she has learned from Carry, Mrs. Bry explains to an acquaintance who happens to be passing by why the wealthy group has not yet been able to decide where to eat: "Of course one gets the best things at the *Terrasse* – but that looks as if one hadn't any other reason for being there: the Americans who don't know any one always rush for the best food" (192). Mrs. Bry's comment demonstrates her new grasp of the usually implicit, sometimes no doubt unconscious, strategies by which the old rich achieve the impression of having more "class" even than those with as much or more money than they. If one rushes for the "best food" by going to the *Terrasse*, one commits the vulgar errors, first, of seeming to follow the herd and, second, of appearing driven by hunger for the "best things," rather than guided by less bodily, more esoteric forms of taste. The old rich continuously seek ways to signify their own privileged elevation above the baser forms of appetite that presumably drive other people. Despite the astuteness of Mrs. Bry's explanation of these strategic principles, however, what she fails to grasp is that being *open* about them automatically defeats their purpose. Old-money manners have the implicit goal of communicating a long-standing sense of security and comfort regarding wealth and social position, a goal that is directly undercut by any obvious angling for more of either. To Carry Fisher's "despair," Louisa Bry has not yet acquired "the air of doing things because she wanted to, and making her choice the final seal of their fitness" (193).

Saving face for the group, another character follows Mrs. Bry's ill-timed remark by suggesting they all dine at a "little place at the Condamine" because "it's the only restaurant in Europe where they can cook peas" (193). Peas are small and delicate enough (think of "The Princess and the Pea," a fairy-tale first published by Hans Christian Anderson in 1835) that seeking perfectly cooked ones seems more of an aesthetic than an appetite-driven quest: one does not desire the perfect pea in order to fill one's hungry belly. At the same time, peas are so common and their preparation would appear to be so basic that the mere claim of being able to identify the one restaurant in Europe that can properly cook them implies a cultivated ability to recognize and appreciate differences calibrated to such a fine degree that most people would not even notice them. "It's quite that," agrees Lord Hubert, and the group moves off toward the Condamine restaurant (193).

Lily Bart's own fate in *The House of Mirth* takes the form of tragic irony. Early in the book, she recognizes a paradox whose conflicting demands will ultimately paralyze her: "The only way not to think about money is to have a great deal of it" (72). Rosedale, having come a long way in his own cultural education, later echoes her: "I know there's one thing vulgar about money, and that's the thinking about it" (186). The old-money imperative to carry off at all times an air of long-standing and unquestioned material wealth not only ordains a discreet silence about money; it would also require, if taken to its logical extreme, the banishing of money from one's very thought. Yet in a capitalist society not thinking about money requires either superhuman asceticism or a large, dependable cushion of wealth – and, in fact, as Wharton's novel goes on we learn that even its richest, most socially distinguished characters think constantly about money, despite their avoidance of open discussion about it. Lily ultimately perishes because she makes the mistake of internalizing more deeply than she realizes, and without the usual hypocrisy, the injunction that a refined upper-class woman, above all, should never allow her actions to be guided by financial calculation.

Even as Lily develops a deep inner aversion to marrying a man simply for his impressive bank account, her craving for the material luxuries only money can buy remains as intense as ever. The immobilizing result, as her cousin Gerty Farish observes, is that "Lily might be incapable of marrying for money, but she was equally incapable of living without it" (171). Hence, Lily is ambivalent until the end about committing herself to Lawrence Selden, the only man in the novel with whom she feels a deep personal sense of mutual attraction and connection. Socially accepted due to his descent and manners by old-money New York, the dilettantish lawyer is far from rich. Indeed, what most draws Lily to Selden is his "air" of distance from "any assertion of personal advantage" (68). Whether consciously on his part or not, Selden's "air" epitomizes the established rich's chief strategy for distinguishing themselves from the new rich; it marks him as the opposite of vulgar and the epitome of fine taste. Yet Selden's lack of wealth means that marrying him would exclude Lily from what she still regards as "the only climate she could breathe in" (27). Equally unable to bring herself to marry the "shoppy" Rosedale because doing so would involve an essential vulgarity, Lily dies from an overdose of sleeping medicine as the novel closes, with Wharton leaving open the question of whether her death results from suicide or accident. Regardless, Lily's death reveals that "manners" constitute far more than a given society's decorative surface. Defined by Trilling as "that part of a culture which is made up of half-uttered or unuttered or unutterable expressions of value," manners are inextricable from lived social reality – and, in Lily's case, from a reality that finally becomes unlivable.

Ethnography and realism

In literary novels of manners such as *The House of Mirth*, realist authors share in the same project taken on by early sociologists such as Thorstein Veblen: to explore the inner workings of modern American social formations. As I have demonstrated with *The House of Mirth*, in some cases the fiction writer's ability to make use of her creative imagination, which draws from but is not necessarily limited to the writer's own personal experiences, may yield more penetrating results than are produced by the social scientist, who is at least supposed to stick to concrete evidence and recorded observation. The "high realist" novel of manners, focused primarily on the middle and upper classes, was not the only form of literary realism to overlap with social-scientific concerns in the late nineteenth century. Where sociology directed its attention mostly toward the complexities of modern American society, the emergent disciplines of anthropology and ethnography took as their primary objects social orders they regarded as more "primitive," whether Native American tribal cultures in North America or other supposedly less advanced cultures abroad. Similarly, the mode of realist fiction called regionalism, also known as "local color," explored geographic and cultural settings outside of and marginal to America's centers of economic, political, or cultural power, with a particular focus on economically disadvantaged rural areas.

Local-color fiction was often published by the same prestigious publishing houses, and in many of the same magazines, as the "high realist" work of authors such as Howells, James, and Wharton. Yet while high realism featured characters and "manners" largely drawn from the same social groupings that constituted its intended reading audiences – the educated middle, upper-middle, and upper classes – the characters populating works of local color were mostly rural, usually poor, and often lacked formal education. As we will see in our next chapter, such differences between the people portrayed in local-color fiction and the readers for whom this fiction was primarily written raise difficult questions about exploitation, and about whether realist writing functions primarily to bridge social divisions between people of different regions and classes or to reinforce them.

Chapter 5

"Democracy in literature"? Literary regionalism

"Sally Parson's Duty," a short story by Rose Terry Cooke, appeared in the *Atlantic Monthly*'s debut issue of November 1857, almost ten years before the young William Dean Howells would begin his official association with the magazine. Cooke's story opens, "The sun that shines on Eastern Massachusetts ..." The first bit of dialogue a reader encounters is spoken by 'Zekiel Parsons, who addresses an old friend: "I expect, Long, you sailors hev a drefful hard, onsartain time navigatin', don't ye?" (24). In specifying from the start the region in which her story will occur (not simply Massachusetts, but *Eastern* Massachusetts) and in using non-standard phonetic spelling and symbols such as apostrophes (even in 'Zekiel's name) to convey not only what her rural characters say but what they *sound* like, Cooke immediately marks the story as belonging to an emerging genre in the United States, known at the time as local color and subsequently also called regionalism (we will return to the question of nomenclature below). Put simply, a local-color or regionalist story is one in which place – that is, the story's geographic setting – not only serves as background but also plays a prominent role in the story's foreground. A reader is always aware of the setting: it becomes an inextricable part of the story's texture, influencing such elements as plot, theme, atmosphere, characterization and characters' speech. Local-color settings, moreover, are usually depicted as someplace outside the mainstream, at a distance from national centers of financial, political, or cultural power.

Though local-color fiction was being written and published at least twenty-five years before a self-conscious movement for literary realism existed in the United States, it enjoyed its greatest public and critical success in the 1870s and 1880s during the period when literary realism became prominent. In those post-Civil War decades, younger writers such as Mary Murfree (who used the pseudonym Charles Egbert Craddock), Mary Wilkins Freeman, and Hamlin Garland moved away from the local-color genre's antebellum association with humorous stereotypes and aligned their own regionally focused writing with realist principles as they were being practiced by figures such as Howells. Sarah Orne Jewett, for example, told her readers in 1877 that to enjoy her portrayal of "a quiet old-fashioned country town" on the Maine coast, they must care to look closely at "every-day life," and take "an instinctive, delicious interest in what to other eyes is unflavored dullness" (*Novels and Stories (Deephaven)* 37).

Recognizing the overlap with his own developing ideas about American literature's need to provide realistic treatment of commonplace people and mundane everyday lives, William Dean Howells promoted local-color authors in his role as a powerful magazine editor and book reviewer. Local-color writing, he believed, would help to better acquaint people in different regions of the country with each other. It would forward what he described as literary realism's most important goal: to teach people that they "are more like than unlike one another ... [to] make them know one another better, that they may be all humbled and strengthened with a sense of their fraternity" (*Criticism and Fiction* 188). Howells came to view local-color writing as a leading aspect of the American realist movement. At the height of local color's popularity during the 1870s and 1880s, high-profile US magazines such as the *Atlantic Monthly*, *Harper's*, and the *Century* assiduously sought out and published fiction set in various corners of the United States. Kentucky writer James Lane Allen asserted in 1886 that "local color is one of the latest aims and highest refinements of modern fiction," and reading audiences agreed ("Local Color" 13). Howells emphasized in 1887 that short stories using local-color elements were in constant demand by "the readers of our best magazines" ("Editor's Study," 1887 [74.441] 484).

In this chapter, we will ask why local-color writers found such a welcoming audience in post-Civil War America. Did such writing truly help to advance, as Howells claimed, "democracy in literature" (*Criticism and Fiction* 187)? Or, did it serve mostly as a form of literary tourism for middle- and upper-class readers, as some recent critics have charged? What historical and social factors are relevant to the notable success of fiction featuring out-of-the-way pockets of America published in magazines aimed primarily at metropolitan audiences?[1] In considering these questions, we will touch on a variety of local-color works as we explore key elements of the genre, including its frequent use of dense regional dialects and the presence in many local-color stories of an outsider visiting the region. We will then turn our focus to the writer whose fiction has become a flashpoint of recent critical debates about regionalist fiction in late-nineteenth-century America: Sarah Orne Jewett. Jewett's lyrically compelling stories set in a rural Maine coastal village raise issues that range from gendered modes of relating with other people to possible links between local-color writing's popularity and the United States' increasingly aggressive imperialism in overseas venues such as Cuba and the Philippines.

Regionalism, dialect, and the "folk"

As already remarked, local-color fiction was an identifiable genre prior to the Civil War. After the war, however, literature that placed in its foreground a geographic or cultural setting outside the nation's centers of financial and political power became much more plentiful, as well as more diverse. Writers set stories in Western mining camps and upstate New York towns; among Appalachian mountain people, Cajuns and Creoles in Louisiana, and farmers on the Great Plains; in declining fishing villages on the New England coast and on former slave plantations in Virginia and North Carolina. Despite the diversity of locales it treated, however, the majority of post-Civil War local-color writing shared, first, that it passed through editors and a publishing industry centered in New York and Boston; second, that the readers whom its narrative voice seemed primarily to imagine were well-educated middle- and upper-class city dwellers; and, third, that the localities it depicted were more impoverished and less economically diversified (that is, they offered fewer ways of earning a living) than the urban centers where the literature was at least initially published. (Due to its unique role in post-Civil War racial politics, Southern "plantation" fiction will be considered more fully in Chapter 9.)

Virtually all post-Civil War local-color fiction included literary dialect as a central feature. Literary dialect refers to an author's attempt to communicate on the written page what a speaker's non-standard English sounds like to the ear. For example, Mary Murfree begins an 1883 short story set in Tennessee's remote Cumberland Mountains with the following remark by a character:

> "I hev hearn tell ez how them thar boys rides thar horses over hyar ter
> the Settlemint nigh on ter every night in the week ter play kyerds …
> an' thar goin's-on air jes' scandalous, – jes' a-drinkin' of applejack, an'
> a-bettin' of thar money." ("A-Playin' of Old Sledge" 544)

Murfree uses phonetic spellings to convey her regional characters' pronunciations, such as "hev" for "have" and "ez" for "as." Some of the phonetic spellings are so extreme, such as "kyerds" for "cards," that readers may find it difficult to identify the words without first reading the entire sentence aloud. Murfree further introduces her audience to regional words that may be new to them, such as "applejack" (apple brandy made with a still), employs local idioms ("hearn tell," "them thar"), and attempts to capture her characters' speech rhythms with the interposition of the extra syllable "a-" ("jes' a-drinkin' … an' a-bettin'").

Many realists writing after the Civil War viewed literary dialect as an art. They took pride in their ability to capture even very fine regional distinctions, as is indicated by an "Author's Explanatory" note that Mark Twain included with his *Adventures of Huckleberry Finn*:

> In this book a number of dialects are used, to wit: the Missouri negro dialect; the extremest form of the backwoods Southwestern dialect; the ordinary "Pike County" dialect; and four modified varieties of this last. The shadings have not been done in a haphazard fashion, or by guess-work; but painstakingly, and with the trustworthy guidance and support of personal familiarity with these several forms of speech.

Scholars studying Twain's many handwritten changes to the original manuscript of *Huckleberry Finn* have shown that, in creating the dialect spoken by various characters, Twain "constantly revised and corrected syllables, sounds, and phrasing," and linguists have concluded that, just as Twain claimed, there are indeed a number of related but distinct dialects represented in the book (Schmidt, "Review").

Readers and reviewers also took the question of dialect accuracy seriously, and often commented on the level of skill with which a writer had depicted the speech of a particular locality. Some of those evaluating the accuracy of literary dialects did so on the basis of their own familiarity with the region in question; others based their judgments on comparisons between a given writer's portrayal of a specific dialect and portrayals of the same or similar dialects by other writers. On occasion, two readers, each of whom could claim long personal knowledge of a given region's speech, would disagree with one another on whether or not a writer had captured it accurately. This latter fact reminds us that, as with realism more generally, a key issue in how readers responded was the *effect* of realness that a writer could give to the dialect in her fiction; that effect should never be regarded as identical with "reality" itself. (See Chapter 3 for a more detailed discussion of reality effects.) Readerly perceptions of an author's dialect-related qualifications, for example, would often help shape their judgment of a given dialect portrayal as "authentic"; hence, Twain was far from the only dialect writer to include a preface emphasizing his own expertise in regional forms of American speech.[2]

The popularity of local-color fiction in the United States coincided with a more general interest in "folk" cultures and languages, on the part both of scholars and of that portion of the public that considered itself well educated. Collectors accumulated folk tales, songs, and proverbs, as well as culturally distinctive objects, from Native American, African-American, and isolated white communities, among others. The American Folklore Society was founded in 1888 and immediately began publishing a quarterly journal. It stressed authenticity as a key value. Anthropology and ethnography emerged as academic disciplines and began to send researchers out to observe customs, study kinship arrangements, and witness important ceremonies, both within the United States and in other parts of the world. Philologists traced the relationships among various languages and dialects, as well as transcribing "samples" of them. Ironically, researchers not infrequently turned to fiction by local-color writers such as Joel Chandler Harris – author of the "Uncle Remus" stories – for data.

Locals and cosmopolitans in a changing nation

Recent scholars have advanced several explanations for Americans' increasing interest in acquiring at least some exposure to a range of different cultures during this period, especially those they viewed as outside the rushing stream of modernity. Some researchers, for instance, have pointed to a desire among the status-conscious middle and upper classes to gain prestige by appearing sophisticated and cosmopolitan. Noting that the anthropological meaning of the word "culture" (to refer to a group's shared way of life or worldview) was only just beginning to come into use at the end of the nineteenth century, Brad Evans plays on two different meanings of "culture" when he argues that "the circulation of something like 'cultures' became a sign of 'Culture' in the late nineteenth century; the contact with or appreciation of this kind of multiplicity was a mark of being 'cultured'" in the capital C sense (*Before Cultures* 7). In other words, a cosmopolitan interest in other cultures during this period could help to elevate one's own status as Cultured – just as, for instance, an individual's refined knowledge of Western classical music or imported wine might do. The boost to a person's own culturally sophisticated status associated with his or her informed appreciation of diverse "folk" cultures – whether Scottish, Appalachian, or Native American – does not automatically invalidate the sincerity of such an interest, of course. No doubt many late-nineteenth-century Americans' desire to be exposed to assorted "folkways" (a term coined by sociologist William Graham Sumner in 1906) also derived, at least in part, from an authentic wish to expand their own perspectives within a diverse world.

Although individual regionalist authors were identified with distinct parts of America (e.g., Jewett with Maine, Hamlin Garland with the great plains of the Midwest, George Washington Cable with Louisiana), commentators of the period often interpreted the genre as such within the larger context of US nationalism. A literature reflecting geographical differences of terrain, manners, and pronunciation – as long as such differences fit, as we will see, within certain boundaries of perceived otherness – embodied the United States' unique identity better than literature emanating from any one region could. As Charles Dudley Warner explained in an 1892 "Editor's Study" column for *Harper's New Monthly Magazine*,

> We have been expecting the American Literature to come out from
> some locality, neat and clean, like a nugget … [instead] there are
> coming forth a hundred expressions of the hundred aspects of
> American life … And all these writers … are animated by the free spirit
> of inquiry and expression that belongs to an independent nation, and
> so our literature is coming to have a stamp of its own that is unlike any
> other national stamp.   (150)

Along related lines, Howells praised what he referred to as "our literary decentralization" as a reliable source of freshness and revitalization for American literature and language.

Some Americans seem to have valued exposure to cultural pockets of the United States that they regarded as distinct from the mainstream – whether through attending concerts where African-American performers sang slave spirituals, joining a "folklore" club, or reading local-color literature – precisely because these sorts of differences signified authenticity and rootedness within a context in which modern consumerism and corporate homogenization seemed to be colonizing ever-expanding portions of the nation and people's individual lives. Coca-Cola, Pillsbury Flour, Quaker Oats, Campbell's Soup, Hershey's Chocolate, and Standard Oil, among many others, grew into nationally marketed brands during this period, wiping out small local competitors along the way (Edwards, *New Spirits* 43). Of course the nation still had a long distance to travel before it would reach our current level of commercialized homogenization, in which the pervasive presence of national and international business chains, from restaurants to hotels to retail stores, makes virtually every American town look alike when approached by car. Nonetheless, modernization was changing the very texture of life, eliminating local wrinkles and peculiarities and threatening to dissolve all of American culture into bland homogeneity. Even people's relationship with daily objects seemed to be changing, as mass-produced, commercially available commodities replaced objects made at home or purchased from local craftspeople. An increasing number of Americans, for instance, particularly in cities, purchased off-the-rack clothing made in standardized sizes – such sizes, just like uniformly accepted time zones, did not exist prior to the Civil War.

In regionalist fiction, by contrast, everyday objects such as dishes, gowns, rugs, and rocking chairs tend to be presented as unique. Individual objects often have a history and a specific emotional significance for their owners. From this perspective, we might see this literature as presenting an alternative, even subversive vision opposed to the relentlessly commercializing and commodifying effects of post-Civil War American capitalism. From another perspective, however, we might also see local color's depiction for its middle-class urban audiences of one-of-a-kind regional objects as itself commodifying those objects for readers, not unlike, perhaps, the business of buying and selling American antiques, which also thrived in the latter part of the nineteenth century.

In the next section, we will examine how selected local-color texts themselves portray the relationship between metropolitan visitors and the rural localities they visit.

Regionalism's implied reader

Late-nineteenth-century regionalist fiction is frequently told from the point of view of an outside visitor, with the narration registering what the visitor to the region sees, hears, and feels. If the outsider is not literally a character in the story, his or her presence is often recognizable by the obvious differences between the language of the local inhabitants and that of the narrative voice that describes them. The visitor from the outside world acts, in effect, as a textual representative for readers. After all, such readers are themselves paying a temporary visit to the locality through the very act of reading about it. If the outside visitor serves as a surrogate for metropolitan readers, then analyzing the visitor's relationship with the locals can help to give us a sense of the possible forms of relation to the region and its inhabitants that a given work seems to envision for its readers. What perspectives do regionalist works themselves offer on Howells's hope that realist literature could help to bridge social divides by showing people that they are "more like than unlike one another"?

The protagonists of Mary E. Wilkins Freeman's short stories are often women considered marginal even in their rural New England societies: unmarried, eccentric, and sometimes so poor as to come close to starving. "A Mistaken

Charity" (1887) begins by introducing us to two elderly sisters, Charlotte and Harriet Shattuck, the former blind, the latter mostly deaf, who live alone in a decrepit cottage. Harriet picks dandelions in the cottage's front yard as the story opens; the first line of dialogue is Charlotte's question to her: "Air there enough for a mess, Harriét?" (41). Although the partially deaf Harriet does not initially hear Charlotte's question, the third-person narrator comments, "Besides the question denoted by the arrangement of her words and the rising inflection, there was another, broader and subtler, the very essence of all questioning, in the tone of her voice itself ... One would have known by the voice that the old woman was blind" (41). Here, the narrative voice grants a seriousness, even a profundity, to the blind Charlotte's "cracked, quavering" dialect voice (41). At the same time, in asserting its own ability to recognize in that quavering voice "the essence of all questioning," the omniscient narrator also implicitly claims a perspective that is larger and deeper than that Charlotte herself possesses, at least at a level consciously available to the old woman. The narrative voice also establishes its own vocabulary as more sophisticated and more analytic than Charlotte's dialect, with the use of such words as "denoted," "subtler," and "inflection."

Finally, the narrator's strategic use of the word "one" in this passage – "one would have known by the voice the old woman was blind" – invites the reader to align him or herself with the narrator's omniscience. If "one" – by implication, somebody reading this story – were present in the cottage's yard with Harriet, then he or she would have been perspicacious enough immediately to grasp Charlotte's blindness merely by the sound of her voice. Importantly, the "one" the passage alludes to, the implied reader, is by definition an outsider visiting the cottage for the first time, as any local neighbor or friend would already know about Charlotte's lack of vision. The narrative voice further identifies both itself and the text's imagined readers as outsiders to the region, with wider and more modern experiences, by telling us that until recently the sisters had "gone about from house to house doing tailor-work after the primitive country fashion" (44). As a cultural practice different from our own implicitly urban habits, the "country fashion" may interest us, but the omniscient narrator's designating the customary behavior as "primitive" indicates that we the readers are presumed to inhabit a more advanced or developed cultural space.

"A Mistaken Charity" begins by marking subtle but clear boundaries between the sophisticated reader of the story and the two "primitive" sisters, who hope to eat a "mess" of dandelions for dinner. But the text's positioning of its readers takes a turn when Mrs. Simonds, a prosperous local woman "bent on doing good," but rigidly set on doing "it in her own way," arranges to move

Harriet and Charlotte to a privately funded "'Old Ladies' Home' in a neighboring city" (49). Unlike Mrs. Simonds, who has known the sisters for many years, the reader can already recognize that they will be miserable in the city-based "Home," despite the care and relative luxuries offered there. In spite of the fact that their own house has been patched so often that it no longer fully protects them from the wind and rain, Harriet and Charlotte cherish their independence. With the narrator, we have overheard Charlotte describing the "chinks" that seem to allow light to shine through her blindness, which appear to her only when she is at home with her sister, usually when she is eating the apples, currants, and pumpkins that grow next to the cottage.

At the Old Ladies' Home, by contrast, both women detest what Charlotte calls the "vittles" served because, as the narrator explains, the food is of a "finer, more delicately served variety than they had been accustomed to" (51). Forced to wear lacy caps and urged to curb their speech, they are so "at variance with their surroundings," that "the two poor old women looked like two forlorn prisoners" (51). Charlotte confesses to Harriet that she has felt "slantendicular to heaven" ever since arriving: "it's been so awful dark. I ain't had any chinks" (52). By this point, the reader clearly recognizes the "mistaken charity" the title refers to, and is eager to dissociate him or herself from it. The same sensitivity and perspicacity by which, as the narrator has told us, we would have known Charlotte was blind simply by hearing "the cracked, quavering notes" in her voice now urge us to reject the supposed "benevolence" practiced by Mrs. Simonds and an unnamed "gentleman" who officially represents the home as a foolish and arrogant attempt to impose an alien culture on the old ladies.

Mrs. Simonds and the "gentleman," as well as a minister and a wealthy widow from the city who also help enforce the "mistaken charity" toward the sisters, are undoubtedly closer to the socioeconomic and educational status of the reader whom the narrator has presumed and addressed throughout the story. These characters – as the reader already has done, but as the two old women never could or would – might even purchase volumes published by the prestigious Harper & Brothers house, similar to the Harper-issued volume of Freeman's short stories in which "A Mistaken Charity" first appeared (*A Humble Romance*, 1887). Nonetheless, we as readers find ourselves aligned against the characters who are closest to our own presumptive social class – we now perceive them as in a sense more "blind" than Charlotte – and thoroughly *with* the two sisters as they stage a dramatic escape from the "Home." We inwardly cheer them along as they slip out a back door and then tell a lie to get a wagon to drive them to their cottage nearby. With the elderly sisters, we "chuckle maliciously" when a buggy carrying a search party from the institution drives by so quickly that it does not see them crouching in the wagon.

Once they reach "their tottering old home," we feel deeply gratified when Harriet is able to inform Charlotte, "the currants air ripe … *an'* them pumpkins hev run all over everything." We share the pure joy of both sisters when Charlotte responds, in the story's last line, "thar is so many chinks that they air all runnin' together!" (56).

The relationship that Freeman's regionalist story works to establish between its readers and the impoverished, dialect-speaking Shattuck sisters is in certain ways similar to the strong emotional identification sentimental literature strives to evoke in its readers (see Chapter 1). But there is a key difference. Readers of "A Mistaken Charity" are never encouraged to imagine themselves in the sisters' circumstances, to feel as they are feeling. For instance, Harriet and Charlotte's escape from the "Old Ladies' Home" resonates with Eliza's famous flight from the slave plantation in *Uncle Tom's Cabin*. Stowe, however, invites readers to place themselves literally in the shoes of the beautiful, gentle, and highly articulate Eliza at this fraught moment, carrying their own child in their arms and running from brutal slave catchers: "How fast could you walk?" Stowe demands of readers. By contrast, throughout "A Mistaken Charity" the omniscient narrator describes "the two old women" as they would appear to an outside observer. Charlotte's use of the word "slantendicular" toward the end of the story is comical and, along with other elements of the sisters' description, works against direct identification with her on the part of the educated and sophisticated readers the narrator has assumed. Still, by the end of the story any reader would admire the women's strong will and stubborn independence, as well as the tight bond they have with one another. It is also not difficult to imagine an urban reader envying their closeness to nature, the largely "good friendly folk" who are their neighbors, and the simple, fresh food they eat. Indeed, because the owner of the land their cottage sits on does not charge the sisters rent (it would be, the narrator says, like "charging a squirrel for his tenement in some old decaying tree in the woods"), they seem to live outside of the nation's modern capitalist economy, with its rampant commercialism and commodification.

Does Freeman's text work to promote the true communication and understanding Howells envisioned for local color and thereby help establish mutually strengthening bonds that traverse class and regional differences? A caution is provided by a satiric sketch written by Constance Fenimore Woolson, which appeared fifteen years prior to "A Mistaken Charity" in *Harper's Monthly Magazine* (issued by the same publishing house that would also bring out the bulk of Freeman's work). Published at the very beginning of local color's boom in popularity, Woolson's "In Search of the Picturesque" (1872) anticipates and plays with many of the genre's features, including the implicit parallel between metropolitan visitors to a rural region inside a story and readers who are also "visiting" the region through choosing to immerse themselves in fiction set there. In gradually uncovering both the desires and the fallacies embedded in its first-person metropolitan narrator's expectations of what she will find when she goes to spend a few days in the "country" (162), Woolson's story helps clarify at least some of the reasons readers may have been drawn to local-color fiction in an industrializing, ever-more urban nation, even as her satire strives to undercut a touristic, fantasy-based approach to rural life.

Searching for the picturesque

As readers, we start "In Search of the Picturesque" by sharing the point of view of the highly articulate first-person narrator Priscilla, her cousin Sue, and their grandfather as they leave their comfortable home in a big industrial town for a brief country vacation. (The fact that Woolson does not specify the locality or even what part of the United States the story is set in indicates that she wishes to critique a general set of attitudes that well-off urbanites bring to the very idea of the rural.) Eager to be refreshed by what Priscilla refers to as "the naïve simplicity of country life," the three travelers all desire a break from the complex stresses of "modern society" (162). Priscilla and Sue desire to fit in with the "simplicity and rustic politeness" of the "farming population," so they wear their "plainest attire" ("old" dresses from two years ago) (162). Their grandfather looks forward in particular to "the good plain fare of the village inns" at which they will sleep and eat (162).

In seeking the "picturesque," the three travelers hope to find more than a lovely view. They hope to enter into a "pure ... atmosphere" unsullied by modernity, a "real Arcadia" (162). Woolson's use of the term "Arcadia" slyly connects late-nineteenth-century urban Americans' new interest in their nation's rural regions with a long tradition of romantic idealizations. Arcadia was a farming region of Greece idealized by ancient Greek and Roman poets writing in the highly conventionalized pastoral genre, which portrayed it as the isolated home of shepherds and shepherdesses who spent their days watching sheep, playing the flute, and singing to one another of love and beauty. Woolson's characters do discover a rural region populated by farms and small villages, where manners and speech are somewhat different from their own, but they are repeatedly forced to recognize how fully incorporated it is into the same "modern society" in which the urban visitors reside. Rather than a separate realm existing in a static past, where life is simpler and closer to nature, the "country" is connected to the city economically and culturally, as well as by a railroad line and teamsters' wagons (which the visitors, who have chosen to travel in a horse-and-buggy, try their best to ignore). The economic interpenetration of the city and country becomes most evident as the urban travelers search for the plain, farm-fresh food that they had expected would be easily available wherever they stopped. They find that they cannot buy milk at a roadside stand because, as a "half-grown youth" explains matter-of-factly, "we sell it all in Marathon" (the name of the fictional city the travelers had set out from) (163). The grandfather asks what beverage they *do* sell. "The best lager made in Marathon; it came out by rail this morning," the boy proudly announces (163). When they spend the night at a farm, the farmer's wife gives them only fried pork and coffee, telling her guests that she markets all her milk and eggs to a distributor who sells them in the city. The modern economy's circulation of goods from farms to city markets and then sometimes back again also means that the farmer's wife doesn't use her garden to grow produce for her family, since "she could get it cheaper from the canal-boats coming down from the city" (167).

Nor does the supposed "Arcadia" have a homespun folk culture that retains its purity separate from the city's rapid changes. The farmer's wife reads a sensationalistic newspaper to keep up with all "the fires and fights up to Marathon" because "it's something lively to think of in this dull place" (168). A "gaunt young woman" the travelers encounter in a small village pumps them for information about urban fashions. Apparently not duly appreciating that the young ladies purposefully chose their "plainest attire" as most appropriate for their visit to the country, the fashion-conscious young village woman asks them if they are "female suffragers" because "the suffragers mostly pays no attention to the fashions" (165).

By the end of Woolson's sketch, it has become clear that the rural "picturesque" the tourists go in search of is largely a fantasy. This fantasy imaginatively projects "rural life" as the obverse of urban modernity. That is, if urban modernity is complex, removed from nature, and corrupted by marketplace values that have left city dwellers, as Priscilla complains, in pursuit of "follies and false ideas of pleasure," then by contrast "rural life" should be simple and self-contained. People should live closer to nature and their enjoyments should be innocent and "pure" (162). Woolson's sketch implies, however, that to fit this fantasy onto an actual late-nineteenth-century rural locality and the people who live there, a tourist – or, by implication, a local-color author or reader – will find it necessary to obscure the effects of large-scale systems of trade and distribution that, with accelerating speed after the Civil War, linked the economies of varied communities ever-more closely together. Sustaining the pleasing fantasy of a "real Arcadia," untouched by the modern world, would also require a tourist, author, or reader to avoid recognizing how the desires and even tastes of rural people, such as the "gaunt young woman" who seeks up-to-date information on urban fashions, are themselves constructed within a changing society, rather than existing in some set-apart realm of nature.

Woolson's "In Search of the Picturesque" effectively satirizes late-nineteenth-century urban fantasies of rural simplicity, which lay behind at least some local-color writing (and reading). The satire suggests that local-color fiction – to the extent, at least, that it functions as a form of literary tourism for middle- and upper-class urban audiences – will do little to help its readers, or other Americans, again in Howells's words, "know one another better, that they may all be humbled and strengthened with a sense of their fraternity" (*Criticism and Fiction* 188). If anything, Priscilla, the narrator of "In Search of the Picturesque," seems to feel a deeper sense of division from the "farming population" than before she took her trip. Her very last words to us are, "Aimez-vous les beautés de la Nature? Pour moi, je les ABHORRE!" (Do you like Nature's beauties? Me, I detest them!) (168). The content of the line emphasizes Priscilla's disillusionment with the fantasy of the "picturesque"; the fact that it appears in French, which she sees no need to translate, also reminds *Harper's* readers of her – and, by implication, their own – superior status as sophisticated cosmopolitans.

Hamlin Garland, Regionalist of the "Middle Border"

Hamlin Garland grew up in a hardscrabble farming family that his restless father repeatedly uprooted and moved further west in a mostly fruitless search for more profitable land. For Garland, the "sense of fraternity" Howells hoped realist writing could help to achieve among Americans of different regions and walks of life was a painful personal issue. He wrestled with guilt for having left his family to the "privations and hardships" that characterized their lives and those of their neighbors on "the enormous sunburned, treeless plain[s]" of what he dubbed the Middle Border (*Main-Travelled Roads* 21,19). The setting for his earliest and most memorable regionalist stories (collected in his 1891 book *Main-Travelled Roads*), Garland's Middle Border was the Midwestern agricultural frontier homesteaded by pioneers who, like his own family, found themselves plagued by recurrent droughts and insect infestations, as well as by fluctuating crop prices and exploitative shipping rates. Reflecting Garland's impassioned involvement in political movements such as the Farmer's Alliance (later the People's Party), some of the stories in *Main-Travelled Roads* have clear political goals. For example, "Under the Lion's Paw" utilizes a conflict between the desperately hard-working Haskins family and a ruthless land speculator in an attempt to motivate sympathetic readers to support specific national policies (above all Henry George's proposed Single Tax) designed to help small farmers squeezed by speculators, bankers, and railroad monopolists. Even as "Under the Lion's Paw" pleaded the western farmer's cause to the largely metropolitan audience of *Harper's Weekly*, however, in stories such as "Up the Coolly" (unpublished until its inclusion in *Main-Travelled Roads*) Garland expressed pessimism about the challenge of retaining or constructing anew any form of connection between urban professionals, such as he had become, and struggling rural farmers who still remained, at least in name, part of the same national family.

Critical controversy: Sarah Orne Jewett and women's regionalism

The local-color fiction of the late nineteenth century that seems closest to shar-ing Howells's hopeful vision that literary encounters with otherness might lead to genuine connection and mutual strengthening, and perhaps even provide a model for positive social change, is a sub-genre of regionalist writing, written by women and primarily (but not exclusively) set in New England. This fiction emphasizes relationship and community among women characters who differ in one or more significant ways, which among other factors may include social class, taste and habits, personal histories, or an actual past conflict. Scholars of women's literature have linked a number of regionalist women writers to this tradition, including both Freeman and Woolson. But the beauty and complex-ity of Sarah Orne Jewett's writing – her powerful ability, for instance, to create a compelling mood and draw readers into it – have led to her work being the object of particular attention. Jewett grew up the daughter of a doctor in the town of South Berwick, Maine, about thirty miles from the Atlantic coast. Wil-liam Dean Howells accepted one of her short stories for the *Atlantic Monthly* before Jewett was twenty years old, and her first book, *Deephaven*, was pub-lished in 1877. Although she continued to spend some of her time in South Berwick, Jewett ultimately devoted the bulk of each year to living with her companion Annie Fields in Boston, as well as traveling with her in the United States and Europe.

Almost all of Jewett's fiction is set in coastal Maine, from her earliest stor-ies to the book that is generally regarded as her masterpiece, *The Country of the Pointed Firs* (1896). *The Country of the Pointed Firs* has for its first-person narrator an unnamed Boston writer of comfortable means, who arrives in the village of Dunnet Landing one summer looking for a peaceful, restorative atmosphere in which to complete a writing project. Her original writing project gets put to the side, however, as she begins to develop a friendship with her landlady, Mrs. Almira Todd. Ultimately, she writes *The Country of the Pointed Firs*, which focuses on that friendship, instead. A widow, Mrs. Todd sells medicinal and other herbs from her home. She takes the narrator with her on herb-gathering trips, as well as on visits to Mrs. Todd's many friends and relations in and around the village, including her impressive mother Mrs. Blackett, who lives alone on Green Island with Almira's 62-year-old reclusive brother William. The narrator, whose name we never learn, soon develops relationships of her own with several of the village's eccentric inhabitants. Dunnet Landing was once actively involved in the international shipping and whaling industries, before steamships replaced sailing ships, and before petroleum replaced whale oil. By the period of the narrator's visit, the town is in economic decline. With many of its young men having died at sea or in the Civil War, and more having moved to the West in search of new economic opportunities, Dunnet Landing seems populated primarily by women, with a few elderly men who occasionally go out fishing in small weathered boats.

The novel's strong women characters and the web of relationships among them have embodied for some recent readers an alternative value system to such "classic" American themes as individualism, competition, and domination over nature, women, and people of color (starting with American Indians). For some critics, Jewett's work defines "identity as collective, connected, and collaborative," as does the writing by other female authors re-published in the influential 1992 anthology, *American Women Regionalists, 1850–1910*, edited by scholars Judith Fetterley and Marjorie Pryse (xvi). For critic Elizabeth Ammons, even the narrative structure of *The Country of the Pointed Firs* moves away from a traditionally masculine (at least in white Western culture) trajectory of linear build-up to a climax, followed by release. By contrast to this conventional narrative structure, Ammons argues, *The Country of the Pointed Firs* is formed more along the lines of such traditionally "feminine" patterns as the circle and the web. Grounded in the core relationship of the narrator and Mrs. Todd, the book's story grows outward from this center, incorporating other characters "in concentric waves of relationality and community" (Ammons, *Conflicting Stories* 46).

Fetterley and Pryse assert that it is primarily male-written "local-color" fiction that encourages snobbish divisions between metropolitan visitors on the one side and, on the other side, primitive, ignorant, or comic locals. They reserve the term "regionalism" for female-centered works which, they argue, characteristically show women – including female narrators visiting from outside the region – growing as they learn from one another in a locally grounded "community of women" (*American Women* xvi). Regarding Jewett's *The Country of the Pointed Firs*, Fetterley and Pryse explain that not only does the text's unnamed narrator from the city reshape her own identity in relation to the older Dunnet Landing women with whom she develops bonds but, in putting her experiences on paper, she also "passes on what she learned from Mrs. Todd and Mrs. Blackett to the successive generations who will read her fiction" (xvi).

Many of the feminist scholars involved in the work of recovering forgotten or marginalized regionalist fiction by women share the goal that Fetterley and Pryse attribute to the narrator of Jewett's *The Country of the Pointed Firs*: that of continuing to pass on the values and wisdom cultivated in "communities of women" such as that Jewett depicts to later generations of readers. Hence, significant controversy erupted when a new wave of scholarship, initiated in the early 1990s and in many cases also produced by feminist scholars, used *The Country of the Pointed Firs* as a prime example in developing a revisionist interpretation of the entire genre of late-nineteenth-century regionally focused literature. For instance, although expressing admiration for both the canon-expanding recovery effort and the "practical-critical" work on Jewett and other regionalist writers performed by scholars such as Fetterley and Pryse, Richard Brodhead's book *Cultures of Letters* (1993) goes so far as to contend that the very category of "women's culture," though of signal importance in feminist canon-recovery scholarship since at least the early 1970s, is overly general, even naïve: "This criticism has tended to forget that no culture is ever specified by its gender dimension alone: that in the real historical world there has been no 'women's culture' but plural and divergent women's cultures, each defined by a host of other social determinants" (144).

Regionalism's revisionist critics generally reject the differences Fetterley and Pryse argue for between condescending, male-authored "local color" writing of the late nineteenth century and a supposedly anti-hierarchical women's regionalism: as a result the genre's revisionist critics use the terms "local color" and "regionalism" interchangeably. For the most part, these critics agree with Brodhead's contention that the "social determinant" most relevant for an understanding of late-nineteenth-century US regionalist writing is not gender but instead the post-Civil War growth and consolidation of the urban middle and upper-middle classes, who defined their cultural identity – and implicitly claimed cultural superiority – in large part through their leisure habits. Such habits included going to the new art museums that were opening in cities across the country, reading "quality" magazines such as the *Atlantic Monthly* and *Harper's*, and taking regular summer vacations either in Europe or in "scenic" areas of America. Brodhead insists that literary regionalism by both male and female authors played into the same "class logic" as these other leisure practices (*Cultures* 145). He points out how frequently the sketches and stories of writers such as Jewett, Freeman, and Murfree made their first appearances in "quality" magazines right next to non-fiction articles and illustrations introducing potential vacation areas to well-off readers, such as New York's Adirondack Mountains and Kentucky's "Blue Grass Country" (131) and giving advice on such matters as how to interview a potential cook for one's yacht (125).

Critics such as Brodhead pick up, but also extend further, the implicit critique local-color writer Constance Fenimore Woolson had already made of the then-young genre in her satiric "In Search of the Picturesque." Brodhead contends that Jewett's fictional Dunnet Landing is "a world realized in a vacationer's mental image" (145). In Brodhead's view, the village functions as a place of rest and restoration for the narrator, a temporary break from her own "world of stressful modernity and its social arrangements" (145). In practice, this means that Jewett's text defines Dunnet Landing "not in its independent reality," but instead as a place that, for the space of several weeks in her life, effectively devotes itself to filling the narrator's psychological, emotional, and even recreational needs (146). In telling her readers at the end of the book that she writes for other travelers who "have a Dunnet Landing of their own," Brodhead claims, the narrator appropriates the rural village, turning it (or any other rural locales metropolitan readers have vacationed in or read about) into an exploitable resource that urbanites can, at least imaginatively, "own."

Revisionist interpreters of regionalism – including Elizabeth Ammons in a new essay on *The Country of the Pointed Firs*, in which she explicitly revises her earlier celebration of Jewett's text – have further argued that racism and nativism (that is, anti-immigrant xenophobia) also lay behind the appeal of regionalist writing set in such largely white rural enclaves as coastal Maine and the Appalachian mountains of Tennessee. In the decades after the Civil War, millions of immigrants arrived in the United States from eastern and southern Europe, from Latin America, and from Asia. These "new" immigrants (as opposed to those from western European countries) spoke unfamiliar languages, had religions different from the nation's prevailing Protestantism, and presented uncertain possibilities for assimilation into mainstream America. Many established Americans also feared that the new immigrants were bringing radical political ideas with them, including socialism, trade unionism, and anarchism. (See Chapter 10 for a discussion of realist writing by "new" Americans.)

The revisionist critics suggest that literary regionalism's rural white communities did represent "difference" to white metropolitan readers, but a difference these readers found more comforting, less threatening than that embodied by the waves of new immigrants settling in their own cities. Consider, for example, how Jewett has the narrator of her first book, *Deephaven*, describe for readers the people she sees in the church of a small Maine village on a Sunday morning:

> Have you never seen faces that seemed old-fashioned? ... These faces were not modern American faces, but belonged rather to the days of the early settlement of the country, the old colonial times. We often heard quaint words and expressions which we never had known anywhere else but in old books ... Among the people who live on the lonely farms inland we often noticed words we had seen in Chaucer, and studied out at school in our English literature class. (44)

For nativist readers who nursed fears that the large influx of new immigrants might be in the process of altering the very meaning of "America" and "American," this passage from *Deephaven* offers a consoling image. It depicts the rural folk who inhabit the small New England village as safely preserving, as if in some repository untouched by social change or by even the passage of time, what many established white Americans regarded as the nation's "true" racial, ethnic, and cultural identity: that of a former English colony which may have become politically independent but still retains deep cultural ties to the "mother country" and its traditions.

Amy Kaplan's influential essay "Nation, Region, and Empire" in *The Columbia History of the American Novel* (1991) takes an even further step in the revisionist reading of Jewett and of regionalism. Kaplan sets the genre within the context of the heightened, often jingoistic nationalism of the late-nineteenth-century United States. Kaplan focuses on a scene toward the end of *The Country of the Pointed Firs*, when the extended Bowden "clan" (of which Mrs. Todd, the narrator's host in Dunnet Landing, is a leading member) holds their large yearly reunion. Family members attend from towns throughout the area, and some from even further away. Kaplan points out that Jewett's narrator compares the reunion to "the great national anniversaries our country has lately kept" (Kaplan, "Nation" 150). Explicitly mentioning the "soldiers' meetings" that were held throughout the 1880s and 1890s, in which Civil War veterans North and South affirmed their shared devotion to the reunified nation, the narrator sees the Bowden family reunion as one of those occasions when "the altars to patriotism, to friendship, to the ties of kindred are reared" (Jewett, *Novels and Stories* 457). The reunion proves "the old saying that blood is thicker than water" and that "clannishness is an instinct of the heart" (469). For Kaplan, the narrator's framing of the Bowden reunion as a celebration of patriotism, shared blood, and a "common inheritance" indicates that regionalism had a role in constructing a prevalent view of the "real" America as a reunified, homogeneous white nation prepared to assert its power against racial others in overseas territories such as the Philippines, at the same time as it also subordinated and excluded from the national "family" racial and ethnic others at home (Kaplan, "Nation" 145).

Revisionist readers of Jewett, including Brodhead, Kaplan, Ammons, and others, do not necessarily contend that Sarah Orne Jewett was a conscious and active supporter of imperial conquest, xenophobia, or class-based elitism. Rather, these critics find assumptions, propositions, and meanings embedded in *The Country of the Pointed Firs* that are consonant with, and may have worked subtly to reinforce, those objectionable perspectives, which others during Jewett's period expressed and acted on more directly and harmfully. (There were also people at the time, however, who courageously denounced and resisted these perspectives, including ethnic regionalist writers such as Zitkala-Ša and Charles Chesnutt, whom we will discuss in later chapters.) Still, it should not be surprising that critics who had been integrally involved in the recovery of Jewett as a major American author, in large part because of her preeminent position in what they view as an "alternative and oppositional" women's regionalism, would object, in some cases forcefully, to these new interpretations of her writing and its cultural meanings (Fetterley and Pryse, *Writing Out of Place* 222).

Fetterley and Pryse's response to the recent revisionist criticism of both Jewett and late-nineteenth-century regionalism itself came in their jointly authored book, *Writing Out of Place: Regionalism, Women, and American Literary Culture* (2003). They accuse critics such as Brodhead, Kaplan, and Ammons of unfairly targeting regionalist writing by women, and particularly Sarah Orne Jewett, in order to return literature by men to its traditionally dominant place in the US literary canon. Regarding the Bowden reunion scene, they argue against Kaplan's and Ammons's claims that it illustrates the reunification of a "white" nation preparing for imperial conquest abroad. Fetterley and Pryse observe, among other things, that it is the narrator, not Mrs. Todd or the other local characters, who portentously claims that the event marks a moment in which "the altars to patriotism, to friendship, to the ties of kindred are reared." The narrator, Fetterly and Pryse argue, has not yet fully internalized the alternative values that regionalism offers, and hence her remarks do not always accurately represent the perspectives of Mrs. Todd or of Jewett herself (238). Similarly, Ammons's revisionist essay detected an underlying militarist tone to the reunion in, among other elements, the presence of a "soldierly little figure of a man," Sant Bowden, who "marshall[s]" the "great family" into ranks and marches them to the large clearing where the picnic itself will be held (Ammons, "Material Culture" 95). Fetterley and Pryse point out, however, that Mrs. Todd and another local woman named Mrs. Caplin gently mock both Sant Bowden and the military impulse as such: "All he thinks of, when he sees a crowd, is how to march 'em. 'Tis all very well when he don't 'tempt too much," Mrs. Caplin remarks (237). At moments such as this, Fetterley and Pryse assert, it is regional women characters, such as Mrs. Todd, Mrs. Blackett, and Mrs. Caplin, who "propose region as a site of resistance to empire and offers the region's values as alternatives to those of the nation" (235).

The continuing controversy over regionalism has helped reveal multiple strands of meaning that contribute both to our interpretations of individual works and to our understanding of the local-color movement as such. It now seems clear that the touristic fantasy-based approach to the rural that Woolson's 1872 "In Search of the Picturesque" satirizes – additional dimensions and implications of which are pointed out by Kaplan's, Brodhead's, and Ammons's critical analyses of Jewett – did play a major role in the genre's success, particularly among the audiences to whom elite magazines such as the *Atlantic Monthly* and *Harper's* addressed themselves. Yet this does not mean that Howells's vision of regionalism helping to foster greater sympathy and solidarity among different segments of the American public went entirely unfulfilled. We can see an instance of such solidarity in, for example, the respect that Freeman's "A Mistaken Charity" builds for Charlotte and Harriet's determination to remain independent. The story may partake of certain metropolitan fantasies regarding the "primitive" simplicity of rural existence, as argued above. Yet it also encourages readers to root for and admire the sisters as they make a conscious choice to live their own lives as they always have, rather than surrender to the supposed modern improvements of the nearby city's "Old Ladies' Home."

As for Jewett's *The Country of the Pointed Firs*, nativist white readers of the comfortable classes may well have found Jewett's depiction of Dunnet Landing as a stable, deeply-rooted white community reassuring. Dunnet Landing appears to exist almost in another world from the ongoing conflicts surrounding industrialization and immigration that were so palpable elsewhere in the country. However, if we recall the "complexity of motive" Howells insists is essential to realism ("Editor's Study," 1886, 972), even the racist underpinnings of Dunnet Landing society may not prevent the internal structure of the community itself, which consists, as Fetterley, Pryse, and others have demonstrated, of a network of empathic, relatively non-hierarchical relationships among women, from yielding glimpses of a more egalitarian, peaceful, and caring social order. In other words, Jewett – and arguably white women's regionalism more generally – does offer a vision of an "alternative" social order, but it is a vision sustained through certain opacities and exclusions.

Our next chapter considers what might be viewed from one perspective as another form of regionalist realism: fiction that foregrounds an explicitly urban setting. Among the issues raised by realist writing set in cities is whether metropolitan areas such as New York were indeed best portrayed as distinct "regions" along the same lines as, for example, coastal Maine or, instead, as national centers made up of migrants and immigrants with diverse racial, ethnic, and national identities. Furthermore, as we will see, the social class divisions that regionalist writing often pictured between poorer local charac- ters and economically privileged visitors from outside the region were more immediate, intense, and unavoidable within the intimate geographies of late- nineteenth-century cities, where slums often abutted wealthy neighborhoods. Did a region such as New York even have a coherent cultural identity? If not, what did it mean for a writer to try to represent the city?

Chapter 6

"The blab of the pave": realism and the city

Describing downtown Chicago (birthplace of the modern skyscraper in 1884) in his novel *The Cliff-Dwellers* (1893), Henry Blake Fuller metaphorically compared its cityscape of tall buildings and narrow streets to the spectacular cliffs and canyons of America's rugged Southwest, whose natural formations scientists working for the US Geological Survey were only just beginning to study. "Each of these cãnóns," Fuller wrote, referring to the city streets,

> is closed in by a long frontage of towering cliffs [i.e., tall buildings], and these soaring walls of brick and limestone and granite rise higher and higher with each succeeding year, according as the work of erosion at their bases goes onward – the work of that seething flood of carts, carriages, omnibuses, cabs, cars, messengers, shoppers, clerks, and capitalists, which surges with increasing violence for every passing day.   (1–2)

Though playful, Fuller's comparison of Chicago's business district to an imposing geologic phenomenon registers the startling magnitude of the transformation American cities underwent during the late nineteenth and early twentieth centuries. The Chicago metropolitan area's growth was especially stunning – from not quite 110,000 people in 1860 to over 1,700,000 by 1900 and then to 2,366,000 people by 1910. During the same period, New York City's population more than quadrupled, from just over a million people in 1860 to a total of 4,766,883 inhabitants in 1910 (Gardner and Haines, "Metropolitan Areas"). Fuller's comparison with canyons and cliffs provides his readers with a natural lens through which to view the changing visual profile of the modern city. Just as moving water erodes and reshapes rock, a "seething flood" of mixed crowds and modern conveyances has forced the cityscape into a striking new form. For Fuller, the "increasing violence" of its "surges" suggests a frighteningly destructive potential. The torrential urban flow sweeps up everything in its path, jumbling together objects and people, even wealthy "capitalists" who might normally be thought of as somewhere above, controlling the flow. Late-nineteenth-century realist writers took as one of their primary challenges to represent in literature a phenomenon – that of the rapidly changing, rapidly expanding American city – that in the eyes of many Americans combined menacing dangers with new and exciting, if disturbing, forms of spectacle.

The United States moved briskly in the direction of becoming an urban nation in the decades following the Civil War. By 1900, more than two-thirds of all Americans living in the Northeast resided in large urban centers, as did 40 percent of the nation's entire population. Throughout the country, the growth of cities – where 90 percent of manufacturing now took place – was fueled by migrants from rural areas, who came in search of jobs (efficient new machinery made agricultural jobs increasingly scarce) and the promise of change (Trachtenberg, *Incorporation of America* 114). In the years between 1880 and 1920, twenty people from farming regions moved to cities for every one urban inhabitant who moved to a farm, while ten children of farmers departed for every one who stayed (Mizruchi, *Rise of Multicultural America* 77). City populations were swelled even more by tens of millions of immigrants who arrived from eastern and southern Europe, from Latin America, and from Asia, all areas that had previously sent relatively few people to America. (Chapter 10 will discuss immigrants and other "new" Americans who employed literary realist techniques to portray their experiences.)

American cities weren't only exploding in size; they were also changing in character. The United States' expanding economy created many new millionaires as well as hundreds of thousands of new positions both for members of what has been called the "managerial-professional" middle classes (including engineers, doctors, college professors, stock brokers, lawyers, mid-level executives, and civil service administrators) and also for lower-middle-class "white-collar" workers, such as store clerks and traveling salesmen. Numerically speaking, however, the most rapidly growing group in the nation was the urban poor. In addition to the dramatic increase in the numbers of immigrants arriving from abroad and of migrants from rural areas coming to cities and looking for work, the boom and bust cycles of American capitalism led to major economic panics in 1873 and 1893, which produced immense armies of unemployed men and women. As the poor crowded into cities, vast slums developed, often overlapping with industrial neighborhoods where sweatshops, larger factories, and freight transportation hubs were located. While many middle-class professionals still continued to live in cities (though rarely in industrial areas), some were already beginning to move out to the suburbs, served by an increasing number of commuter trains and trolley lines. Meanwhile, the wealthy had lavish homes both in fashionable resort areas such as Newport, Rhode Island and in exclusive city neighborhoods that may have been located only a short geographic distance from the slums, but that were immensely different in style of habitation, density of buildings and population, and the level of public services (such as sanitation) provided.

As we saw in Chapter 4, "high realist" writers such as Henry James and Edith Wharton focused their fiction primarily on the middle and upper classes, characteristically pushing poor and working-class people to the margins or even off their pages. By contrast, works discussed in the current chapter engage the challenge of realistically portraying city spaces in which the urban poor constitute a tangible, visible presence.[1]

The "other" half

The Gilded Age, as historians often call the decades following the Civil War (the phrase comes from the title of a satiric novel by Mark Twain and Charles Dudley Warner), witnessed the greatest disparity in incomes since the nation's founding. The gaps between the poor and the well-off went beyond money, however. As urban slums grew in size and density, and as their populations became increasingly dominated by people whom established whites of the time called "foreign stock" (meaning at least one parent was born outside of the United States), a sense of cultural estrangement grew as well. Many middle- and upper-class Americans viewed burgeoning urban slums as a sort of mysterious foreign territory, inhabited by strange others whom they regarded with varying mixtures of fear, disdain, compassion, philanthropic zeal, and voyeuristic curiosity. The slums, many Americans believed, were centers of sin and vice replete with drug and alcohol abuse, juvenile delinquency, illicit sexual activity, and casual violence. A series of labor strikes in cities and industrial areas throughout the nation during the 1880s, several of which culminated in violent clashes between strikers and strike-breakers (the latter often backed by private militias hired by company owners), further contributed to a feeling on the part of many middle- and upper-class Americans that the modernizing nation's explosively growing cities were the epicenter of precisely those social and cultural changes they found most frightening.

In 1890, social reformer and pioneering documentary photographer Jacob Riis published a highly influential book, *How the Other Half Lives*. Riis used photographs (which had to be converted to line drawings for printing in the book's earliest editions), statistical charts, and journalistic prose in an attempt to introduce the nation's comfortable classes to the poorest inhabitants of its largest city, New York. Though *How the Other Half Lives* is technically a non-fiction text, scholars often discuss it in the context of literary realism, not only because of its direct influence on realist writers such as Stephen Crane, but also because the book's claim to offer a combination of documentary accuracy, reliable objectivity, and a uniquely intimate perspective on slum dwellers and their lives closely matches literary realist aims. Riis strove to convince readers that all of American society was implicated in the overcrowded and unsanitary slums, from tenement owners who themselves lived on Fifth Avenue to apathetic lawmakers to middle- and upper-class citizens who ignored the problem even while wearing clothes manufactured in immigrant sweatshops – clothes, Riis emphasized, that might still carry germs picked up from their slum origins.

Impact and Implications of *How the Other Half Lives*

In many respects, Riis's work had a positive impact. His book's detailed exposé of the harsh and damaging environment in which millions of New York City's poor people were forced to live, which Riis further illustrated in narrated slide shows he presented around the state, helped instigate reforms involving such issues as tenement design and the provision of public parks and playgrounds in poor neighborhoods. At the same time, however, several features of *How the Other Half Lives* also conveyed a sense that impoverished slum dwellers truly were "other" from the established Americans to whom Riis addressed the book. Although some of Riis's pictures focus on individuals, in many the people depicted seem to meld into one another and into their cluttered backgrounds, as if there is no real distinction between them and the dirty, disorganized slums in which they live. Even in some of the pictures where individuals are clearly visible their bodies appear as shapeless masses. It is true that the relatively new technology Riis was using may, in certain cases, have contributed to a photograph's depersonalizing effects. Regardless, the depersonalization remains. Moreover, relatively few of Riis's pictures show us full-on individual faces, looking at the camera, as was common in the studio photographs many middle-class Americans had taken of themselves during this period. In the written portions of *How the Other Half Lives*, Riis assumes the persona of a tour or perhaps jungle guide, warning his readers not to (metaphorically) "stumble" as he shepherds them through a deep, dark, and very alien territory, full of unexpected sights and unfamiliar beings (38). In sum, although *How the Other Half Lives* encouraged its readers to "see" the urban poor, it did little to promote a sense of solidarity, kinship, or imaginative identification with them.

Figure 1 *Tenement House Yard*, c. 1890. Museum of the City of New York, Jacob A. Riis Collection.

But what of fictional treatments of the nation's new urban realities? William Dean Howells's *A Hazard of New Fortunes*, published in 1890 – the same year as Riis's *How the Other Half Lives* – was the first extended attempt by a literary realist to grapple with both the stark class contrasts and the striking ethnic diversity of the post-Civil War American city. As we will see, Howells elected to approach this material via the experiences of a fictional professional-class couple who have just moved to New York and who, as they try to establish a life in the city, observe and speculate about the urban population that surrounds them. Later in the decade and into the early twentieth century, a younger generation of "naturalist" writers including Stephen Crane, Upton Sinclair, and David Graham Phillips offered representations of urban poverty often considered to be more direct and immediate than those of older realists such as Howells. After a detailed consideration of *A Hazard of New Fortunes*, we will turn to Stephen Crane's "naturalist" portrayal of New York's slums in *Maggie: A Girl of the Streets* (1893). We will consider literary naturalism more fully in Chapter 7, but the current chapter will ask, to what extent does – or doesn't – *Maggie's* attempt to portray slum life from the "inside" provide a deeper, richer understanding of the urban poor than Howells's novel with its explicit emphasis on the perceptions of middle-class characters?

Howells's *Hazard*

Howells began writing *A Hazard of New Fortunes* in the winter of 1888–89, around the same time that he moved his home from Boston to the larger and more metropolitan New York City. During this period, even as he was enjoying greater professional success (and making more money) than ever before, Howells also found himself increasingly dismayed by what he saw as growing inequalities and injustices in America's social system. Among prominent American artists and intellectuals, Howells alone publicly opposed the hanging of Chicago's Haymarket anarchists for their alleged murder of police officers during a labor demonstration. Howells correctly believed that the arrested men, most of whom were immigrants, had been framed by panicked authorities eager to show themselves in control of potentially explosive class conflict in the city.

In open letters to newspapers and in a passionate plea to the Governor of Illinois, Howells insisted that the state was going to execute the anarchists on the basis of their unpopular opinions and not for any acts the men had committed or been involved in committing (Goodman and Dawson, *William Dean Howells* 282). His protests failed, but Howells's lonely stance against the hangings was a brave one. In an atmosphere of public fear and anger, he risked his income by knowingly displeasing his employer, even after being warned that speaking out on the issue violated the terms of his contract with the Harpers firm (Goodman and Dawson, *William Dean Howells* 281). Because of his public agitation in defense of the anarchists (whose political goals he did not support) Howells was vilified in the mainstream press as, in his own words, an "imbecile and bad citizen" who encouraged threats to public order (*William Dean Howells* 283). Howells's involvement in the Haymarket events correlated with his immersion during the same period in the powerful social writings of Russian novelist Leo Tolstoy, who drew inspiration from the New Testament in advocating a radical social equality. In New York, the nation's largest city, Howells was struck more deeply than ever before by the discrepancies between actual American life and the nation's promises of liberty, justice, and equality for all. During this period, his earlier optimistic belief that literary realism could help to unite Americans of different backgrounds by showing them that they were "more like than unlike one another" (see Chapter 5) was severely shaken, if not fully abandoned.

Howells sets *A Hazard of New Fortunes* within a New York City that is, as characters in the book describe it, "vast," "frantic," and "heterogeneous" (301, 184, 301). The story cuts back and forth among several significant characters, but primary among these is Basil March, the husband from Howells's first realist novel, *Their Wedding Journey*, which he had written almost two decades earlier (see Chapter 2). Now well into middle age and with two teenaged children, Basil and his wife Isabel accept an offer to leave Boston for New York as the story opens. Basil will be the literary editor of a new magazine, *Every Other Week*, which hopes to distinguish itself by soliciting fresh contributions from around the entire country, as well as by paying its writers and artists according to a cooperative system. All of the novel's major characters have some level of involvement with the magazine, which thus serves as a shared point of connection for a web of disparate people, most of whom would otherwise have little in common.

Despite its author's increasingly radical ideas, in many ways *A Hazard of New Fortunes* reassures middle-class, Anglo-identified readers that they and people like them still retain their cultural centrality and power even in the midst of newly unsettling urban cityscapes. Within the novel, the fictional *Every Other Week* brings together a group of mostly middle-class white characters who are new to New York City, which the novel represents as significantly larger, more confusing and multifarious, and in certain respects more dangerous than its characters' previous communities (including the Marches' Boston). Their experiences of and attitudes toward the city vary, and in some cases clash, but the social and professional network the characters form around the project of creating a new periodical helps them to experience the sprawling metropolis as navigable, graspable, a space that can after all be at least cognitively assimilated, if not fully tamed, by members of the middle classes (see Kaplan, *Social Construction* 55).

Beyond the centering presence of *Every Other Week*, Howells's novel and its main character Basil March model additional strategies by which middle-class readers might acquire a sense of control over a city that many Americans imagined as an anarchic mass, growing at an ever-faster pace and bursting with angry, mostly foreign proletarians. Basil, for example, likes to explore the city's diverse neighborhoods, but he habitually distances himself from much of what he sees by turning it into an aesthetic spectacle, a tactic the text relays with gentle irony. For instance, riding the elevated railroad through a working-class neighborhood, Basil "said it was better than the theatre, of which it reminded him, to see those people through their windows … What suggestion! what drama! what infinite interest!" (76). Sitting on a bench in a Greenwich Village park full of immigrants, Basil and Isabel, who have traveled in Italy and Spain, "met the familiar picturesque raggedness of Southern Europe with the old kindly illusion that somehow it existed for their appreciation, and that it found adequate compensation for poverty in this" (55). Basil enjoys the mixed "ethnical character" of the Mott Street neighborhood, which was an early border of New York's Chinatown (186). His strolls around the city inspire him with the idea of composing a series of New York "local studies" for magazine publication (184). (We might envision Basil's proposed literary "studies" of the city's immigrant neighborhoods, which he never gets around to actually writing, as urban parallels to the local-color sketches of rural areas satirized by Constance Fenimore Woolson's "In Search of the Picturesque" – see Chapter 5, above.) Basil and Isabel come to pride themselves on having developed a distinct taste for the city's diverse ethnic character, so long as it is presented in a form that can be aesthetically appreciated. They become American literature's first middle-class New Yorkers, for example, to cast their pleasure in the city's ethnic restaurants (Italian, French, Spanish) into a unique sort of cosmopolitanism, one that distinguishes them from the more staid eating habits of other, less sophisticated members of their class (Barrish, *American Literary Realism*, 42).

As scholar Amy Kaplan points out, Basil, Isabel, and the novel's other middle-class characters try to restrict the city's working-class and impoverished immigrant population to the role of providing an interesting metropolitan background for their own dramatic narratives, unified around *Every Other Week*. Despite their best efforts, however, that "background" invades the foreground at key moments, most drastically during the violent streetcar strike that occurs at the end of the novel (Kaplan, *Social Construction* 59). Initially, the strike inconveniences the novel's main characters without directly affecting their lives. Even when the owners hire scabs (non-union replacement workers) and violence begins to occur at outlying points along the tracks, March retains "his character of philosophical observer" by comparing the struggle between the workers and the owners (supported by the police) to the medieval street wars fought between powerful families in such cities as Florence and Verona (Howells, *Hazard* 412, 407). *Every Other Week*'s publisher, Mr. Fulkerson, goes so far as to suggest that March should "go round" with the magazine's art editor to "take down" the strike's "aesthetic aspects" (409).

One afternoon, however, Basil absent-mindedly boards a trolley operated by replacement workers only to find it brought to a sudden halt by "a tumult of

shouting, cursing, struggling men" – a crowd of strikers and their sympathizers –
who try to force the replacement workers from their posts (421). A contingent
of police, meanwhile, battle the strikers. From his perch on the trolley car, Basil
notices Lindau, an elderly, erudite German-American radical who has done
some translating for the magazine, grabbing a policeman's arm to prevent him
from clubbing a striker. In the same instant, March sees the magazine owner's
son, Conrad Beaton, running forward in a futile attempt to stop the policeman
from instead clubbing Lindau, who is a Civil War veteran: "He's an old soldier!
You see he has no hand!" (422). A shot rings out and Conrad falls to the pave-
ment, dead, while Lindau sustains what will later prove a fatal blow from the
policeman's club. These deaths, tragic as all of the novel's characters feel them to
be, impart a sobering tone to the final pages of *A Hazard of New Fortunes*. Yet
the deaths still do not substantially affect the lives or views of the network that
has formed around *Every Other Week*. If anything, that community becomes
more solid, with the marriage of Fulkerson to Madison, the daughter of con-
servative essayist Colonel Woodburn, strengthening their interconnections.
Meanwhile, *Every Other Week* drops Fulkerson's original idea for sharing profits
among its staff and contributors and adopts a regular business model.

Urban poverty, middle-class rationalization, and self-criticism

A Hazard of New Fortunes provides models for managing middle-class anxieties about America's changing urban spaces. At the same time, the novel reveals
and perceptively critiques certain techniques used by middle-class urbanites to
rationalize the poverty, human suffering, and cultural alienation experienced
by many of the city's poorer inhabitants. Such techniques of rationalization
became more necessary as the close quarters of city life rendered dramatic differences in social class and material comforts highly visible, causing feelings
that we might today call "liberal guilt" on the part of well-intentioned citizens,
including not only the fictional Marches but also, as we will see, their creator.
In restricting his novel's point of view to that of his middle-class characters,
Howells keeps a group that is already socially and culturally empowered at the
center of his picture, as we have seen. But in doing so Howells also displays this
group's moral failings in regard to the urban poor – failings that he identified
first and foremost in himself.

A Hazard of New Fortunes uses a mixture of omniscient and focalized narration (see Chapter 3's discussion of narrative techniques), with a narrative
voice that goes in and out of various characters' consciousnesses: Basil most

frequently, but also Fulkerson and Conrad, among others. Notably, the narration never attempts to give the reader a view from inside the consciousness of a striker. Nor do we ever see slum life from the perspective of somebody who lives there. Even the erudite translator Lindau, who resides in the slums as a matter of political principle, we know only from the outside, through descriptions by the omniscient narrator and the perceptions of other characters, as well as by the fiery socialist's public declamations. The Marches are especially disturbed one evening not long after they have arrived in the city to observe what seems to be a "decently dressed person" searching the gutter for bits of food and cramming what he finds into his mouth (70). When Basil approaches to offer him a coin, the man tearfully thanks him and grasps Basil's hands. Basil is uncertain what to do or say after that. As he turns to Isabel, the man goes around a corner and disappears: he has "lapsed back into the mystery of misery out of which he had emerged" (71). Neither Basil nor Howells's novel attempts to follow him.

Howells's decision in *A Hazard of New Fortunes* not to give readers direct access to this starving man's experience of his own "misery" might from one perspective be seen as a failure of his realism. As we will see in later chapters, some writers and critics active in subsequent years scoffed at Howells as a so-called "founder" of American literary realism who was apparently too timid to explore in any detail the nitty-gritty, day-to-day experiences of the urban underclass. But I would argue that such criticism misses what is most original about Howells's realism here. It is true that the novel does not make even an ostensible attempt to open the inner experiences of the urban poor to readers. What *A Hazard of New Fortunes* does expose with notable acuity and candor, however, are the various psychological mechanisms by which intelligent and sympathetic people such as the Marches are able to accept, to live with, social conditions that include material deprivation and physical suffering for other human beings whose paths they cross on a regular basis.

In a letter that he wrote to Henry James the same year that he moved to New York, Howells bitterly announced that "'America'" (Howells places the country's name in quotation marks) now seemed to him "the most grotesquely illogical thing under the sun." "After fifty years of optimistic content with 'civilization' and its ability to come out all right in the end," Howells tells James, "I now abhor it, and feel that it is coming out all wrong in the end, unless it bases itself anew on a real equality. Meantime, I wear a fur-lined overcoat and live in all the luxury my money can buy" (quoted in Anesko, *Letters* 262). The letter expresses Howells's new disillusion with modern American society, crystallized by the Haymarket events. The quotation marks he puts around "America" signify Howells's perception of glaring contradictions between, on the one hand, the nation's self-image as a uniquely virtuous bastion of free-dom, equality, and justice and, on the other hand, the social and economic realities he saw around him, Similarly, the quotation marks around "civiliza-tion" signify Howells's doubt that late-nineteenth-century United States soci-ety deserves that name.

In the strike and in many of its street scenes, *A Hazard of New Fortunes* does make visible some of the uglier realities of late-nineteenth-century American capitalism: the pool of impoverished people accumulated in cities, the alliance between wealthy capitalists and the executive branch of government (repre-sented by police and, in many cases, state and federal militia) to fight unions and keep working-class wages low. Yet Howells devotes *A Hazard of New Fortunes* at least as much to unfolding the implications of the final sentence in the passage quoted above from his letter to James, where Howells admits that, despite his bitter criticisms of American capitalism, he continues to enjoy the luxuries (the fur coat) it makes available to people of his class. Summoning the honesty he felt realism demanded, Howells used his novel about New York City to explore, among its other themes, a set of contradictions he recognized in himself and in others he knew.

In *A Hazard of New Fortunes*, after Basil gives money to the man who had been eating scraps from the gutter, Isabel announces to him that she will not live in New York: "I shall not come to a place where such things are possible, and we may as well stop our house-hunting here at once." Basil responds with a rueful challenge: "Yes? And what part of Christendom will you live in? Such things are possible everywhere in our conditions." "Then we must change the conditions– " Isabel exclaims. Basil interrupts her, "Oh no; we must go to the theatre and forget them. We can stop at Brentano's for our tickets as we pass through Union Square" (71). Basil implies that the problem is too big for them to solve and, since they can't do anything about it, they may as well enjoy themselves at the theater. At the same time, Basil is self-aware enough to recognize such rationalizations for precisely what they are: excuses for accepting a socioeconomic system ("our conditions") where "such things are possible" – such things, that is, as a starving man eating scraps from the gutter as others hurry by for an evening at the the-ater. After driving through an especially impoverished slum street, which they view through a carriage window, Isabel offers another rationalization: "I don't believe there's any *real* suffering – not real *suffering* – among those people; that is, it would be suffering from our point of view, but they've been used to it all their lives, and they don't feel their discomfort so much" (69). Basil accepts and agrees with her assertion, but he does so with a perceptible degree of self-irony; "I shall keep that firmly in mind," he tells Isabel with a laugh (70). Basil's ironic laugh, directed just as much at himself as at Isabel, indicates his understanding that holding to a belief that "those people" don't feel suffering in the way that "we" would is a way to alleviate his and Isabel's feelings of guilt about their own relatively luxurious lives.

Howells's realism in regard to a city sharply divided by extremes of poverty and material comfort, as well as by ethnicity, race, and status as "native" or "foreign," does not attempt to show readers "how the other half lives," as the title of Jacob Riis's book promises to do. As we saw above, Riis's depiction of harsh conditions in the slums did help to prompt some reforms, but the manner in which *How the Other Half Lives* actually presents poor urban immigrants relies on ethnic stereotypes and other distancing (and at times dehumanizing) devices to convey a view of them as definitively "other" from established white Americans (see text box above). By contrast to Riis, Howells makes no claim that either *A Hazard of New Fortune*'s main characters or the book's narrative voice sees the city's slum inhabitants as they "really" are – or for that matter that the middle-class characters can have any idea of how they themselves appear from the vantage-point of those living in the slums. Instead of trying to penetrate the lives, experiences, or consciousnesses of urban poor people, the novel explores the complex but ultimately self-serving responses its middle-class characters have when brought face to face with the effects of urban poverty or of struggles between capital and labor. In other words, the realism of *A Hazard of New Fortunes* exists more in its nuanced portrayal of Basil March's conflicted psychology, including his psychological evasions and rationalizations, in the face of the urban poor than in the book's admittedly external portrayal of the urban poor themselves.

People of the streets: *Maggie*'s slums

In 1893 Stephen Crane, a 20-year-old college dropout, used a small inheritance to print just over a thousand copies of his first novel, *Maggie: A Girl of the Streets.* The book found few readers, however, until after the 1895 publication of Crane's second novel. *The Red Badge of Courage* narrates the experiences, emotions, and thoughts of the fictional Henry Fleming, a common infantryman, during the Civil War's three-day Battle of Chancellorsville. When Crane wrote *Red Badge* he had never seen a battle; instead, he had learned about Chancellorsville and other Civil War clashes by reading non-fiction accounts written by veterans. Despite Crane's lack of personal experience, however, numerous readers found the book's depiction of what war feels like to its participants compellingly realistic. Veterans who had fought at Chancellorsville insisted that *The Red Badge of Courage* could *only* have been written by someone who had participated in the battle, and the work quickly became an international bestseller. Its precocious young author was transformed, almost overnight, into a literary celebrity. Crane's new fame led *Red Badge*'s New York publisher to issue a new edition of *Maggie* in 1896. Although *Maggie* would never approach the dazzling level of sales or public attention achieved by *The Red Badge of Courage*, this time around Crane's book about life in the urban slums was widely reviewed in periodicals and newspaper and enjoyed respectable sales. As we will see, most reviewers offered strong praise of the novel's realism.[2]

Like Howells's *A Hazard of New Fortunes*, Crane's *Maggie: A Girl of the Streets* takes place in late-nineteenth-century New York City. But the novels differ dramatically. Where *A Hazard of New Fortunes* views the urban poor entirely through the eyes of its middle-class protagonists, Crane's text contains no middle-class characters at all, except for a few nameless individuals who brush past his slum characters in the street. *Maggie* takes readers directly inside tenement apartments, into Bowery saloons, and among working-class audiences as they consume cheap popular entertainments made available to them by the new mass culture industry. In marked contrast to Howells's representation of the urban scene, *Maggie*'s omniscient narrator makes us privy to slum inhabitants' perceptions and thoughts, often inviting us to look through their eyes at events and other characters in the novel.

Does Crane's choice to offer readers direct access of this sort mean that *Maggie* provides a fuller and more accurate view of the slums and those who inhabit them than Howells's *A Hazard of New Fortunes*, which continuously makes readers aware that they are seeing urban poor people only through the eyes of the novel's middle-class characters? *Maggie*'s depiction of life in the slums certainly succeeded in conveying what Henry James would call "the air of reality" (see Chapter 3) to many of its early readers and reviewers. Reviewing Crane's *Maggie* in *The Arena*, for example, realist writer Hamlin Garland called it "the most truthful and unhackneyed study of the slums I have yet read" (Weatherford, *Stephen Crane* 38). Howells himself admired *Maggie* more than he did Crane's better-known *The Red Badge of Courage*, asserting that *Maggie*'s "greater fidelity" as a representation of actual life "cannot be questioned" (Weatherford 47). Edward Marshall, editor of the New York *Press*, claimed that *Maggie* "approaches nearer to realizing it [slum life] than any other book written by an American ever has" (Weatherford 39), while an anonymous reviewer for *Munsey's Magazine* announced to the publication's more than half a million subscribed readers that Crane's novel demonstrated "a scrupulous regard for veracious description" (Weatherford 53).

Figure 2 *Giving the Girl a Show. Also in Playground,* c. 1895. Museum of the City of New York, Jacob A. Riis Collection.

Current scholarly treatments of *Maggie* have continued to develop the theme initiated by early reviewers of the novel's "veracious description" of slum life. One especially rich and compelling vein of contemporary scholarship, for example, has focused on expanding our understanding of the depth and acuity with which Crane's text engages with late-nineteenth-century urban American culture. Critic Keith Gandal, for instance, has explored Crane's depiction of New York's Bowery neighborhood as a place in which the assumptions of middle-class morality jostle uneasily against alternative ethical codes in such areas as sexual behavior, interpersonal violence, and the earning and bestowing of respect (Gandal, *Virtues of the Vicious* 52–55). Crane's non-judgmental stance toward the alternative ethical codes visible in the Bowery, Gandal emphasizes, offers a notable contrast with the overtly moralistic perspective taken by most other post-Civil War writing about the slums during the post-Civil War period

(*Virtues of the Vicious* 56). Scholar Andrew Lawson has highlighted how well *Maggie* captures the intense pressure felt by urban inhabitants to "perform" different identities in a variety of new public spaces ("Class Mimicry" 597–98), a phenomenon emphasized by recent cultural historians of the period as well. Such spaces included not only the many cheap theaters situated in the Bowery, which offered vaudeville shows and popular melodramas, but also crowded and brightly lit nighttime avenues. For working-class people employed in the city's burgeoning service sector, whether as showy bartenders, retail sales staff, or streetwalkers, projecting an image was a crucial part of the job – just as it was, Lawson points out, for those slum dwellers who hoped to receive assistance from the many charitable and philanthropic organizations operating in New York's poorer neighborhoods, which often sent investigators to ascertain whether a given tenement family was "virtuous" enough to deserve help (see Lawson, "Class Mimicry" 599–610).

Approaches such as Gandal's and Lawson's reveal *Maggie*'s intimate connections with specific aspects of late-nineteenth-century urban cultures. When early reviewers of *Maggie* wished to underline Crane's "scrupulous regard for veracious description," however, more often than not they emphasized his depiction of lower-class urban *speech* (Weatherford, *Stephen Crane* 53). Representations of "slum" dialect play a prominent role throughout the book and can legitimately be said to dominate several important scenes. Howells's review asserted that *Maggie* offered readers "the best tough dialect which has yet found its way into print" (Weatherford 40). The *New York Times* dubbed Crane "a master of slum slang" and described the dialogue between slum characters as "surprisingly effective and natural" (Weatherford 42). The *Morning Advertiser*, also published in New York, echoed the *Times*'s judgment that the speech of Crane's characters was "natural" (a term of high praise in the context of literary realism) (43). For Hamlin Garland, quite simply, the book embodied "the voice of the slums" (Weatherford 38). In short, Crane's representation of slum speakers' dialogue, as with his representation of the slums more generally, yielded a persuasive "reality effect" for influential authors and reviewers of his day; the dialect led them to feel that, in reading *Maggie*, they were virtually listening in on how "real" slum inhabitants converse.

It does not take away credit from Crane's achievement as the first American fiction writer even to attempt a serious portrayal of life in the New York slums – a portrayal offered without either the heavy-handed moralizing, the excessive sensationalism, or the cheap attempts at humor characteristic of other writing about the slums – to recall at this point that a literary artist's successful production for an audience of the *effect* of reality is never (and by definition cannot be) the equivalent of providing that audience with unmediated access to an *actual* free-standing reality.[3] Any writer's representation of reality requires the writer to make choices, from the diction and syntax the writer will use to the perspective(s) from which a work's story will be narrated (see Chapter 3). When looked at closely, the particular stylistic choices Crane makes in constructing *Maggie*'s many passages of dialogue imply severe limits to urban poor people's intelligence: limits, more specifically, to their capacity to perceive, process, and communicate (whether to peers or others) important information about their environment and themselves. Above all, the use of language becomes a glaring indicator of difference between the cognitive capacities of the book's characters and the cognitive capacities of its narrator and assumed readers.

When giving copies of *Maggie* to friends, Crane often included the following handwritten inscription: "Environment is a tremendous thing in the world and frequently shapes lives regardless" (*Maggie* 132). Crane's inscription would seem to suggest that the slum environment into which Maggie was born bears responsibility for her descent into prostitution and her sordid death. If so, the logical implication would be that if the material deprivations and dangers of the slums could only be eliminated or even lessened – perhaps by concerted action on the part of *Maggie*'s middle- and upper-class audience – then the individuals growing up within the slums would change as well, in ways that would enable them to live more satisfying lives and potentially integrate with and contribute to the larger society. Although we have no record of Crane ever discussing social or political policy in relation to the slums – as a realist he preferred to show rather than tell – such indeed may have been his personal belief. There are certainly aspects of the novel suggesting that Maggie's self-destructive errors of judgment, and even the violent physical and psychological abuse she and her brother suffer from both parents, are at least indirectly caused by the anger and desperation of a grinding poverty that offers few opportunities for escape, especially for a woman. Indeed, Maggie's tragic misjudgment of her brother's friend Pete, the Bowery "tough" who first seduces and then abandons her to a streetwalker's life (and early death) is fed by her fantasy that Pete represents a way out from the material harshness of her life. At one level, then, it is indeed possible to interpret *Maggie* as issuing an implicit call to reform inequitable economic and social structures that impoverish the lives and choices of inner-city populations. To the extent that the details of Crane's novel bear out the assertion in his private inscriptions to friends that environment is a "tremendous thing" and "shapes lives regardless," the book can be read as a significant refutation of Social Darwinist thinking. (Social Darwinism, as will be discussed further in Chapter 7, was a body of thought prevalent in public discourse during the 1890s that blamed poverty entirely on the laziness, vices, and inherent weaknesses of the poor.)

Yet despite the elements of *Maggie* that seem consonant with the assertion in Crane's handwritten inscriptions that environment often "shapes lives
regardless" of other factors, another strand of representation in the text offers
support for – indeed illustrates and fleshes out, as only literature can – Social
Darwinist beliefs regarding slum inhabitants' inherent inferiority, an inferiority that renders them by definition unfit for the complexities of modern
American life. This textual strand is most visible in the choices Crane makes
about representing the slum characters' speech, but it extends as well to what
he conveys about their interior thought processes. For instance, here is a boast-
ing anecdote related to Maggie by Pete. Pete tells Maggie that a well-dressed
man bumped into him as they were both crossing the street and then called
him an " 'insolen' ruffin' ":

> " 'Oh, gee,' I says, 'oh, gee, go teh hell and git off deh eart',' I says, like
> dat. See? 'Go teh hell an' git off deh eart',' like dat. Den deh blokie he got
> wild. He says I was a contempt'ble scoun'el, er somet'ing like dat, an' he
> says I was doom' teh everlastin' pe'dition an' all like dat. 'Gee,' I says, 'gee!
> Deh hell I am,' I says. 'Deh hell I am,' like dat. An' den I slugged 'im.
> See?"   (19–20)

Although Crane no doubt wishes us to recognize the self-righteous pomposity
manifested by the well-dressed man's diction, far more striking in the passage
is the literal impoverishment of Pete's language. Almost none of his words, with
the exception of those he mangles in trying to quote the well-dressed man, are
longer than one syllable. His repetitive recourse to the same few words and
phrases suggests rigid limits not only in his linguistic but also, implicitly, in his
cognitive resources. Even the missing final consonants in Pete's speech (whose
absences are underlined for readers by apostrophes) contribute to the impression he gives of a shrunken ability to process and convey information. In this
context, Pete's immediate recourse to his fists merely confirms the impossi-
bility of his navigating successfully in a modern world composed of complex
signs and meanings.

Pete's reduced language contrasts markedly with the extravagant, even purposefully overdone linguistic resources the narrator calls upon to convey to
readers Maggie's admiring view of Pete.

> Maggie marvelled at him and surrounded him with greatness. She
> vaguely tried to calculate the altitude of the pinnacle from which he
> must have looked down upon her ... Here was a formidable man who
> disdained the strength of a world full of fists. Here was one who had
> contempt for brass-clothed power; one whose knuckles could defiantly
> ring against the granite of law.   (19–20)

Throughout the book, the narrator uses a varied, often multi-syllabic vocabulary abounding in words of Latinate origin. Unlike the book's slum characters, the narrator also employs sophisticated, even elaborate, figures of speech, as when, in paraphrasing Maggie's worshipful view of Pete, the narrator uses figural language to describes Pete as someone not afraid to ring his "knuckles" against the rock-hard "granite" of the law. The text's representation of its slum characters' speech makes it obvious that they possess neither the vocabulary nor the linguistic skills even to understand the narrator's language. By the same token, the narrator's confident use of that language conveys a flattering assumption that *Maggie*'s reading audience shares the narrator's linguistic sophistication.

In most works of literary realism, point-of-view narration – that is, the device of narrating from within a particular character's perspective – helps readers gain a more intimate understanding of the fictional character in question. Readers may even temporarily merge their own perceptions with the character's perceptions, as in Isabel Archer's famous nighttime meditation on the significance of a scene she had earlier observed between her husband and Madame Merle in James's *The Portrait of a Lady* (see Chapter 3). In *Maggie*, by contrast, readerly access to the characters' own processing of experience emphasizes glaring differences between the reader and the character. In the passage just cited, Maggie may marvel at Pete's greatness, and try to "calculate the altitude of the pinnacle" on which he stands, but her foolishly inflated vision of him diminishes both Maggie and Pete, and it increases the reader's sense of superiority over them. When Pete curses out a waiter for not bringing Maggie a large enough glass of beer, "Maggie perceived that Pete brought forth all his elegance and all his knowledge of high-class customs for her benefit. Her heart warmed as she reflected upon his condescension" (23). The irony with which we are encouraged to view the characters' perceptions and thought processes has the effect of placing not Pete, but the reader and narrator, on a "pinnacle" from which we look down at both Pete and Maggie – and, elsewhere in the book, at Maggie's father and mother, at her brother Jimmy, and at Jimmy's friend Billy.

Again, the novel's plot and several of its descriptive passages help to illustrate the implication in Crane's inscription that Maggie's physical and social environment bears responsibility for her self-destructive life choices and, ultimately, her sordid death. At the same time, Crane's portrayal of his characters' stunted speech and defective thinking processes supports Social Darwinist claims about the inborn mental inadequacies of the urban poor. Does the seeming contradiction mean that Crane was simply confused when he wrote *Maggie*? For that matter, a school of critical thought on the novel I have not had space to discuss argues plausibly that the dismal fate of its heroine, whom Crane describes early in her life as a flower that "blossomed in a mud puddle," is caused by Maggie's having been *in*sufficiently influenced by her environment; she is more naïve and vulnerable to a man like Pete than most girls who have grown up in the slums would be. Does the possibility of defending different and conflicting interpretations of *Maggie* suggest that it is a weak, at bottom even incoherent work that does not deserve the detailed analysis scholars have devoted to it? Recall that it was an important goal for American literary realists from Howells, James, and Sarah Orne Jewett to Charles Chesnutt, Kate Chopin, and Edith Wharton to produce literature that resisted translation to a one-dimensional social meaning (see Chapters 3 and 5). If Crane's novel could easily be boiled down to a single message it would have been forgotten long ago – whether it were a message endorsing the philosophy of environmental determinism, a message supporting Social Darwinist beliefs about the urban poor, or a simple suggestion that some individuals are more affected than others by their environments.

Our next chapter considers a group of literary works written around the turn of the century and subsequently labeled "naturalist" by literary scholars. Many naturalist works are set within gritty cityscapes. Even those without urban settings follow *Maggie* in bringing to the forefront questions about the forces – interior and exterior – that shape human lives.

Chapter 7

Crisis of agency: literary naturalism, economic change, and "masculinity"

"Naturalism" is a peculiar term in American literary studies. Although it arises frequently in discussions of late-nineteenth-century literature, the term's meaning is not a settled question. Equally unsettled in critical and scholarly discourse is the term's precise relevance to the works most often called "naturalist." The four American authors whom scholars most frequently associate with late-nineteenth- and early-twentieth-century naturalism are Theodore Dreiser, Frank Norris, Jack London, and Stephen Crane. Over the years, critics have also suggested numerous other fiction writers from the same period whom they believe should be considered literary naturalists as well, including, for example, Kate Chopin, Upton Sinclair, Hamlin Garland, Edith Wharton (in some of her novels), Paul Laurence Dunbar, David Graham Phillips, and Abraham Cahan. With the important exception of Frank Norris, however, almost none of the period's writers whom critics have subsequently dubbed literary naturalists used the word to describe their own writing. Writers such as Crane and Dreiser, for example, preferred to identify themselves as literary realists, with Crane specifically designating Howells as his most important literary influence. For that matter, as Nancy Glazener has pointed out, no evidence exists that critics or reviewers of their own era regarded the specific works written between 1890 and 1910 that today often get linked together as "naturalist" as belonging to any sort of distinct grouping, whether within or separate from the more general category of realism (*Reading for Realism* 6).

Further complicating matters, when US literary critics of the 1920s and 1930s did start using the term "naturalism" to distinguish certain turn-of-the-century fiction writers from the larger American realist movement that had become prominent in the 1870s and 1880s, these critics tended to adapt their understanding of naturalism from the more easily recognizable French "school" of naturalism, whose widely acknowledged chief was Émile Zola. In France, naturalism was associated with dispassionate or "scientific" depictions of the more lurid aspects of everyday urban and industrial life, with a special focus on lower-class criminality, sexuality, and alcoholism. The view of human existence that Zola sought to convey with his fiction was, as summarized by critic George Becker in 1960, "pessimistic materialistic determinism" ("Modern Realism" 35). This concept was used fruitfully for several decades by US literary critics as a key to understanding American writers they grouped together as naturalists – in particular, Norris, Crane, Dreiser, and London – and it is still considered the standard view of the category. Since at least the 1970s, however, major scholarly works have appeared on a regular basis making persuasive arguments for substantially overhauling the long-standing interpretation of American naturalism as pessimistic materialistic determinism. Rather than settling on a new definition, these revisionist works have advanced conflicting visions even of how to define "naturalism" (see, e.g., Michaels, *Gold Standard*, Seltzer, *Bodies and Machines*, Fleissner, *Women, Compulsion, Modernity*, Link, *Vast and Terrible Drama*).

In light of critical quarrels about what "naturalism" even means, as well as the fact that most of the turn-of-the-century American writers to whom the term has subsequently been attached did not themselves find it useful for describing their work, it might seem as if the entire idea of naturalism should simply be jettisoned. Indeed, more than one recent critic has indicated skepticism regarding the existence of "paradigmatic distinctions between realism and naturalism" (Gregg Crane, *Cambridge Introduction to the Nineteenth-Century American Novel* 217). In my view, however, as long as we do not attempt to make rigid distinctions between individual works – as if literary texts could be classified according to some Linnaean taxonomy, with each assigned to a carefully defined species, genus, and family – then "naturalism" can still serve a productive function. The mere fact that critics and scholars still argue so vigorously over naturalism's meaning and relevance tells us that the concept remains generative for those seeking to understand American realistic fiction of the late nineteenth and early twentieth centuries. In this volume, retaining naturalism as a multifaceted and contested category will help us to frame some provocative questions both about the writers regarded as naturalist and about how their work relates to important historical developments at the turn of the century. We will begin by using Frank Norris's novel *The Octopus* (1901) to explore literary naturalism's fascination with deterministic biological and social forces, which occurred in the context of large corporations' growing dominance in American economic life and the related popularity of Social Darwinist thinking. Next, we will consider the close relationship between Theodore Dreiser's *Sister Carrie* (1900), which critics often place at the top of the naturalist canon, and the pervasive spread of consumer culture in late-nineteenth-century America. Finally, a focused examination of Jack London's *The Sea-Wolf* (1904) will help illuminate naturalist works' participation in a broader movement in American culture to develop a new ideal of aggressive, elemental masculinity – a movement that arose largely in response to perceived threats to individual (male) agency caused by the corporate restructuring of the workplace, the increasing importance of female consumerism to the US economy, and other related developments.

Naturalism and determinism

Literary works that critics have traditionally identified with naturalism depict characters whose lives are controlled or "determined" by immense, impersonal forces that the characters themselves can barely understand, let alone effectively resist. In these works, possibilities for free will, for individual choice or human agency, are minimal at best, and more often entirely illusory. By contrast to ancient Greek epics such as *The Iliad* and *The Odyssey*, where heroes' fates rest in the hands of the gods, the forces that control human lives in naturalist literature are not divine or supernatural. Literary naturalism's determining forces derive from nature, including human biology and even weather; from "society" understood as itself a large, ungovernable entity; or from some combination of the two. Characters' fates are determined, for example, by their inability to resist their own innate "animalistic" or "primitive" instincts (usually sexual or violent), as well as by what some scientists at the time saw as strictly hereditary traits handed down within families, including alcoholism and criminality. The impersonal social forces that wreak havoc in naturalist fiction often correspond with conspicuous features of late-nineteenth-century capitalism in America, including not only the rise of monopolistic corporations but also capitalism's periodic economic "crashes" or depressions – particularly painful crashes occurred in 1873 and then again in 1893 – in which millions of farmers, workers, and small-business owners suddenly found their livelihoods gone through no action or fault of their own. In naturalist literature, moreover, mere chance often plays a role in triggering eruptions of destructive biological or social forces in individual lives.

In their conception of the all-powerful forces that impact their characters' lives, naturalist writers frequently blur together the natural and social orders.

For example, the first volume of Frank Norris's planned three-volume "Trilogy of the WHEAT," *The Octopus* (1901), depicts a Railroad Trust, the Pacific and Southwestern (based on the real-life Southern Pacific Railroad Trust), which destroys myriad individual lives in an insatiable search for increased profits. The Railroad Trust is headed by ruthless businessmen, who not only direct the large corporations that own the trains and tracks, but also extend the Trust's wealth and power by bribing politicians and judges, deceiving those who depend on the railroad to ship goods, and calling upon armed thugs when they deem it necessary. Yet though the railroad and the Trust that directs it would seem entirely man-made, a business organization created by powerful individuals making ruthless use of others, Norris uses a metaphor drawn from the animal kingdom – a giant octopus – to imagine the Trust's strangling reach and power.

Even the president of the Pacific and Southwestern, Mr. Shelgrim, whom other characters throughout the book regard as an evil genius responsible for all of the Trust's machinations, describes himself (in a speech Norris seems to endorse) as merely the instrument of an unstoppable natural force. The Railroad Trust, Shelgrim asserts, "is a force born out of certain conditions, and I – no man – can stop it or control it" (576).

> The Wheat is one force, the Railroad another, and there is the law that governs them – supply and demand. Men have only little to do in the whole business. Complications may arise, conditions that bear hard on the individual – crush him maybe – *but the Wheat will be carried to feed the people* as inevitably as it will grow. If you want to fasten the blame of the affair … on any one person, you will make a mistake. Blame conditions, not men. (576; italics in original)

In addition to representing specific social structures as having the force of natural law (see discussion of Social Darwinism, below), literary naturalism also drew upon the imagistic potential of the impressively powerful machines used by US industry to help picture the irresistible potency of impersonal forces that diminished, perhaps even evaporated human agency. After speaking with Shelgrim about the combined force of the Railroad Trust and the wheat crop, *The Octopus*'s literary intellectual Presley, loosely modeled after Norris himself, finds himself thinking of

> a gigantic engine, a vast cyclopean power, huge, terrible, a leviathan with a heart of steel, knowing no compunction, no forgiveness, no tolerance; crushing out the human atom standing in its way, with nirvanic calm, the agony of destruction sending never a jar, never the faintest tremour through all that prodigious mechanism of wheels and cogs. (577)

So too, in Stephen Crane's *The Red Badge of Courage* (based on the Civil War's three-day Battle of Chancellorsville) war is as an "immense and terrible machine," which methodically tears up the human bodies that happen to become "entangled" with it (43, 45); such mauling also occurred on a regular basis in fast-paced factory and agricultural labor of the period when workers' clothing or limbs would get caught in a machine. Literary naturalism's characteristic evocation of such machines, most often as a metaphor for other vast forces – machines with "a heart of steel," infinitely more powerful than individual humans, killing and crushing without compunction – has led critic Mark Seltzer to refer to naturalism as "the terminator-version of the realist project" (*Bodies and Machines* 108).

Naturalism's historical and intellectual contexts

Literary naturalism's emphasis on large forces that determine (and often destroy) the lives of its characters correlated with widespread cultural anxieties about fading possibilities for self-reliant individualism in late-nineteenth-century America. Such individualism, despite its long-standing status as a national credo, began to feel for many people more like a myth than a reality under the new economic, industrial, and social structures that rose to dominance during the period. For example, although some Americans envisioned a future in which machines would liberate human beings from onerous labor, thereby making possible previously undreamed individual and national progress, many also feared that, as social reformer Henry George wrote in 1883, Americans would become degraded by and dependent on industrial machinery, ultimately "lessening" the individual's "control over his own condition and his hope of improving it" (quoted in Trachtenberg, *Incorporation of America* 43).

A growing number of Americans were also troubled by the role large corporations and business trusts were playing in the nation's economy and, by virtue of their wealth and power, in political and judicial processes. Courts of the era issued many decisions that favored corporate interests over individuals and even over government entities. For example, the legal doctrine of "corporate personhood," ratified in 1886 by the Supreme Court in Santa Clara County vs. Southern Pacific Railroad Company, gave large corporations many of the same legal rights and protections historically afforded only to private individuals. With the cooperation of the courts, corporations took on a size, reach, and power far greater not only than that of their individual founders but of virtually all other individual citizens in the nation. Business historians have calculated that, as early as 1904, corporations had become responsible for three-fourths of all industrial production in the United States (Leverenz, *Paternalism Incorporated* 26). Large corporations, trusts, and so-called political "machines" also played an increasingly significant role in the distribution and marketing of goods, as well as in the provision of basic services ranging from streetcars to power to water. The increasing dominance of large corporate structures in the US economy affected the lives of every American, as well as many people overseas, as corporations aggressively sought to fill their ever-increasing needs both for raw material and for new markets.

Defenders of corporate power drew frequently on Social Darwinism, a body of thought that attempted to translate Charles Darwin's analysis of evolution and natural selection to the social sphere. Although English philosopher Herbert Spencer's phrase "the survival of the fittest" (a phrase Darwin himself did not originate but eventually adopted) became the guiding principle of Social Darwinism, the belief system was embraced more widely by prominent figures in the United States than it ever was in Spencer's and Darwin's England. Especially among American business leaders, Social Darwinism provided "scientific" confirmation that the growing concentration of power and wealth in a relatively small elite was not immoral but instead inevitable; in fact, such developments contributed to the nation's overall health and strength, just as natural selection made biological species stronger and more likely to survive. As John D. Rockefeller, president of the Standard Oil Trust, explained to an audience of Sunday school students, "The growth of a large business," which depended on squeezing out weaker competitors, "is not an evil tendency ... It is merely the working out of a law of nature and a law of God" (quoted in Hofstadter, *Social Darwinism* 45).

Nature's "laws," for Social Darwinists such as Rockefeller, Andrew Carnegie, and other big businessmen of the day, dictated that the strong and fit would rise naturally to the top of society, while the weak and unfit would sink helplessly to the bottom. Hence, poverty was not perpetuated by social, legal, and business structures designed to benefit those who already possessed power and wealth – and which, by the same token, the truly powerful could disregard or abuse when convenient, as when private corporations secretly "bought" legislators or judges. Instead, Social Darwinists insisted that poverty and the suffering attendant upon it were due to poor people's own inherent flaws, including their supposed laziness and stupidity and their purported tendency to vices such as excessive drinking and sexual promiscuity. High rates of mortality among the poor were sad, Social Darwinists conceded, but they were also unavoidable and, in fact, strictly required if society were to evolve to higher stages. As we saw in Chapter 6's discussion of *Maggie*, naturalist portrayals of the poor can carry conflicting implications. Many naturalist novels sought to bring public attention to the often grievously difficult lives of impoverished Americans. At the same time, however, it is manual laborers and the urban poor whom naturalist works characteristically depict as most fully subject to the crushing forces of social and biological determinism, which the characters themselves are frequently too stupid to understand, let alone resist. Such characters are often represented as brutes, whether savage wolves fighting for scraps or dumb oxen who understand nothing beyond working, sleeping, and eating (Howard, *Form and History* 102).

Literary naturalism's portrayals of the increasing power of big business in the United States could also be interpreted in more than one way. Naturalist writers' use of fiction to dramatize the pathos of individuals crushed by the ruthless actions of corporations and trusts had the potential to add to the public sentiment for reform that investigative or "muckraking" journalists of the period also helped mobilize. This public sentiment culminated in the limited trust-busting the federal government engaged in during the Theodore Roosevelt era, as well as in tighter government regulation of certain industries. One of these was the Chicago-centered meat-packing industry, whose horrific abuse of workers and shockingly unsanitary practices had been exposed by Upton Sinclair's naturalist novel *The Jungle* (1906), which traced the destruction of a family of Lithuanian immigrants laboring in Chicago's "Beef Trust" slaughterhouses. Yet the federal regulations sparked by *The Jungle* focused on making meat safer for consumers, not on changing the meat industry's treatment of its laborers (let alone reducing the suffering of the slaughtered animals). As Sinclair famously complained, "I aimed at the public's heart, and by accident I hit it in the stomach" (351). More broadly, to the extent that works of literary naturalism portrayed certain business practices – the creation of giant corporate trusts, unceasing attempts to wrench more efficiency and productivity out of workers – as possessing the same unstoppable (if destructive) force as, say, earthquakes and volcanic eruptions, such literature indirectly supported Social Darwinist efforts to "naturalize" the harshest dimensions of American capitalism.

In our next chapter section we will explore literary naturalism's engagement with another key development in late-nineteenth-century US capitalism: the proliferating growth and new sophistication of what historians have called America's "culture of consumption" (Fox and Lears, *Culture of Consumption*).

Naturalism and consumer culture: the case of Dreiser's *Sister Carrie*

With America's productive capacity increasing by leaps and bounds in the decades following the Civil War, business leaders and economists came to view perpetual increases in consumption – that is, ever-expanding purchases of the ever-expanding array of goods the nation's factories were churning out – as imperative for the country's ongoing economic growth. As manufacturers sought to stimulate consumption of their products, the marketing and advertising industries gained a previously unprecedented importance in the United States. Large pictorial advertisements appeared in new mass-market periodicals and newspapers, as well as on billboards conspicuously placed in cities, towns, and villages, including on railroad and streetcar routes. New forms of shopping made purchasing easier and more enticing than ever, whether in the lavish new department stores opening in cities such as Chicago, Philadelphia, and New York or through vividly illustrated mail-order catalogues circulated throughout the entire country by Montgomery Ward, Sears, and other companies. The lower prices of some goods made possible by mass production meant that the phenomenon of "conspicuous consumption," as early-twentieth-century sociologist Thorstein Veblen dubbed it, became an important signifier of status not only among the very rich but at lower levels of the nation's class structure as well (*Theory of the Leisure Class* 43).

First published in 1900, Theodore Dreiser's *Sister Carrie* is the best-known naturalist novel directly to engage with this new culture of consumerism. Initially controversial because its heroine engages in extramarital relationships with two men on her way to becoming an actress, Dreiser's novel gained in popularity and status in the 1920s and 30s and today remains at the top of the naturalist canon. *Sister Carrie* focuses on a young woman who, as millions of other Americans were doing at the time, leaves her small village in search of work and excitement in the city. In Chicago, Carrie agonizes over the clothes and accessories she cannot afford to buy. Although she longs to work as a department-store sales girl where she would be surrounded by beautiful commodities, the only job she can find is as an underpaid assembly-line worker in a dingy, airless shoe-making factory. After she has escaped the factory by moving in with a traveling salesman, Carrie meets George Hurstwood, a wealthy and successful (and married) resort manager. Overcome with passion for her and pressured by the demands of his own wife, Hurstwood steals money from his employer's safe and sweeps Carrie off to New York, where they adopt the aliases of Mr. and Mrs. Wheeler and begin to live on the stolen money. Failing to find a satisfactory job in the city, however, and depressed at what he has lost, Hurstwood gradually enters what proves to be an irreversible decline. Once he has spent all of the stolen money, the former resort manager sinks to the level of working as a strike-breaking "scab" during a streetcar strike (recalling the strike portrayed at the end of Howells's *A Hazard of New Fortunes*, discussed in Chapter 6) and finally commits suicide in a cheap Bowery flophouse.

Forced to search for work herself, Carrie finds a place in New York's thriving popular culture industry. Beginning as a titillating chorus girl in extravagant music and dance productions, she ultimately becomes a star of Broadway's musical stage and moves into a luxurious hotel suite, for which she pays no rent because the hotel owners believe her presence will serve as an advertisement to attract other customers. Throughout her rise, just as she did when she was poor, Carrie desires possessions and a lifestyle above whatever her means allow at that moment. No matter what clothing, luxuries, and public recognition Carrie garners over the course of the novel, she never goes long without finding something else to crave, as she yearns for the one last thing that will finally make her success and indeed *herself* complete. Even at the novel's end, when she can "look about on her gowns and carriage, her furniture and bank account," when she is surrounded by "those who would bow and smile in acknowledgment of her success" – even then Carrie remains longing and dissatisfied, newly conscious of a sphere of serious artistic achievement which she has not yet entered (353).

Theodore Dreiser

Unlike most writers active in the development of American literary realism, Theodore Dreiser (1871–1946) grew up in genuine poverty. His father, a passionately religious immigrant from Germany and a strict disciplinarian, was chronically unemployed, and the large Indiana-based family moved numerous times (and sometimes split up) in an ongoing attempt to find stable living arrangements. In his early twenties Dreiser worked as a journalist in Chicago and St. Louis, specializing in covering the police station and criminal court (Loving, *Last Titan* 57). In 1894 he relocated to New York to join his older brother Paul, who had become a successful writer of hit songs – including "On the Banks of the Wabash, Far Away," still the state song of Indiana. There, Dreiser worked as editor of *Ev'ry Month*, a woman's magazine put out by Paul's music-publishing company (Riggio, "Biography of Theodore Dreiser"). Dreiser's first novel, *Sister Carrie* – in part inspired by the experiences of his sister, Emma, who had fled Chicago in 1886 with a married embezzler – was accepted by the New York publishing firm of Doubleday, Page in the spring of 1900 while the firm's primary owner, Frank N. Doubleday, was away vacationing in Europe. In what subsequently became an infamous episode, Doubleday read the manuscript upon his return and, outraged not only by *Sister Carrie*'s extramarital relationships but even more so by Dreiser's non-judgmental, matter-of-fact approach to them, declared the work indecent and immoral. The publisher attempted but was ultimately unable to extricate his firm from its legal agreement to publish the book. In revenge, Doubleday made sure that only a bare minimum of 558 copies was produced, which he then refrained from advertising.[1] Ironically, the work attracted significant attention in the American literary world only after a cluster of enthusiastic reviews appeared in England, where another publisher had issued it in 1901.

Although married twice, Dreiser himself practiced what he later called sexual "varietism," by which he meant that he engaged in simultaneous affairs, both long and short term, with different women (Fishkin, "Dreiser and the Discourse of Gender" 291). His heavily autobiographical novel *The "Genius"* (1913) caused the New York Society for the Prevention of Vice to threaten its publisher with criminal prosecution for distributing obscenity, whereupon the publisher withdrew the book from sale; it was not reissued until 1923 (Loving, *Last Titan* 259). Combined with the earlier attempt to suppress *Sister Carrie*, the incident made Dreiser a heroic symbol to progressive artists and intellectuals of an ongoing battle between creative freedom and the nation's Puritan heritage. Dreiser's biggest critical and popular success (and his only bestseller) during his lifetime was *An American Tragedy* (1925), whose protagonist stands trial for murdering his pregnant working-class girlfriend and is ultimately executed in the electric chair. The book was later made into the Academy-Award-winning movie *A Place in the Sun* (1951), starring Elizabeth Taylor and Montgomery Clift.

Early scholars of literary naturalism, oriented toward the theme of pessimistic determinism, found the primary source of *Sister Carrie*'s ongoing relevance and power to lie in the book's grueling depiction of the once well-off Hurstwood's destruction by inhumane economic forces, whose effects are compounded by Hurstwood's progressively more paralyzing passivity. More recently, however, critics of the novel have turned their attention to *Sister Carrie*'s deep engagement with – and ambivalent attitude toward – the consumerist ethos that had become so pervasive in the United States by the end of the nineteenth century. In what ways does Dreiser's book help us to understand how the abundance of new mass-produced goods, the remarkable growth of advertising, and the striking changes to the shopping experience during the period (represented, for example, by the alluring new department stores) had on individuals' personal conceptions of satisfaction, pleasure, and success? How does the novel help us to grasp, for example, what a coveted consumer object represents to the person longing to buy it? Questions like these have led recent critics of *Sister Carrie* to focus more closely on Carrie herself and, in particular, on her intimate relationship with the plethora of material goods – clothing and jewels, furniture and decorative objects, edibles – that at times seem literally to speak to her. A lace collar Carrie tries on at a department store, for example, whispers tenderly, "My dear ... I fit you beautifully; don't give me up" (72).

Critical concentration on matters such as female consumerism in *Sister Carrie* – as well as on a constellation of related issues in other naturalist works (Jennifer Fleissner, for instance, has identified a recurrent association in naturalist texts between women and compulsively repetitive behavior) – indicates that some of the most provocative recent writing about American literary naturalism has shifted away from the traditional emphasis on the tragic pathos of individuals crushed by deterministic forces. Indeed, some recent critics have reached conclusions about naturalist works strikingly at odds with long-standing interpretations. For example, in a 1986 book that helped to inaugurate the still-ongoing wave of revisionist critical approaches to American naturalism, Walter Benn Michaels developed the still contro-versial argument that, whatever Dreiser's political opinions may have been later in life (he joined the Communist Party USA in 1945), *Sister Carrie* as a text thoroughly accepts, even endorses, consumer capitalism's underlying dynamic of unending desire. In Michaels's reading, *Sister Carrie* depicts insatiable desire as integral both to leading a successful life and to creating important art. Hurstwood's downward spiral in New York has its root cause, Michaels convincingly shows, in the former manager's waning wants – for business success and social status, for Carrie's love, for fine clothes, ultimately for anything at all. Conversely, even Carrie's final impulse to leave Broadway and the world of showy accumulation behind in favor of creating more mean-ingful art expresses the same principle of perpetual dissatisfaction, of the constant craving for something new and improved, that consumer capitalism both instills and depends on.

Chapter 8 will focus on realism's engagement with the sense of new possi-bilities, as well as the conflicts, that accompanied increasing opportunities for middle-class women to enter the salaried work force and other arenas of pub-lic life previously reserved for men. For the remainder of this chapter, however, we will explore literary naturalism's participation in a broad cultural move-ment around the turn of the century to elaborate a new, more "muscular" ver-sion of middle-class masculinity.

Naturalism and masculinity

The impulse to redefine middle-class masculinity – led by figures such as Theodore Roosevelt, among others – arose as a response to many of the same historical developments with which we have already seen literary naturalism engage. Ironically, anxieties about such developments as the increasing domination of the economy by large, vertically organized corporations, as well as the new economic centrality accorded to the traditionally female-identified sphere of shopping and consumerism, hit white middle- and upper-class men with special acuity – despite the fact that such men did then and would long continue to enjoy more freedom and greater personal empowerment, on average, than virtually all other members of American society. On the one hand, as the economy expanded, work opportunities and earnings for middle-class men grew, as did middle-class standards of living. On the other hand, however, the changing structure of the economy meant that more and more men found themselves employed within bureaucratic systems of management and hierarchy. Not only men who worked for private corporations but also those employed in the government's rapidly expanding workforce were affected. Clerical, sales, and minor administrative positions, which would soon come to be called "white-collar" jobs, proliferated. In large bureaucracies, chances for significant promotion, especially for mid-level white-collar workers, were tightly restricted not only by such factors as formal education but also by the simple fact that positions grew fewer in number the higher up one looked in a hierarchy. Such conditions favored the masterful "captains of industry" at the top of corporate ladders. The heads of large business enterprises, though at times decried as "Robber Barons," often became public celebrities, toasted for their vision, intellect, and force of will. (Dreiser's novels *The Financier* [1912] and *The Titan* [1914] were inspired by one such figure, Chicago streetcar magnate Charles Tyson Yerkes.) But even if they admired the achievements of bigger-than-life business tycoons, many men with mid-level positions in such businesses experienced their own dependence on and "explicit self-subordination" to bureaucratic superiors as "feminization" (Leverenz, *Paternalism Incorporated* 21).

In short, the new dominion of corporate principles of organization in the structure of men's working lives undercut the ideal of the "self-made man" that had been so vital to American male identity since the Revolutionary period. The model of self-reliant independence that had seemed to work for their fathers and grandfathers began to feel remote for many men, almost a relic of the past. White Protestant middle-class men sensed as well that their traditional claim to self-sufficiency and individual autonomy, as well as their traditional modes of asserting social and political power, were further threatened by factors including immigrant Catholic men's development of powerful political machines in urban areas, the period's strident and sometimes violent working-class labor movement, and the visible success of the New Woman in certain professional roles previously reserved for men (Bederman, *Manliness and Civilization* 14; Chauncey, *Gay New York* 111–17). All of these factors, along with, for example, the 1890 announcement by the US Census that the American "frontier," as traditionally understood, no longer existed (an announcement famously amplified by historian Frederick Jackson Turner at the 1893 Chicago World's Fair) led prominent voices to warn that American men were in danger of losing such decisive attributes of manhood as the ability, in President Theodore Roosevelt's words, "to dare and endure," to "wrest triumph from toil and risk." American men, Roosevelt feared, suffered from being "overcivilized." They were becoming soft ("Strenuous Life"). As if confirming such fears, scientific and popular discourse about "neurasthenia" – a nervous disease supposedly brought on by the stresses of modern life, including too much brain-work – proliferated widely, in reference at least as often to modern men as to modern women (Lutz, *American Nervousness*).

The ability to earn a good living and support one's family still remained an important component of manly self-definition, even if one worked as a mere cog in a corporate machine, but to many it no longer seemed nearly sufficient. For middle-class men, reinforcements to their sense of manhood therefore came to depend more heavily than ever before on activities outside the workaday experiences of earning their livelihoods. Such phenomena as weekend athletics, which middle-class men participated in both as competitors and as spectators, assumed new significance in many men's lives. Prize-fighting, for example, "long associated with the working class – became fascinating to middle- and upper-class men" (Bederman, *Manliness* 17). College football, especially that played at elite institutions such as Harvard and Yale, became a national passion. Hundreds of national and local organizations from the Boy Scouts to the YMCA devoted themselves to the project of "making men." Theodore Roosevelt and others urged "strenuous" support of America's overseas imperialist ventures as a way of confirming manhood both for individuals and for the nation as an entity. Roosevelt set the model himself with his highly publicized leadership of a cavalry regiment dubbed "Roosevelt's Rough Riders" during the Spanish American War of 1898.

Beginning in the 1890s a noun new to the English language, "masculinity," began to appear with more and more frequency in discussions referencing male identity. If the adjective "masculine" had previously meant simply "of or related to men," without any other specific values attached to it, the newer word "masculinity" evoked virility, aggressive sexuality, and not only a capacity for, but an attraction toward, physical risk or violence (Bederman, *Manliness* 19). Mid-century ideals of manhood, by contrast, had clustered around the term "manliness," and had emphasized such traits as self-control, industriousness, and morality. The attributes of Victorian manliness did not lose their cultural value at the turn of the century. But traits associated with masculinity gained an increasing weight in socially dominant conceptions of the ideal man. The two sets of traits – those evoked by masculinity and by manliness – were often viewed as complementing one another, especially in conceptions of upper-class manhood. But there was also a degree of tension between them. For example, while Victorian manliness implied a cultivated distance from, indeed distaste for, the primitive "savagery" that the period's racism and class prejudices linked with both working-class men and men with darker skins, the newer ideology of masculinity promoted the idea that even an upper-class white man had a "primitive" or "savage" self lurking not too far beneath his more "civilized" values and manners. Retaining some degree of contact with that more primal self was an important part of what allowed a "gentleman" also to be a real man (Bederman, *Manliness* 16–20).

Associating themselves and their writing with these newer ideals of masculinity is one key way in which the 1890s generation of authors who would subsequently be called literary "naturalists" differentiated themselves from the slightly older generation of writers whom the public had come to identify with realism in the 1870s and 1880s. As discussed in Chapter 1, leading members of this earlier generation of realists, in particular William Dean Howells and Henry James, defined their own literary projects in part against what they construed as the excessive emotionality of women's sentimental literature. Their own writing, by contrast, would embody the manliness of disciplined artistic professionalism; for material, it would draw from their expert observations of complicated individuals engaged in subtle social interactions.

Without acknowledging the ironic extent to which they were repeating their predecessors' own gesture, the younger generation of male naturalists rising to prominence in the 1890s criticized Howells's and James's realism, in turn, as overly domestic, too concerned, as Frank Norris dismissively put it, with "dramas of the reception-room, tragedies of an afternoon call, crises involving cups of tea." The older men's realism was, in short, over-civilized. By contrast, as Norris insisted in transparently phallic language, naturalists such as himself were drawn to the "world of big things; the enormous, the formidable, the terrible, is what counts; no teacup tragedies here" (Burgess and McElrath, *Apprenticeship Writings of Frank Norris*, "Zola" 71). Today, it is easy to recognize that Sinclair Lewis's early-twentieth-century novels attacking the repressions and hypocrisies of middle-class American life owe a great deal to Howells's model of realism. But in his speech accepting the Nobel Prize for Literature in 1930, Lewis celebrated so-called naturalist writers such as Theodore Dreiser, Upton Sinclair, and Hamlin Garland for their "harsh and magnificent" realism, while dismissing Howells and his writing as insufficiently masculine: "Mr. Howells was one of the gentlest, sweetest, and most honest of men, but he had the code of a pious old maid whose greatest delight was to have tea at the vicarage" (Lewis, "American Fear of Literature" np).

Naturalist Jack London was perhaps the first significant American novelist to make his personal embodiment of virile masculinity a major part of his literary-celebrity persona (a tradition carried on by later writers ranging from Ernest Hemingway to Norman Mailer). He and his publishers emphasized the links between London's fiction and his experiences prospecting for gold in the harsh Yukon, serving before the mast on a bloody seal-hunting ship, sailing across the Pacific in a tiny boat, and engaging in oyster piracy on the San Francisco Bay, all of which he drew on for his writing. Scholar Jonathan Auerbach has gone so far as to suggest that London often "courted adventure merely to have something to write about" (*Male Call* 17). In any case, the much-publicized link between London's fiction and his iconic masculinity helped to make London's work enormously successful. London's novel *The Sea-Wolf*, published in 1904 and subsequently made into one of the first feature-length American movies, with London himself appearing in the film as "a sailor," takes as its overt theme the necessary re-masculinization of an over-civilized American writer. In its characters, plot, and descriptions London's book articulates what was coming to be mainstream American culture's dominant vision of ideal manhood: a combination of mid-nineteenth-century manliness, with its emphasis on self-discipline and traditional morality, and the newer concept of primitive, even savage masculinity. At the same time, as we will see, *The Sea-Wolf* also illuminates how turn-of-the-century US culture's increased emphasis on the muscular male body as an icon of real manhood could allow a dimension of homoeroticism between men to gain visibility, even though London's novel works to divert and suppress it.

Because *The Sea-Wolf* is so intimately involved with the realist period's shifting and sometimes contradictory ideas about male identity, we will examine it in some detail.

The sissy and the wolf

Protagonist and first-person narrator Humphrey Van Weyden is a "finely organized, high-strung man" whom we first meet on the deck of a ferry crossing the perennially foggy San Francisco Bay (London 511). Van Weyden is pleased to notice a "stout gentleman" reading an "analysis of Poe's place in American literature – an essay of mine, by the way, in the current *Atlantic*"

(482, 481).[2] We learn later that Van Weyden is known in established literary circles as "the Dean of American Letters, the Second" (637), a clear reference to Howells, whose long-standing literary prominence (including his editorship of the *Atlantic Monthly*), in combination with his middle name, led to his frequently receiving the sobriquet Dean of American Letters during the latter part of his career. In what can only be understood as yet another jab by a naturalist writer at Howells's masculinity, the younger "Dean" portrayed by London's novel is called "Sissy" by his friends, a nickname London's character seems almost to boast of: "I had not been called 'Sissy' Van Weyden all my days without reason," he tells us; "Violent life and athletic sports had never appealed to me" (553, 512).

When Van Weyden's ferry is struck by another ship in the fog, he passes out in the water with a life preserver on, only to awaken much later on the deck of a schooner that has saved his life by plucking him from the Bay. Ominously named the *Ghost*, the boat is already en route to seal-hunting grounds off the coast of Japan. The *Ghost*'s captain, Wolf Larsen, gives Van Weyden no choice but to come along for the voyage in the demeaning position of cabin boy, insisting that it is "for the good of [his] soul" (500). Wolf Larsen embodies the traits summoned up by the new term "masculinity" at the turn of the century: he possesses the physical "strength we are wont to associate with things primitive, with wild animals, and the creatures we imagine our tree-dwelling prototypes to have been – a strength savage, ferocious, alive in itself, the essence of life" (494). Wolf exudes potency – "all powers seemed his, all potentialities" – and takes for granted his right to dominate others weaker than he (558). Even Wolf's powerful intellect takes an ostentatiously masculine form. When he reads or thinks about complex issues, "the elemental simplicity of his mind" allows him to drive "directly to the core of the matter, divesting a question always of all superfluous details" (533).

Horrified as he is at Wolf's brutality toward his own crew, Van Weyden is also deeply drawn toward him. Under the harsh tutelage of Wolf, the 35-year-old author becomes "aware of a toughening or hardening which I was undergoing and which could not be anything but wholesome for 'Sissy' Van Weyden" (603). Echoing the attempt by key naturalist writers to claim that their realism was at once more forcefully masculine and more in touch with authentic reality than that of older "drawing-room" realists such as Howells and James, Van Weyden, the second Dean of American Literature, asserts that the masculine roughening he undergoes thanks to Wolf Larsen has finally given him access to "the world of the real, of which I had known practically nothing and from which I had always shrunk. I had learned to look more closely at life as it is lived" (603). The latter lesson, of course, is most crucial of all for a writer of realist literature – and recall that Van Weyden himself will go on to "write," or at least to narrate, *The Sea-Wolf.*

Humphrey Van Weyden is particularly drawn toward the "savagery" of Wolf's "beauty" (beauty, he is quick to add, "in the masculine sense") (557). Van Leyden comments upon Wolf's physical features frequently and at great length. Wolf's "mouth, his chin, his jaw" show "all the fierceness and indomitableness of the male – the nose also" (558). Wolf's eyes – "it was my destiny," Van Weyden informs us, "to know them well" – demand a full paragraph of description, permeated with romantic language (499). A lengthy meditation upon their "protean ... shades and colorings" culminates in Van Weyden's assertion that though Wolf's eyes "could snap and crackle points of fire like those which sparkle from a whirling sword," they could also "warm and soften and be all a-dance with love-lights, intense and masculine, luring and compelling, which at the same time fascinate and dominate women till they surrender in a gladness of joy and of relief and sacrifice" (499).

When he first sees Wolf "stripped," following an episode in which "the primitive fighting beast" has put down a potential mutiny with his own hands, Van Weyden tells readers that "the sight of his body quite took my breath away" (593, 594, 593). "As he moved about or raised his arms the great muscles leapt and moved under the satiny skin" (593). Watching Wolf's "bicep move like a living thing under its white sheath," Van Weyden observes that "the bronze ended with his face. His body, thanks to his Scandinavian stock, was fair as the fairest woman's" (593). Unable to "take my eyes from him," Van Weyden tells us, "I stood motionless, a roll of antiseptic cotton in my hand unwinding and spilling itself down to the floor" (593–94). Under the circumstances, the roll of white cotton spilling from Humphrey Van Weyden's hand evokes an image of masturbatory ejaculation. For his part, Wolf Larsen, when he notices Van Weyden staring at his muscles, commands the latter to "feel them," which Van Weyden does, slowly moving his hands "about the hips, along the back, and across the shoulders" (594). Calling Van Weyden a "handy man" (595), Wolf then invites him to take the position of "mate" on the ship, despite Van Weyden's complete lack of knowledge regarding navigation (see Auerbach, *Male Call* 206). On the most immediate level the term "mate" refers here to a ship's officer whose rank is just under the captain's, but in *The Sea-Wolf* the term "mate" is also used to refer to a sexual or conjugal partner. Late in the book, Van Weyden's favored term for Maud Brewster is "my woman, my mate" (717). In addition, London addressed his own wife, Charmian, as "Mate-Woman" (Reesman, *Jack London's Racial Lives* 243). In this context, Wolf's invitation to Van Weyden – whom he nicknames "Hump" – to become his "mate" inevitably carries at least something of a sexual resonance underneath its more immediate nautical meaning.

Conveniently, just a few chapters after this scene in which "Sissy" Van Weyden is erotically transfixed by the sight of Wolf's naked body, when the already-intense relationship of the two primary male characters in London's book appears most to verge on the sexual – thus raising the period's newly minted specter of homosexuality – a woman enters the *Ghost*'s previously all-male world. Maud Brewster happens to be rescued from a lifeboat that drifts by. Both "homosexual" and "heterosexual" emerged as socially recognized categories of identity in Anglo-American culture around the 1890s, the same decade in which most of the literary works critics today call "naturalist" were written. Prior to that period, as scholars working in the discipline of gay, lesbian, and queer studies have shown, heterosexual and homosexual acts of course occurred, and anti-sodomy laws criminalized some of the latter, but sexual orientation did not carry the weight it would subsequently develop in psychological, legal, and popular discourses as a key part of who somebody "is."[3] Starting in the 1890s, so-called "normal" men began to experience it as imperative "to define their difference from queers on the basis of their renunciation of any sentiments or behavior that might be marked as homosexual" (Chauncey, *Gay New York* 100). Theorist Eve Kosofsky Sedgwick has used the term "homosexual panic" to convey the phobic fear that most English and American men at the time (with the exception of the relatively few who were openly gay) came to feel at any possibility that they might be perceived by others as – or for that matter might in fact be – homosexual (Sedgwick, *Between Men* 89).

Some men's response to this anxiety would take the form of violent gay bashing. As Sedgwick shows, however, another strategy with a long cultural pedigree for keeping the specter of homosexuality in intense male–male relationships at arm's length is for the two men to position a woman between them, whether literally or figuratively, as an object to be shared, exchanged, competed for, or even fought over. Unsurprisingly, works by Jack London and Frank Norris – the two turn-of-the-century naturalist writers most explicitly concerned with recovering a supposedly more authentic form of virile masculinity – often include an intense, almost conjugal masculine friendship involving bodily intimacy that is "saved" from the appearance of homosexuality by a woman who comes between the two men. She becomes each man's most direct focus of erotic interest, while also allowing the men to express the intensity of their feelings for one another indirectly, sometimes by nobly sacrificing her to the other man and sometimes by fighting over her (first one, then the other, occurs in Frank Norris's *McTeague* [see Cruz, "Reconsidering McTeague's 'Mark' and 'Mac'"]).

When Maud Brewster comes aboard the *Ghost*, she immediately becomes an object of strong interest to both Wolf Larsen and Humphrey Van Weyden.

Previously, Hump admits to the reader, he has never been "amative to any considerable degree" toward women (582). But obsessed with the fear that Wolf will try to rape Maud (justified, it turns out), Hump announces to the reader, "The knowledge that I loved her rushed upon me" (649). As herself an unmarried independent writer with yearly earnings of $1,800 (Van Weyden has written an admiring review of her work without ever having met her in person), Maud might be construed as a New Woman. Yet Van Weyden continually emphasizes his perception of her as "a delicate, fragile creature" (620). It is only after Hump and Maud have abandoned the *Ghost* and its captain for a deserted island, however, that Van Weyden is able to claim as fully his own both heterosexual desire and the "primitive" masculinity previously aligned with Wolf Larsen (711; see also Derrick, "Making a Heterosexual Man" 126).

The key moment on the island occurs when Van Weyden and Maud set out looking for seals with the idea of using their skins to construct shelter. When they find themselves among an angry herd, Maud's body trembles with fear as she confesses to Van Weyden that she is "dreadfully afraid" (711). Van Weyden "instinctively" places his arm "protectingly" around her:

> I shall never forget, in that moment, how instantly conscious I became of my manhood. The primitive deeps of my nature stirred. I felt myself masculine, the protector of the weak, the fighting male ... She leaned against me, so light and lily-frail, and as her trembling eased away it seemed as though I became aware of prodigious strength.   (711)

Using a club and then a knife, he manages to "slaughter" and skin a sufficient number of seals to roof not only one hut for Maud to sleep in but also a second hut for himself, so that he may respect her privacy (712). By the end of London's book, the reader is clearly meant to perceive that despite Wolf Larsen's unmatched physical strength and courage, as well as the near "perfectness" of his body (593), Humphrey Van Weyden has become the better man: he retains key traits of Victorian manliness even as he also incorporates into his repertoire the virile "savagery" that turn-of-the-century America was coming to view as an essential part of manhood (713). As a "magnificent atavism," Wolf Larsen has "no conscience" (557). By contrast to Larsen, and in spite of the numerous seals he clubs to death, Van Weyden's savagery never crosses the line into wanton animality. Above all, where Wolf tries to rape Maud (he is stopped only by a violent headache presaging the brain disease that ultimately kills him), Van Weyden manfully resists his growing physical desires for her. Having once put his arm around her when they were threatened by the herd of seals, he forces himself not to do so again; filled with, as he puts it, desire "swaying the very body of me," he refrains from touching her in any way other than a "father or brother" would (765). Only after their rescue has been assured does Van Weyden allow himself openly to express his feelings. Even then, after they both have communicated their love for one another, on the novel's last page he graciously requests only "one kiss, dear love" (771).

The revised ideal of white middle-class male identity that literary works such as *The Sea-Wolf* helped to shape, which combined traditional nineteenth-century "manly" virtues such as sexual self-control with a notable increase in supposedly primeval masculine attributes, was mostly embraced across the Anglo-American cultural spectrum. By contrast, turn-of-the-century attempts by women to revise the prevailing nineteenth-century ideology of "true womanhood" tended to be met with a far more hostile response. Our next chapter considers works by women writers who used fiction both to suggest the damaging falsity of many conventional ideas about women and to explore the bitter conflicts, both internal and external, that a woman's challenge to those ideas could provoke.

Chapter 8

"Certain facts of life": realism and feminism

For much of the nineteenth century, a set of codes and conventions defining proper femininity, so-called "true womanhood," was articulated and enforced by culturally authoritative sources such as ministers, politicians, and teachers, as well as by wide-circulation magazines such as *Godey's Lady's Book* and popular domestic fiction. Influential figures and texts defined "true womanhood" by the key values of female purity, submissiveness, piety, and domesticity (Welter, "Cult of True Womanhood"). Directed primarily at middle- and upper-class white "ladies," but also affecting working-class women and women of color, true womanhood ideology held that the nation's public arenas of business, professional life, politics, and governance were and should be reserved for men, who were by nature smarter, stronger, and more competitive than women. A woman's realm was the home, where she was supposed to nurture her children and provide an attractive space of tranquility and spiritual refreshment for her husband when he returned from his difficult work in the outside world of men. True womanhood ideology assumed women's spiritual and moral superiority over men, but at the same time its emphasis on purity, domesticity, and submissiveness was used to justify women's exclusion from the full rights and responsibilities of American citizenship. Instead of participating in democratic debate (including voting) or trying to create private wealth, women should strive to embody the idealized figure that an immensely popular 1854 poem by Englishman Coventry Patmore dubbed "The Angel in the House."

In 1848, the United States' first organized Woman's Rights Convention was held in Seneca Falls, NY. A total of sixty-eight women and thirty-two men signed the convention's Declaration of Sentiments, which was written on the model of the US Declaration of Independence and called for equal rights for women. Such calls grew in number during the latter part of the nineteenth century, as a wide range of women writers and activists actively challenged aspects of true womanhood ideology. For instance, Victoria Woodhull declared herself a candidate for president in the 1872 election (the same presidential election in which both Sojourner Truth and Susan B. Anthony made unsuccessful attempts to vote) and wrote articles supporting "free love" in a newspaper she and her sister edited. Woodhull and other feminists argued that marriage was simply a form of legalized prostitution too hypocritical to recognize itself as such. They made the radical assertion that, in Woodhull's words, "ownership and control of her sexual organs" should belong to a woman herself both before and after marriage, and never to a man, including even her husband (Woodhull, *Reader* 40).

The mid-nineteenth century's tight ideological association between women and domesticity was put under even more pressure in the decades following the Civil War by the increasing number of middle- and upper-class women who, although they may not have considered themselves women's rights activists, nonetheless pursued an unprecedented range of activities outside the home, including professional careers and other paid work. While working-class women, both white and of color, had long been forced to labor outside their own homes, both in domestic occupations and in factories (the latter primarily in New England), the later nineteenth century saw a multiplication of clerical jobs, sales positions, and openings for women in such increasingly professionalized fields as teaching and social work. An expansion of higher education opportunities for women, both in newly founded women's colleges and in coeducational public institutions (particularly in the West and Midwest), helped to prepare them for careers in these fields and others. Women also became more active and visible in the public sphere through increased membership, including leadership positions, in formal organizations devoted to a wide variety of causes, from female suffrage to municipal reform to alcohol prohibition. They increased their participation in athletic and recreational activities as well. Women cyclists became a major focus of public controversy when some of them started wearing "bloomers," baggy pants-like garments that were more practical for pedaling than the full-length skirts ladies were supposed to wear. Pants were for men, not women, and many conservatives were horrified. By the early 1890s the term "New Woman" was used to encapsulate the changes both large and small that many women were making in their lives. Although in fact the majority of American women around the turn of the century still organized their personal aspirations around the traditional roles of wife and mother, the figure of the New Woman loomed large in the popular imagination and occasioned a great deal of often fierce debate in the periodical press.

Realism and the New Woman

Even prior to the public circulation of the term New Woman in the early 1890s, American literary realism both reflected and shaped cultural conversations about women who did not fit the mold of traditional expectations for their gender. For example, a sub-category of important realist works in the 1870s and 1880s, including William Dean Howells's second novel *A Chance Acquaintance* (1873) and Henry James's first popular success, "Daisy Miller" (1878), as well as his masterpiece of three years later, *The Portrait of a Lady* (1881), treated the post-Civil War phenomenon of the so-called new "American girl." The term referred to middle- and upper-class white female adolescents reputed to be bolder, more iconoclastic, and more resistant to overly rigid restrictions than girls of the antebellum period had been, albeit just as scrupulously chaste in mind and body. Moreover, as we saw in Chapter 5, female local-color writers such as Rose Terry Cook and Mary Wilkins Freeman featured rural women, often unmarried and often middle-aged or older, struggling to carve out at least relatively independent lives, typically in the face of opposition or scorn by male authority figures. From the 1880s onward, realist works also depicted middle-class women choosing professional careers over traditional domesticity. For example, regionalist writer Sarah Orne Jewett's character Nan Prince in her 1884 novel *A Country Doctor* eschews marriage in order to continue her father's work as a physician in a rural neighborhood, while the ambitious illustrator Alma Leighton of Howells's *A Hazard of New Fortunes* (1890) announces to her disconcerted mother that she will probably choose not to marry: "I'm wedded to my Art, and I'm not going to commit bigamy, whatever I do" (211). Alma later adds that if she ever does get married she will "pick and choose, as a man does" and not "merely be picked and chosen" (477).

The prospect of a woman picking and choosing a mate raises the possibility – or specter – of female sexual autonomy. In doing so, it hints at an area of life that Howells saw as too dangerous for American novelists, even realist writers, to explore in any but the most delicate, indirect fashion. Despite Howells's mostly positive portrayal of independent-minded female characters, he used his position as unofficial spokesperson for American realism to draw a line that he urged American writers not to transgress, involving above all "certain facts of life which are not usually talked of before young people, and especially young ladies" – the "facts," that is, of sex ("Editor's Study," 1889 [79.469] 151). Realist novels could deal with social strife, with business betrayals, even with the still scandalous topic of divorce, as did Howells's own 1882 novel *A Modern Instance*. Yet because the novel-reading audience in the United States included many young unmarried women, American writers would break a public trust if they included in their books anything other than that which "could be openly spoken of before the tenderest bud at dinner" (151). For Howells, American girls "are none the less brilliant and admirable because they are innocent" of sexual knowledge (152). Realist writers have an obligation not to violate that innocence. There were many other facets of modern life both more important in themselves and more deserving of realist literary attention, Howells insisted, than "guilty love" (152). Howells's commitment to keeping young American women both innocent and ignorant of sexuality indicates the sway that true womanhood ideology, with its emphasis on female "purity," still held over the late nineteenth century's most influential representative of American literary realism (151).[1]

Feminist realisms: the "facts" of female lives

Women writers associated with literary realism used fiction to explore what they saw as vital dimensions of women's lives left mostly untouched by mainstream male authors such as Howells. The remainder of this chapter will focus on three important works of what might be thought of as "feminist realism": Charlotte Perkins Gilman's "The Yellow Wallpaper" (1892), Kate Chopin's *The Awakening* (1899), and Pauline Hopkins's *Contending Forces: A Romance Illustrative of Negro Life North and South* (1900). As we will discover, the gender-inflected "reality" emphasized by each of these three works differs in accord with the writer's distinctive life experiences, ideological investments, and aesthetic aims. Yet all three texts dramatically challenge the assumed and enforced innocence of body and mind that most men of the nineteenth century, including realists like Howells, took for granted as essential to the very existence of "true" womanhood. Ironically, in order to probe actual women's realities, these works also find it necessary to combine realism with other genres that writers such as Howells and Twain dismissed as "unrealistic," including the gothic, French symbolism, melodrama, and domestic sentimentalism.

In "The Yellow Wallpaper" Gilman calls on classic elements from the gothic tradition to help her delve into the impact on a young mother's psyche of her doctor husband's paternalistic impulse to "protect" her from overly vigorous intellectual activity. *The Awakening* uses a lyrical symbolist style influenced by Kate Chopin's extensive readings in French literature to explore her married upper-class protagonist Edna Pontellier's "awakening" to the sensuality of nature, everyday bodily experiences, and previously buried emotions, including tabooed sexual desires. Finally, the strategic juxtaposition in Hopkins's *Contending Forces* of textual elements and techniques associated both with literary realism and with the romance genres of melodrama, sensation fiction, and sentimentality brings the cultural authority and aura of objectivity associated with realism to her book's portrayal of the appalling, almost literally in-credible experiences still prevalent in "Negro Life" decades after the Civil War had ended, even as her novel also gives life to nineteenth-century African-American women's impressive record of achievements.

Gothic realities: "The Yellow Wallpaper"

Charlotte Perkins Gilman's story "The Yellow Wallpaper" draws, albeit with "embellishments and additions," from Gilman's own experience of "a severe and continuous nervous breakdown tending to melancholia – and beyond" following her marriage and the birth of her daughter (Gilman, *Yellow Wallpaper* 86). Her condition would today probably be considered severe postpartum depression, but the term was unavailable during an era when women were supposed to regard marriage and motherhood as the ultimate forms of personal fulfillment, the twin glories of their existence. Gilman's depressive breakdown was exacerbated by a lack of understanding and sympathy on the part of her husband, the artist Charles Stetson. Despite Stetson's protestations to the contrary during courtship, he did not take seriously Gilman's feminist ideas, nor did he respect her desire to have an intellectual, social, and politically active life beyond the domestic sphere (Judith Allen, *Feminism of Charlotte Perkins Gilman* 27–42). A desperately unhappy Gilman put herself in the hands of one of the nation's best-known physicians for treating so-called "nervous" diseases, Dr. S. Weir Mitchell. In the spring of 1887, Mitchell treated her in his Philadelphia clinic with his famous "rest cure," which involved extensive bed rest, isolation, and a controlled diet. After declaring her much improved, Gilman later recalled, Mitchell sent her home with strict instructions to "live as domestic a life as possible," to "have but two hours' intellectual life a day," and "never to touch pen, brush, or pencil again as long as I lived" (Gilman, *Yellow Wallpaper* 86). "I went home and obeyed those directions for some three months," Gilman wrote, "and came so near the border line of utter mental ruin that I could see over." It was only when, "using the remnants of intelligence that remained," she started to work again – "work, the normal life of every human being" – that she began to recover (86). She wrote "The Yellow Wallpaper" in an attempt to halt the use of the rest cure for women suffering from depression. Some early readers found the story's portrayal of mental illness so powerful that they thought merely reading it would be dangerous for impressionable readers. "Such literature contains deadly peril," a doctor warned (103). Gilman responded that the work "was not intended to drive people crazy, but to save people from being driven crazy" (86).

"The Yellow Wallpaper" begins with its unnamed first-person narrator, a young mother, telling us that she and her husband John have rented an old country mansion for three months. John, "a physician of high standing," has prescribed isolation, quiet, and rest to help the narrator get over a psychological condition he views as "a slight hysterical tendency" (29). Almost immediately we recognize a divide, which grows throughout the story, between the narrator's and her husband's modes of understanding reality. John "is practical in the extreme [and] scoffs openly at any talk of things not to be felt and seen and put down in figures" (29). When she tells him that she can "feel" "something strange about the house," he responds that what she feels is a draft, and shuts the window (30). Above all, John's aggressively rationalist orientation renders him unable to recognize the kind and degree of her mental anguish: "John does not know how much I really suffer. He knows there is no *reason* to suffer, and that satisfies him" (31). To John, even the words with which his wife attempts to articulate her inner state stem from "excited fancies," "nervous weakness," and a "habit of storytelling," all of which he considers disconnected from measurable reality (32). "You see," the narrator tells us, "he does not believe I am sick!" (29).

If we can say that the character John embodies an especially limited version of Howellsian realism's commitment to the rational over the romantic – to what Howells called "the light of common day" over anything unknown or mysterious – this approach to reality proves increasingly inadequate for understanding the inner experiences of the story's narrator ("Editor's Study," 1889 [79.474] 966).[2] John, who travels into town on professional business every day, has chosen as their bedroom a chamber on the house's top floor. The narrator spends virtually all of her time alone in the room. Based on his claim that it would be over-stimulating, John has forbidden her to see friends, to draw, or to write. The story we read is presented as a day-by-day account the narrator surreptitiously sets down on paper despite John's prohibition because, as she explains, "I *must* say what I feel and think in some way – it is such a relief!" (Gilman, *Yellow Wallpaper* 35). Written in the present tense, this account gives readers access to the narrator's reality. It is a reality that eludes John's limited perspective demanding an openness to emotions, including terror, despair, and painful self-doubt, as well as a sensitivity to the "expression" that even inanimate objects may carry. "I used to lie awake as a child and get more entertainment and terror out of blank walls and plain furniture than most children could find in a toy-store," the narrator tells us (32). Although the narrator is able to understand John's hyper-rational, "practical in the extreme" orientation to the world – and in fact, as we will see, believes that she herself should adhere more closely to it – her own approach to the real is closer to that found in gothic fiction. "Gothic" was a popular literary genre featuring mysterious old houses, menaced or imprisoned women, and an ever-present possibility of madness. With its novelistic heyday in the 1790s and early 1800s, gothic fiction was one of the literary forms that late-nineteenth-century realists criticized as overly removed from everyday plausibility and too dependent upon sensationalistic tricks to stimulate and manipulate its readers.[3]

The narrator's very first entry tentatively raises the possibility that the old mansion is a "haunted house" but, as if having internalized realist criticism of the gothic, she immediately minimizes the thought by turning it into a playful joke: a haunted house "would reach the height of romantic felicity – but that would be asking too much of fate" (29). Similarly, trying to follow John's injunction that she should avoid thinking of disturbing things, she attempts to interpret the bedroom's odd features within the reassuring normality of modern family life by telling herself that it must have been a "nursery first and then playroom and gymnasium ... for the windows are barred for little children, and there are rings and things in the walls" (30). In addition to the bars and the rings in the walls, the legs of the large bedstead, which is nailed to the floor, appear to have been gnawed by human teeth, the floor is "scratched and gouged and splintered," and "the plaster itself is dug out here and there" – actions she attributes to rambunctious children when the space was used as a "playroom" (33). What the narrator cannot normalize, however, is the wallpaper, whose "waves of optic horror" commit "every artistic sin" (34, 31). The paper's color is "repellant, almost revolting; a smoldering unclean yellow," and when the narrator attempts to follow the "sprawling, flamboyant" pattern's "lame uncertain curves," "they suddenly commit suicide – plunge off at outrageous angles, destroy themselves in unheard of contradictions" (31).

Simultaneously repelled and fascinated by the wallpaper, the narrator devotes an increasing amount of time to scrutinizing it, following its lines and curves in search of some "principle of design," some form of "order" in the pattern (34). That is, she tries to make the paper – her surrounding environment – follow the sort of "good sense" and "reason" that John urges on her (32, 31). Indeed, she feels like a failure for being unable to assume the traditional wifely role of domestic helpmeet: "I meant to be such a help to John, such a real rest and comfort" (31). But the paper seems to offer her only such monstrous images as a "recurrent spot where the pattern lolls like a broken neck and two bulbous eyes stare at you upside down" (32). Gradually, however, she starts to notice "a kind of sub-pattern in a different shade" of yellow, which ultimately takes dim shape as a "strange, provoking, formless sort of figure, that seems to skulk about behind that silly and conspicuous front design" (33). After some time, that "formless sort of figure" becomes clearer to her: "it is like a woman stooping down and creeping about behind that pattern" (35). She continues to watch until she sees that, at night, the faint figure in the wallpaper seems "to shake the pattern, just as if she wanted to get out" (36). Soon, she observes that when it is dark out the wallpaper "becomes bars! The outside pattern I mean, and the woman behind it as plain as can be" (37).

By this point in the story, Gilman has led the reader to recognize something the narrator at first cannot quite bring into her conscious awareness: what the narrator sees in the wallpaper visually represents, in horrifying gothic form, the real, underlying structure of her own situation. She is, after all, a woman who has been placed by her husband into a room with bars, where he forbids her to engage in "congenial work, with excitement and change" (29). Beyond the literal bars and explicitly spoken prohibitions, the narrator is imprisoned by a "pattern" she has not been able to separate herself from – the pattern of nineteenth-century gender ideology, which has told her that her most import-ant role is to be a devoted "help" to her husband and a self-sacrificing mother to her offspring (31). Looking at the wallpaper, the narrator is unable to decide how many women are trapped within it; sometimes she thinks there are a "great many ... and sometimes only one." One or many, they are "all the time trying to climb through. But nobody could climb through that pattern – it strangles so" (39). She decides that is why she has seen so many grotesque heads in the patterns: "They get through and then the pattern strangles them off and turns them upside down, and makes their eyes white!" (39).

Only in the final portion of the story does the narrator at last start to iden-tify with the woman she sees in the paper, and to view the supposedly "real" world – in which she is the wife of a successful physician who "loves me very dearly and hates to see me sick" – as less authentic to her own experience than the wallpaper's gothic world of strangled and imprisoned women (35). She decides to aid the woman's escape from the pattern when John is away. They tear together at the paper: "I pulled and she shook, I shook and she pulled, and before morning we had peeled off yards of that paper" (40). By the final day of the lease on the house, the narrator has fully entered the wallpaper's gothic reality – she now sees *herself* as a woman who has "come out of that wallpaper" (41). She gets on her hands and knees and starts creeping around the edges of the room as she has seen the other woman do. When her husband finds her, she informs him, "I've got out at last … And I've pulled off most of the paper, so you can't put me back!" The story concludes: "Now why should that man have fainted? But he did, and right across my path by the wall, so that I had to creep over him every time!" (42). By the standards of John's – and probably the reader's – world, the narrator has clearly had a psychotic break. She has lost the ability to differentiate between reality and delusion. Yet, Gilman's story hints, she may also have gained access to a deeper, underlying level of gendered reality in nineteenth-century America. From the perspective of patriarchal society this "alternate real," as critic Barbara Johnson has written, "can be figured only as madness" (Johnson, *Feminist Difference* 25).

Corporeal realities: *The Awakening*

When Kate Chopin published *The Awakening* on the cusp of the twentieth century in 1899, the 49-year-old St. Louis resident did not realize how much vituperative criticism the book would evoke from contemporary reviewers. She also did not realize that her novel would later be viewed as a landmark of feminist realism. At the time, Chopin was a nationally known writer of local-color fiction, for which she drew heavily on the fourteen years she had spent observing different aspects of Louisiana life while living there as a wife and mother of six children, and then as a young widow. Set in and around New Orleans and drawing on many of the same local-color elements as her short stories, *The Awakening* tells of Edna Pontellier, a 28-year-old married woman with two young children. During a summer flirtation with an unattached young man, Robert, at a seaside resort – a flirtation that ultimately turns to love – Edna feels her very being "awakening." She discovers newly "impassioned" sexual desires and, further, an awareness of her entire body that is new to her (44). She finds herself experiencing a highly intensified sensory awareness of the world around her, encompassing smells, textures, and sounds. She becomes deeply receptive to music and cultivates her own talents as a painter.

At the same time, Edna begins to recognize that as a young girl in Kentucky, ignorant both of herself and of "the world of reality," she had entered into the roles of "devoted" wife and mother without fully grasping their implications (19). She had "blindly assumed" a lifelong, self-engulfing commitment to these roles, but her assumption of that commitment was based on "illusions" from which she is now ready to "wake up" (19, 105). No longer able to understand why she should ever have "submitted" to her husband

Léonce's authority in matters large or small, she develops a powerful urge toward asserting her own personal liberty (31). Robert has left for Mexico before either he or Edna could admit their love for one another. With her husband also away on business and her children visiting at their grandmother's plantation, Edna decides to move into a tiny house whose rent she pays with her own money, some of which she has earned by selling her paintings. To Edna this move, funded by money she has earned, signifies a new "freedom and independence" (76). With Robert still in Mexico, Edna has a brief affair with Alcée Arobin, an attractive man whom she knows she does not love. Although she ultimately finds it unsatisfying, Edna is aroused by the relationship's sexual dimension. Strikingly, she does not feel either guilt or shame at the extramarital sex, emotions which would no doubt have devastated a middle-class female protagonist in almost any other nineteenth-century American novel.

As an author, the bilingual Kate Chopin was strongly influenced by French realist writers such as Gustave Flaubert and, especially, Flaubert's protégé Guy de Maupassant, both of whom depicted sex and sexuality with far more openness than American writers. *The Awakening* also shows the influence of French Symbolist poetry in its evocative use of such primal elements as the sea, which calls seductively to Edna throughout the text and in which she wishes "to swim far out, where no woman had swum before" (27). Yet beyond the influence of nineteenth-century French literature, *The Awakening* can in many ways be read as both a feminist rejoinder to and a further elaboration of the American realism represented by Howells. The "real" to which Chopin's novel seeks to give her readers access is an upper-middle-class white woman's inner experiences and sensations – bodily, intellectual, and emotional – as she, like many other American women around the turn of the century, "begin[s] to realize her position in the universe as a human being, and to recognize her relations as an individual to the world within and about her" (14). Those "certain facts of life" to which Howells insisted the female portion of American fiction's audience should not be exposed – "facts of life" relating to sex and sexual desire – constitute a crucial portion of the sensations and experiences Chopin's realism includes, all related from Edna's female point of view and with a remarkable lack of moral judgment from the author.[4]

In withholding even implicit moral criticism of Edna's unorthodox sexual conduct, *The Awakening* brings the same technique of narrative objectivity called for by Howells and other realists to a form of human experience earlier works of American realism had shied away from. (See Chapter 3 on realism's narrative techniques.) Reviewers did not hold back their own moral judgments. They were disgusted both by the character of Edna Pontellier and by the failure of the novel to offer "a single note of censure of her totally unjustifiable conduct," as the *New Orleans Times-Democrat* complained (Chopin, *Awakening* 167). The *Providence Sunday Journal* accused Chopin of putting "her cleverness to a very bad use in writing *The Awakening*" and worried that the novel would promote "unholy imaginations and unclean desires" among readers (166, 167). As with Howells's insistence that even realist writers should scrupulously protect the "innocence" of young lady readers, these comments express a deep investment in the nineteenth century's ideology of true womanhood. *The Awakening*, meanwhile, has effected a bold realist countermove by aligning the entire set of true womanhood requirements – requirements supposed to produce an idealized "Angel in the House" – with the same history of romantic literary clichés against which Howells himself sets the project of American literary realism.

Edna's best friend and foil, Adèle Ratignolle, exemplifies what Chopin calls the "rôle" (the French term connotes artifice and performance) of "mother-woman." Adèle "idolized" her children, "worshipped" her husband, and would deem "it a holy privilege" to "efface" herself as an individual and "grow wings as [a] ministering angel" (9). Chopin's language about Adèle explicitly aligns her domestic-angel persona with the hackneyed language of outdated literary romance: "There are no words to describe her save the old ones that have served so often to picture the bygone heroine of romance and the fair lady of our dreams": hair of "spun-gold," eyes like "sapphires," lips like "cherries or some other delicious crimson fruit," and hands so "exquisite" it was "a joy to look at them when she threaded her needle or adjusted her gold thimble" (9). Chopin draws on familiar clichés associated with the idealized beauty of fictional heroines to suggest that the figure of the (sewing) angel in the house properly belongs with fairy princesses in the "bygone" realm of romance, rather than serving as a model for real American women at the onset of the twentieth century. Throughout the book, Chopin recurs to the purposefully stereotyped character of Adèle Ratignolle to set into relief both Edna Pontellier's growing disillusion with the traditional "rôle" of devoted mother-woman and her struggle to uncover the reality underneath "that fictitious self" she has unthinkingly "assume[d] like a garment" for most of her life (55).

In associating Adèle with "bygone romance," Chopin seeks to leverage, as it were, literary realism's rejection of outdated idealizations to help dislodge the still powerful American ideology of true womanhood, which continued to receive at least partial support from leading male realists, including not only Howells but also Mark Twain and Henry James (see text box on James's

The Bostonians, below). Even as she sought to dislodge it, Chopin recognized true womanhood ideology's ongoing social force. She understood that, even in the era of the New Woman, to allow Edna an untroubled achievement of social, sexual, and economic autonomy would itself risk straying into the realm of fantasy. Edna remains, after all, a nineteenth-century American married woman with two young children who has had no previous experience in living by herself and almost none in thinking or planning for herself. Even Robert, the young man who serves as a catalyst for Edna's "awakening," is startled when, near the close of the novel, she laughs at the idea of his asking her husband to "set [her] free." Robert's face turns white as she tells him, "I give myself where I choose" (167). Fearing that her radical disregard of seemingly all social rules will bring destructive scandal down on both of them, Robert departs from her at the first opportunity. His desertion leaves Edna despondent and isolated. Even were she to obtain a divorce from her husband (all but unthinkable in Catholic New Orleans), she would not wish "to trample upon the little lives" of her two boys (105). Yet, given the era's virtual cult of self-sacrificing maternity – especially when male children were involved – the only alternative the despondent Edna can envision to trampling upon their little lives is to allow her children "to drag her into the soul's slavery for the rest of her days" (108).

In *The Awakening*'s last chapter, Edna wanders back to the same beach where she had earlier imagined herself swimming further out than any woman has before. The beach is deserted and she removes her clothing: "For the first time in her life she stood naked in the open air" (108). Feeling "like some new-born creature opening its eyes in a familiar world that it had never known," Edna enters the sea and begins to swim. She swims out and out into the distance, until she feels "exhaustion … pressing upon and overpowering her" (109). With her arms and legs too heavy to move and "her strength … gone," in the novel's final paragraph Edna re-experiences the sounds and smells of a seemingly endless meadow she had run through as a small child: "There was the hum of bees, and the musky odor of pinks filled the air" (109). The reader is never explicitly told as much, but the context makes evident that in the moment following the book's final line, Edna will drown. Whether we take her implied death as a suicidal surrender, or whether, as some readers have argued, Edna's choice to swim further and further out embodies her decision never to give up her freedom, despite social and personal circumstances that prevent the full realization of her "awakening," Chopin herself embraces literary realist form in eschewing a pat resolution or simplistic closure for the complex character and situation she has created.

The Bostonians and the "Woman's Movement"

Henry James's *The Bostonians* (1886) is the best-known portrayal by a literary realist of the "Woman's Movement" (a name used at the time for organized feminist advocacy), a phenomenon toward which the novel takes a largely satiric view. At the center of the triangle (both romantic and political) constituted by the book's three main characters is Verena Tarrant, an attractive young girl from the lower middle classes with a remarkable gift for public speaking, a gift she uses to make speeches in favor of women's rights. Verena is passionately supported – funded, tutored, housed, ultimately loved – by Olive Chancellor, an upper-class young woman. Olive believes that Verena's eloquence, channeled and reinforced by Olive, can inspire a nationwide campaign whose "pressure ... shall be irresistible. Causing certain laws to be repealed by Congress and by the State legislatures, and others to be enacted" (139). The triangle's third member, Basil Ransom, competes with Olive for Verena's affection and loyalty. Ransom, a distant cousin of Olive's who falls in love with Verena during a visit and determines to make her his wife, is a Southerner whose family lost its plantation during the Civil War. Ransom is proudly reactionary in his political and social views, especially concerning gender. Should they marry, he informs Verena, her career as a public speaker will stop: "My plan is to keep you at home" (323). Basil's and Olive's competition for Verena's devotion thus also becomes a struggle between feminism and old-fashioned patriarchy over the fate of the nation's most promising women's rights icon. Hence, when Verena finds herself in love with Basil, the narrative itself seems to be endorsing not only Basil's view that "he had read her nature ... the right way," but also his larger belief that the only proper "business" of women "was simply to be provided for, practise the domestic virtues, and be charmingly grateful" (352, 191). Yet, as with all of James's works, the text leaves room for ambiguity. In the book's final scene, Basil succeeds in persuading Verena to come away with him just before she is to give a major feminist speech to her largest audience yet. She claims to be "glad" as he propels her out a back door of Boston's Music Hall, but Verena's eyes fill with tears at the loss and humiliation she knows she is inflicting on Olive and the larger Woman's Movement. Far from a happy or storybook ending, the narrator's last words to us predict that these tears of the soon-to-be traditionally married Verena "were not the last she was destined to shed" (435).

Whiteness and *The Awakening*

Chopin was plunged into depression by the largely negative, uncomprehending, and, in some cases, scathing responses her book had provoked. After having a collection of short stories rejected by a publisher the year after *The Awakening* came out, she wrote little more before dying of a cerebral hemorrhage in 1904, at the age of 54. After Chopin's death *The Awakening* remained out of print and forgotten by all but a few scholars until a new paperback edition was finally published in 1964. It wasn't until feminist literary criticism began to gain traction in the academic world during the late 1960s and the 1970s, as part of the period's larger Women's Liberation movement, that *The Awakening* began to appear on college reading lists and, more broadly, to achieve recognition as the powerful and original work of American literature it is. Feminist literary critics were drawn to the book not only because of its compelling story and precise, lyrical writing, but also because Edna embodied a woman struggling to liberate herself – sexually, economically, socially – from patriarchal oppression. Albeit in a somewhat more modern version, feminists of the 1970s still found themselves trying to escape the ideology of true womanhood. Even with Edna's flaws and her ultimate inability to achieve a successfully liberated existence, she reflected what many women felt to be the realities of their own lives and struggles.

At the same time, however, groups such as the National Black Feminist Organization, founded in 1973, criticized the larger Women's Lib movement as overly focused on the concerns of middle-class white women. Such critics argued that the liberation of black women in the United States could never be accomplished if feminists did not strive to understand the complex interplay of sexism, racism, and class oppression in the lives of women of color. For just one example, even as middle-class white feminists were insisting on the right to work outside of the home and to escape being defined only as wives and mothers, the majority of African-American women in the United States had long been *forced* to work outside their own homes by economic necessity – and earlier, of course, by slavery. Even in the late twentieth century, many women of color were unable to mother their own children in the way they wished because they were helping to care for the children of wealthier white families.

Such insights enabled a post-1970s generation of feminist literary critics to recognize that, rather than reflecting the situation of "women" within a patriarchal social order, as earlier feminist writing about *The Awakening* had assumed, the "reality" the book shows its readers is significantly more partial. *The Awakening* depicts female experience from one position in a complicated web of different relationships, all existing within a multi-dimensional social context that the reader sees almost exclusively from Edna's viewpoint. Yes, Edna is a woman whose struggle for full self-realization is blocked by social, cultural, and economic restrictions tied to gender. But she embarks on this struggle supported by the privileges of her race and social class. For instance, Edna has time and space to cultivate her relationship with Robert at the seaside resort only because a nameless "quadroon" cares for her children. African-American women keep her house clean and cook meals for herself and her family; "a little black girl" carries messages between Edna and Robert. In meaningful ways, the specific forms in which Edna experiences her own awakening depend on the *non*-awakening of these women of color: the continued subordination of their own desires, even their individuality, to Edna's service during her quest to develop an autonomous self (Ammons, *Conflicting* 74–77; see also Birnbaum, "Alien Hands"; Barrish, *White Liberal Identity* 62–70). From this perspective, Edna's description of the life she envisions living after she moves to her own house has an ironic dimension that she, and quite possibly Chopin, does not recognize: "Old Celestine [an African-American servant] will come stay with me and do my work. I know I shall like it, like the feeling of freedom and independence" (76).

A different reality: *Contending Forces*

Even as *The Awakening* left nameless and largely unacknowledged the African-American women whose presence "lubricates … the plot" of Edna Pontellier's journey,[5] the late nineteenth century also saw publication of the first substantial body of fiction in US literary history created by women of color. Pauline Hopkins's novel *Contending Forces: A Romance Illustrative of Negro Life North and South* was published in 1900, one year after *The Awakening*, by Boston's Colored Cooperative Publishing Company. At the time, most African-American women who published fiction were also active in other arenas of the public sphere, from working for wages outside the home (Hopkins was an expert stenographer) to editing magazines to occupying leadership positions in local and national advocacy organizations. Hopkins and her colleagues were New Women who struggled not only against gender-based restrictions, as white women did, but also against the virulent and widespread racism of the period. Although several of these women writers became well known among significant segments of the African-American population at the turn of the century, they were ignored by most white authors, male and female, including the leading literary realists of the period. After having been out of print and largely forgotten for decades, the work of these pioneer writers is still in the process of being recovered by scholars, publishers, and teachers.

Unlike either Gilman or Chopin, Hopkins explicitly addressed both an African-American and a white reading audience. She wrote as part of a concerted project among African-American intellectuals, male and female, after the Civil War and Emancipation to help improve the situation of black people in the United States. This broad project of racial "uplift," as it was known, involved providing African Americans with a stronger, more confident sense of their own individual and racial potential for social, educational, and economic achievements, as well as challenging the debasing stereotypes about them that circulated in the dominant culture.

The subtitle that Hopkins appends to *Contending Forces* – "A Romance Illustrative of Negro Life North and South" – signals from the start that Hopkins will cross generic boundaries as a means of achieving the goal stated in the first sentence of her preface: "to raise the stigma of degradation from my race" (13). The subtitle identifies as "romance" the literary genre with which Hopkins most explicitly aligns her novel, a choice she underlines in the preface when she refers to the book as "my somewhat abrupt and daring venture within the wide field of romantic literature" (13). At the same time, however, the subtitle also asserts that the novel will illustrate "Negro Life" in two geographic regions; by 1900, fiction that presented itself as offering depictions of culturally and regionally specific ways of life was associated more with realism than with romance. The preface affirms the novel's literary realist credentials as well, stating that the author has "tried to tell an impartial story, leaving it to the reader to draw conclusions" and that "ample proof" that key events in the story "actually occurred ... may be found in the archives of the courthouse at Newberne, N.C., and at the national seat of government, Washington, D.C." (15, 14). Hopkins's novel does not merely juxtapose literary elements associated with realism and with "romance" genres: she combines them in new ways to meet the difficult challenge of both vividly and believably conveying the violence, exploitation, and social negation, as well as the resilience and accomplishments, experienced by African-American women, both Northern and Southern, in the decades following Emancipation.

Contending Forces tells the story of Sappho Clark, who is kidnapped and raped at the age of fourteen by her father's white half-brother and then left in a bordello. After Sappho's father threatens to report his half-brother to federal officers, he and his family are killed and their house burnt down by Klan-like vigilantes, leaving Sappho the only survivor. Having been separated from the baby she gave birth to after the rape, Sappho moves to Boston where, under a different last name, she rents a room from the black middle-class Smith family and finds work as a stenographer and typist. Still carrying a deep inner sense of violation, she feels redeemed only after a chivalric courtship and then legal marriage to an educated black man allow her to experience "a love sanctified and purified" (398). Upon reuniting with her young son, Sappho can also finally experience the "holy love" of motherhood (347). Purified love and holy motherhood, of course, invoke the ideology of pure womanhood integral to the "romance" genre of sentimental domestic fiction. But Hopkins gives that ideology a different valence than it carries in such domestic fiction of the 1850s as, for example, Susan Warner's *The Wide, Wide World* (1850).

Hopkins's preeminent strategy for accomplishing her novel's aim of "rais[ing] the stigma of degradation from my race" was to establish Sappho as a heroine who, despite the sexual abuse she has suffered, "is an exemplar of female purity, piety, and the work ethic" (Hopkins, *Contending Forces* 13; Tate, *Domestic Allegories* 8). True womanhood ideology, however confining it may have been to white women such as Edna and the unnamed narrator of "The Yellow Wallpaper," at least brought with it a degree of respect and social protection that the slave system had entirely denied to black women – respect and dignity that white feminist authors such as Gilman and Chopin showed little interest in fostering for black women. The well-known sexual exploitation of disempowered black women by white men did not end when slavery did, nor did the widely disseminated myth of black women as lustful, hyper-sexual beings – a myth first disseminated during slavery as a sort of ideological cover, or excuse, for white men who used their power to take sexual advantage of African-American women. In *Contending Forces*, Sappho's white rapist tries to justify his action by demanding, "What does a woman of mixed blood, or any Negress, for that matter, know of virtue? It is my belief that they were a direct creation by God to be the pleasant companions of men of my race" (261).

In this context, rather than portraying idealized true womanhood as an outdated and retrograde model, more pertinent to "bygone" romance genres than to modern women's actual lives, as Chopin does, Hopkins presents the role of idealized wife and mother as an aspirational goal for black women, one that has been denied them by white culture but which they are no less qualified than white women to occupy. Beyond its meanings for individual women, literary critic Claudia Tate has argued, this role has an important allegorical function in Hopkins's fiction, as it does in the fiction of other African-American women novelists of the late nineteenth and early twentieth centuries. Both for these authors and for their black female readers, black literary heroines attaining the position of idealized "mother-woman" (in Chopin's dismissive phrase) represented the possibility not only of civil equality for the African-American family, which slavery had tried systematically to destroy, but also "the acquisition of authority for the [black female] self both in the home and in the world" (Chopin, *Awakening* 9; Tate, *Domestic Allegories* 8).

In depicting the process through which her heroine comes to acquire a valued self in the home and in the world, Hopkins engages literary realist techniques to convey Sappho's gradual integration into Boston's multilayered African-American community. It is a community that includes doctors, lawyers, and educators, as well as ward politicians, domestic servants, and manual laborers. In particular, Hopkins's text counters the virtual invisibility of middle-class black society to most white Americans by revealing that in Northern cities such as Boston "little circles of educated men and women of color have existed since the Revolutionary War" (145). The novel also pays scrupulous attention to the intermixture of standard English and vernacular dialects among Boston's African-American community, with the former used by the narrator and the book's middle-class black characters, and the latter spoken by characters of lower-class backgrounds, both black and white. Paralleling a similar dynamic in Howells's *The Rise of Silas Lapham*, some of the well-educated younger black characters that *Contending Forces* aligns with social modernity show an affectionate, if condescending, appreciation of the black "folk" speech used by certain older characters.[6]

While white realist writers often scornfully linked idealized feminine heroines similar to Sappho with "romance" genres they wished to transcend, Hopkins grounds Sappho's introduction into Boston's African-American community with realist-style ethnographic details. Such details serve to illuminate what Hopkins's preface calls "manners and customs – religious, political, and social" of various African-American social groupings in the city (13). Readers learn, for example, that "colored churches" offer extra Easter services at night, in addition to daylight hours, for worshipers who work as domestic servants during the day (315). Also in the realist mode, the novel dramatizes many of the historically specific social and economic dynamics that both separated and linked Boston's black and white inhabitants at the end of the nineteenth century. For example, *Contending Forces* shows black laborers being squeezed out of jobs because new immigrants from Southern and Eastern Europe refuse to work at places where "'niggers' are hired" (83) – a tactic the immigrants employ in an attempt to gain recognition for themselves as full-fledged "white" Americans (see Chapter 10). Fleshing out another corner of Boston society that touches Sappho's life, Hopkins offers a nuanced, far from idealized depiction of a mutually beneficial relationship between wealthy white philanthropists and African Americans seeking funds for black educational and other institutions in the post-Reconstruction South. In fact, Sappho finds her "sanctified" love with Will Smith, who plans to found a school for black students interested in the liberal arts and sciences. (Will, who earns a doctorate in Germany, ultimately decides to seek a setting for his school outside of the Southern states.)

Yet even with all of its grounding in dense social description, the plot of *Contending Forces* is full of the twists that mainstream literary realists professed to disdain, including such melodramatic developments as, at the end of the novel, the shocking emergence of a long-lost family connection that leads to the Smith family suddenly inheriting a large sum of money, and the accidental yet glorious reconnection of Will and Sappho after the latter, harassed by the dastardly attempt of Will's best friend John to blackmail her into becoming his mistress, has attempted to disappear into a Catholic convent in another part of the country. A minor character aptly comments upon hearing a brief summary of the book's final plot developments, "It is indeed a fairy tale of love and chivalry such as we read of only in books" (398). We have already seen that there were compelling cultural and political reasons for Hopkins to idealize her African-American heroine as perfectly embodying nineteenth-century America's vision of "true womanhood," despite – or, more precisely, *because* of – Sappho's painful history of degradation and violation. An explanation of Hopkins's unusually striking interweaving of realist detail with melodramatic plot twists may lie in how radically "Negro Life North and South" departed in key aspects from the everyday realities of middle- and upper-class Anglo-American life that well-known realist writers such as Howells and James sought to bring into literary representation.

Hopkins's narrative, as scholar Nancy Glazener points out, features several instances of "whipping, rape, and lynching – events fairly typical within the history of any family descended from slaves" (*Reading for Realism* 119), but which risked seeming sensationalistic or implausible to literary realism's dominant audience of well-off white readers. As we will see in Chapter 9, many such readers, especially in the North, preferred to believe that the Civil War had largely resolved the nation's race problems, with the occasional Southern lynchings reported in Northern newspapers nothing more than an ugly but isolated after-effect of slavery's end (see Chapter 9). For such readers, the very inclusion of such lurid material by Hopkins might seem to violate the "absolute and clear sense of proportion" that William Dean Howells contended was integral to the realist novel. For Howells, realism was a genre that "preserves the balances" (Crane, "Fears"). Glazener aptly observes that Howellsian realism's "constructions of which kinds of events counted as typical and realistic had the profoundly political potential to relegate experiences of violence, suffering, and oppression to the domain of 'cheap' – commodified, manipulative, addictive – fiction" (*Reading for Realism* 119).

Thus, Hopkins's image in the preface of lynch-law "raising its head like a venomous monster" might seem to evoke a cheap horror genre, just as her mention of "cruel … piratical methods" might sound like a cliché taken from popular adventure tales (14, 15). In deploying these images directly next to such realist-coded assurances as that she will "tell an impartial story" verifiable by documentary proofs, however, Hopkins has a delicate double aim. Readers must recognize that "*such things are*" (14; Hopkins's italics), yet this recognition of reality must occur outside the mode of Howellsian realism, with its emphasis on viewing everything with a plausible sense of proportion. Hopkins, that is, strives to convey both that the "venomous monster" of lynch-law is fully as horrifying as the image suggests, and at the same time that it is a daily lived reality for black people in the American South.

In our next chapter we will see that, as with Hopkins's *Contending Forces*, the question of what modes of literary representation, or what combination of modes, will most compellingly convey to readers the disturbing truths of American race relations remains an urgent issue within the work of other writers who seek to convey those truths – and, perhaps, to change them.

Chapter 9

"The unjust spirit of caste": realism and race

In white Southern writer Thomas Nelson Page's short story "Marse Chan," which appeared in New York's prestigious *Century Magazine* in 1884 and was then widely reprinted, an elderly African-American character named Sam waxes nostalgic to a white visitor from the North. The Civil War has ended and Sam's former owner is dead, but he still resides on the once wealthy, now dilapidated, plantation where he used to be a slave. Speaking of his life before the war, Sam insists to his visitor,

> Dem wuz good ole times, marster – de bes' Sam ever see! Dey wuz, in fac'! Niggers didn' hed nothin' 't all to do – jes' hed to 'ten' to de feedin' an' cleanin' de hosses, an' doin' what de marster tell 'em to do; an' when dey wuz sick, dey had things sont 'em out de house, an' de same doctor come to see 'em whar 'ten' to de white folks when dey wuz po'ly. Dyar warn' no trouble nor nothin'.   (935)

The heavily marked rural African-American dialect spoken by Sam identifies this story as part of the local-color movement that became so popular in the 1880s, especially in the short-story form. As we saw in Chapter 5, late-nineteenth-century local-color fiction, later also called regionalism, was characteristically set in places removed from the nation's centers of economic, political, and cultural authority, and it made the speech, manners, and geography local to its setting inseparable from the story being told.

"Marse Chan," however, along with the other stories Thomas Nelson Page collected in a volume he titled *In Ole Virginia* (1887), helped constitute a distinct sub-category of local-color writing often referred to as the "plantation school." Other plantation-school writers included Joel Chandler Harris, author of the immensely popular Uncle Remus stories, the Louisiana writer Grace King, and, in the twentieth century, Margaret Mitchell, whose *Gone with the Wind* achieved blockbuster status first as a novel and then as a movie in the 1930s. Plantation-school writing by these white Southerners painted nostalgic, sometimes humorous pictures of the South before the Civil War. It depicted the so-called "Old South" as a stable world in which the noble values of honor and chivalry thrived and loyal, happy slaves lived on beautiful plantations, where their benevolent owners regarded them as members of their own extended families – as "overgrown children" in the words of one nostalgic author (Avirett, *Old Plantation* iv). We saw in Chapter 5 that critics still heatedly debate the social meanings and cultural functions of regionalist works such as Sarah Orne Jewett's *The Country of the Pointed Firs*. By contrast, there is today little debate regarding the pernicious cultural work performed by most plantation-school writing in the late nineteenth and early twentieth centuries.

The post-Reconstruction South

Plantation fiction emerged at a time when racist white Southerners were taking extreme, often violent actions to restrict the political and civil rights ostensibly guaranteed to the nation's four million newly freed slaves by the so-called "Reconstruction Amendments" to the US Constitution. Passed and ratified in the wake of the Civil War, the Thirteenth Amendment abolished slavery; the Fourteenth Amendment granted citizenship and equal protection under the law to former slaves; and the Fifteenth Amendment guaranteed the right to vote to all male citizens of the United States, regardless of "race, color, or previous condition of servitude." (More than fifty years would pass before female citizens would be granted this same right.) The twelve brief years of Reconstruction (1865–77) witnessed remarkable achievements by African Americans living in former Confederate states. With the support of, among other entities, the Freedmen's Bureau, a government agency launched by President Lincoln in 1865 to assist former slaves, African Americans built schools, churches, and businesses. With their right to the suffrage protected by the full force of the federal government, including the army, black people voted in large numbers and helped to elect many African-American office holders, including two US senators and nineteen members of the House of Representatives.

Opposition to these developments, and to Reconstruction more generally, was intense and widespread across white Southern society, but was perhaps most venomous among those who still owned large plantations or who were involved in efforts to build new factories, often with the help of Northern investors.[1] Though indirectly and far more subtly than, for example, the terrorist actions of the Ku Klux Klan, which first emerged soon after the Civil War, plantation fiction lent support to racist efforts to undercut full implementation of these amendments. An essential, though always unspoken, implication of plantation-school fiction was that the Reconstruction Amendments had been misguided – above all granting full voting rights to African Americans. Along with other racist portrayals of African Americans prevalent at the time, including those found in minstrel shows and in popular illustrations and decorative knick-knacks, plantation fiction depicted black people as too child-like, ignorant, and gullible to make responsible use of the franchise. African Americans in the South would themselves be better off, plantation-school writing implied, if wise and benevolent white people made important decisions for them, just as had occurred under slavery. Importantly, this message of white supremacy was aimed not so much at white Southern readers of plantation literature, many of whom already embraced its premises, but at white Northern readers.

Though white Northerners often shared white Southerners' racist presumptions about black inferiority, some also felt ambivalent, even guilty, about the federal government's increasing unwillingness to continue enforcing civil rights laws in a recalcitrant South, especially as the Civil War receded further into the past. The massive economic depression that struck the United States in 1873 (the largest until the Great Depression of the 1930s) persuaded many white Americans, both Southerners and Northerners, that it was time for the nation to shift its attention away from the divisions and conflicts of the Civil War era toward more pressing challenges (Foner, *Reconstruction* 512–63). In the face of what seemed absolute intransigence by the majority of white Southerners on racial issues, powerful figures in the North, including key leaders both in the business community and in the Republican party (the party in charge of Reconstruction and still most associated with African-American civil rights), became willing to sacrifice the interests of black Americans in the name of national unity. Such unity would only be possible, the white South insisted, if white Southerners were left alone to manage their so-called "Negro Problem" as they saw fit.

In what amounted to a betrayal of several commitments the US government had made to the freedmen after the Civil War, Reconstruction was officially abandoned in 1877. The effect was to give racist elements in the South virtually a free hand, over the following few decades, to attack and try to reverse the political, social, and economic gains African Americans had achieved during Reconstruction. Although the re-institution of slavery as such was never a serious possibility, "Jim Crow" laws enforcing strict racial segregation in schools, on trains and buses, and in many other areas of everyday life, were soon passed throughout the former Confederacy. Voting rights were chipped away both by violence and intimidation, and by local laws specially designed to exclude black voters. Race riots instigated by whites destroyed new black businesses and homes. Lynching was increasingly used as a weapon of terror against black Americans.

Plantation fiction during the post-Civil War decades looked back with nostalgia to the days of slavery before the Civil War when well-meaning white people exercised benign power over faithful, satisfied African Americans. The genre's rosy depictions of slave–master relations subtly helped to assuage any uncertainty or guilt its target audience – white Northerners – might feel about the nation's effective re-empowerment of former slave owners to deal with racial matters in the South. Readers of plantation fiction were encouraged to feel that, yes, re-establishing harmonious relations between the races after the chaotic periods of Civil War and Reconstruction might involve taking away rights; the process might even involve some lamentable violence of the sort depicted in Northern newspapers' coverage of Southern lynchings. But when the fictional black character Sam confides to a white Northern visitor in "Marse Chan" that the days of slavery were "de bes' Sam ever see!" and goes on to praise the affectionate care devoted to his health and welfare by his former master, the indirect message conveyed by plantation writer Thomas Nelson Page is that, with Reconstruction halted and its radical changes reversed, everything will work out just fine for both black and white people in the South. A similar message is conveyed by author Joel Chandler Harris, whose stories utilized as narrator the elderly Uncle Remus, a plantation fixture who has "nothing but pleasant memories of the discipline of slavery" (Harris, *Uncle Remus* 12). The unspoken implication of Remus's "pleasant memories" is that present-day white Southerners could have only good hearts and kind intentions toward the simple people who had formerly been such a valued part of their happy plantation communities.

The context sketched above of Reconstruction, its shameful abandonment, and the bitterly unequal struggle over African-American human and civil rights that ensued is of critical significance for understanding the fiction by Charles Chesnutt and Mark Twain to which this chapter will now turn.

Chesnutt's revision of plantation fiction

Charles Waddell Chesnutt was born in 1858 in Cleveland, Ohio. Two years earlier, his mixed-race parents had left their home in Fayetteville, North Carolina, where they had belonged to a small group of people labeled "free persons of color" by the 1850 census. Chesnutt's family returned to Fayetteville after the war in 1866, when he was eight years old. He continued to live there until 1883, which meant that he directly participated in the important achievements and great promise of Reconstruction in the South; he also experienced first-hand the crushing disappointment of Reconstruction's abandonment in 1877. Although the segregated South's "one-drop rule" meant that his legal status was black, Chesnutt's extremely light skin would have enabled him to "pass" as white once he left Fayetteville, and thus to escape the racial discrimination that hampered certain of his professional ambitions throughout his life.[2] As a matter of personal and political principle, however, he chose not to take this step, pledging in his journal at age twenty, "I will show to the world that a man may spring from a race of slaves, and yet far excel many of the boasted ruling race" (Chessnut, *Journals* 93).

Meditating a career as a writer in a journal entry of 1880, when he was twenty-one, Chesnutt decided,

> If I do write, I shall write for a purpose, a high, holy purpose, and this will inspire me to greater effort. The object of my writings would be not so much the elevation of the colored people as the elevation of the whites, – for I consider the unjust spirit of caste which is so insidious as to pervade a whole nation, and so powerful as to subject a whole race and all connected with it to scorn and social ostracism – I consider this a barrier to the moral progress of the American people.   (*Journals* 139–40)

Planning to address his future writing mostly to white readers, who needed to receive his message far more than African Americans did, Chesnutt goes on in the same journal entry to describe the literary "crusade" against racism that he envisions himself launching as "not a fierce indiscriminate onslaught; not an appeal to force, for this is something that force can but slightly affect; but a moral revolution which must be brought about in a different manner" (*Journals* 140).

Seven years later, Chesnutt made the first of several brilliantly revision-ary contributions to the genre of nostalgic plantation fiction by publishing "The Goophered Grapevine" in the *Atlantic Monthly*, which made him the first African-American fiction writer to have a story accepted by what was at the time the most prestigious magazine in America. As we have seen in other chapters, the *Atlantic Monthly* was also the premier venue for works by many of the nation's best-known realist writers, including Howells, James, Jewett, and others. Fulfilling the plan Chesnutt had articulated in his journal, "The Goophered Grapevine" does not launch a "fierce ... onslaught" against the racism of the *Atlantic*'s readers, nor against their general willingness to acquiesce in the brutal revocation of African Americans' citizenship rights in the post-Reconstruction South. Instead, Chesnutt tries in that story and in his other plantation fiction to adjust his white readers' perspectives more subtly, strategically aiming, "while amusing [his readers], to lead them on imperceptibly, unconsciously, step by step, to the desired state of feeling" (*Journals* 140).

The first pages of "The Goophered Grapevine" parallel the beginning of Thomas Nelson Page's "Marse Chan," while its overall structure resembles that of Joel Chandler Harris's Uncle Remus plantation stories, first published in a book collection as *Legends of the Old Plantation* (1881). Like Page and Harris, Chesnutt uses a frame narrative in which a white listener or listeners settle in for a tale about plantation life before the war told by an elderly former slave. In "The Goophered Grapevine" and thirteen additional stories adapting the plantation formula that Chesnutt would go on to write, the inside-the-frame story is narrated by Uncle Julius, who speaks in heavy dialect and displays ignorance about such matters as whether the earth is round or flat, just as in Page's and Harris's plantation fiction. The white listeners in this series are a middle-class couple who have relocated from the North to a rural area of North Carolina some years after the end of the Civil War. John, who narrates the framing story in a standard style of literary English, informs readers that he and Annie chose to move to the South, despite their unfamiliarity with the local culture, both because a doctor suggested that warmer weather may improve Annie's health and because John has a business plan. He wishes to buy some former plantation land "for a mere song" and, using the "cheap" labor of former slaves, to grow grapes for export to Northern markets (31). Chesnutt does not present John and Annie as unusually greedy, callous, or racially prejudiced; he merely makes clear that the couple has moved to the South not in order to challenge the prevailing racial order but to profit from it.

This well-educated white couple from the North functions within "The Goophered Grapevine," and the related set of stories by Chesnutt (*Conjure Woman*, 1899), as fictional surrogates, or stand-ins, for just the sort of white, educated, and well-off Northern readers who mostly subscribed to the *Atlantic Monthly* and whom Chesnutt hoped to reach. John and Annie are exploring a plantation they are considering buying, where scuppernong grapes were formerly grown, when they come across "a venerable-looking colored man" sitting on a log (34). Informing them that he was "bawn en raise' on dis yer same plantation," Uncle Julius warns John, " 'f I 'uz in yo' place, I wouldn' buy dis vimya'd" (34, 35). When asked why not, Julius narrates a sequence of events that he claims occurred on the plantation "many years befo' the wah" (35). Telling his story in heavy dialect and with a "dreamy expression" on his face, Julius seems to "be living over again in monologue his life on the old plantation" (35). Julius's opening statements follow plantation-fiction conventions as he draws on racist stereotypes, supposed to be humorous to white audiences, to explain to John and Annie why the plantation's slaves used to sneak into the vineyard at night: "Now, ef dey's an'thing a nigger lub, nex' ter 'possum, en chick'n, en watermillyums, it's scuppernon's ... De scuppernon' make you smack yo' lip en roll yo' eye en wush fer mo'; so I reckon it ain' very 'stonishin' dat niggers lub scuppernon'" (35–36). In addition to Julius's repeated use of what was a commonly accepted but even at the time debasing term for African Americans, his emphasis on eye rolling and lip smacking and on a reputed craving for possum, chicken, and watermelons among black people would have fit right in with popular minstrel-show portrayals of the so-called "darky." In other words, Julius begins his story with what appears to be yet another reiteration of plantation fiction's image of Southern blacks as childlike, often slightly comical creatures.

After establishing this familiar set-up, however, the rest of Julius's story subverts the nostalgic plantation formula in key ways. First, Julius reveals what amounts to an ongoing battle between the then owner of the plantation, "Mars Dugal McAdoo," and the plantation's slaves over the literal fruits of the slaves' labor, the scuppernong grapes. McAdoo wishes to turn every single grape grown by the slaves into money for himself, and posts spring guns, steel traps, and armed guards in an attempt to prevent the slaves from making nighttime raids on the vineyard they labor in during the day. Featuring a runaway slave hunted by dogs and a master who pays for medical care only when his own economic interests are at risk, what begins as a seemingly light-hearted sketch about grape-loving slaves ultimately illuminates the underlying realities of a system that depended on violence and the threat of violence to extort labor from human beings whose freedom had already been stolen from them.

The powers of conjure

By casually inserting details of slavery's horrors into what would initially strike readers as a conventional plantation narrative, Uncle Julius's stories undermine the idealized vision of pre-Civil War racial hierarchies that, during the post-War period, helped provide justification for attempts to re-subordinate black people to their supposedly good-hearted former masters. Julius shares his stories about "slab'ry times" to achieve more immediate, more personal aims as well, usually related to the current well-being of himself and those close to him. In "Mars Jeems's Nightmare," for instance, Julius seeks to have a grandson of his rehired as a worker on the plantation, after

John has fired him for "laziness" (*Conjure Woman* 56). Julius never attempts to gain these more personal aims through direct persuasion. Instead, he achieves them through the effect his narratives about plantation life "befo' de wah" have on his listeners.

More specifically, Julius's achievement of his personal aims almost always hinges on the role played in individual stories by "conjure," also called "goopher," which refers to acts of metamorphosis and transformation performed by one of several local conjure women (and, occasionally, a conjure man). In a practice whose elements can be traced back to Africa (as Chesnutt contends in a later essay called "Superstition and Folklore of the South"), the conjure women in Julius's tales combine roots, herbs, and miscellaneous personal effects belonging to intended targets to turn people temporarily into animals; to help reunite family members who have been separated by slavery; and, on one occasion, briefly to transform a cruel plantation owner into a black person forced to work under the harsh overseer he himself has hired. Although conjure functions as a form of power alternate and, in brief flashes, superior to the overwhelming power of white masters over their slaves, Julius's stories make plain that it is never sufficient fully to mitigate slavery's destructive impact on individuals and families.

In "Po' Sandy," among the most powerful of the conjure tales Chesnutt wrote (and the second one he published in the *Atlantic*), Julius desires John and Annie's permission to turn an old schoolhouse building on the former plantation into a makeshift church for his Baptist splinter group, despite John's existing plan to tear the schoolhouse down and reuse the lumber for a new kitchen. Julius tells his white employers a story in which Tenie, a conjure woman, turns her husband Sandy into a tree so that he can evade the compulsory and unending mobility forced on him by an "easy-gwine" master (47). "One of dese ... folks w'at wanter please eve'ybody," Sandy's master regularly lends him out to relatives and friends in the neighborhood for weeks and months at a time (47). As a tree, the exhausted Sandy can rest in one place (his master thinks he has escaped to the North), and he has the pleasure of Tenie turning him back to himself every now and then so that they can talk together. But on a day when Tenie has herself arbitrarily been lent out to her "easy-gwine" master's daughter-in-law and so is off the premises, the master needs some lumber for a new kitchen and happens to select the very tree into which Sandy has been transformed. When Tenie returns home the following morning, Julius continues, and "seed de stump standin' dere, wid de sap runnin' out'n it, en de limbs layin' scattered roun', she nigh 'bout went out'n her min'" (50). The conjure woman rushes to the local sawmill, arriving just as the tree is about to be carved into planks. She throws herself in front of the large saw, crying and desperately apologizing to Sandy, but it is no use. The new kitchen is built from the lumber. But the structure "wuzn' much use" to the master, Julius explains, because the slaves supposed to cook and clean in it "could hear sump'n moanin' en groanin' 'bout de kitchn in de night-time, en w'en de win' would blow dey could hear sump'n a-hollerin' en sweekin' lack it wuz in great pain en sufferin'" (52). The plantation's slaves soon refuse to work there, even when whipped, and Mars Marrabo is finally forced to tear the kitchen down. He reuses the wood to build a schoolhouse for the neighborhood's white children, who attend it until the war breaks out. The building has "be'n stannin' empty ever sence," Julius concludes, adding that folks still believe the lumber it was made from "is gwine to be ha'nted tel de las' piece er plank is rotted en crumble' inter dus'" (53).

Julius's story convinces Annie that the wood in the schoolhouse is indeed haunted, whether literally or metaphorically – haunted by the pain, suffering, and mutilating losses inherent in, as she puts it, a "system ... under which such things were possible" (53). When John asks her in amazement if, by "such things," she means the possibility of "a man's being turned into a tree" (53), Annie evades the question. Yet, she insists that she will not accept a kitchen made from the lumber and instead gives Julius permission to hold his church meetings in the structure. That such was his aim all along is hinted by the ready response he has when asked if the ghosts won't present a problem to his church group. He says that ghosts never disturb worship and adds, in Annie's paraphrase, that "if Sandy's spirit *should* happen to stray into a meeting by mistake, no doubt the preaching would do it good" (54). Through his narrative of "conjure," Julius conveys a grim picture of African-American life under slavery and, at the same time, attains a present-day meeting space for his community. To the extent that Julius's stories transform the listening John and Annie – or at least lead them to take actions they wouldn't otherwise have taken (such as, in another case, setting free a man whom John caught stealing meat from his smokehouse and initially intended to send to prison as "an example") – we can say that the stories become Julius's own form of "conjure." Using verbal skills to circumvent those with more power connects Julius to ancient African folk stories about trickster figures, even as it helps him and his people to navigate the brutal realities of the South after Reconstruction.

Once we turn to the world outside the text, by contrast, it becomes much more difficult to measure the extent to which "Po' Sandy" or the other tales conjured any sort of meaningful transformation in white readers who encountered them either in the *Atlantic Monthly* or, twelve years later, in Chesnutt's story collection *The Conjure Woman*. Perhaps, in the case of some individual readers, Chesnutt's slyly subversive plantation fiction did achieve the goal he had set for himself when first imagining his career as a writer: to amuse his readers but also, at the same time, "to lead them on imperceptibly, unconsciously, step by step, to the desired state of feeling" (140). Whether or not he succeeded in changing the hearts or minds of individual readers, however, Chesnutt was only too aware that conditions for African Americans in the South grew, if anything, worse as the twentieth century began. Rights continued to be stripped away. Lynching became more frequent. Gruesomely, in some cases lynching also became a popular spectacle: bleachers were set up and special trains were run to accommodate audiences in the thousands. Despite urgent requests from black leaders, the federal government refused to intervene in any meaningful way. In the face of such developments, and of his own growing ambitions as a writer, Chesnutt ultimately found the plantation-fiction format of his Uncle Julius stories too restrictive and moved on to other modes of writing, including essays and novels.

The last section of this chapter will discuss the most radical of Chesnutt's novels, *The Marrow of Tradition* (1901), written in direct response to a race riot (or, more accurately, a racial massacre) that occurred in Wilmington, North Carolina, not far from where the writer had grown up. First, however, the chapter's middle portions analyze the treatment of race in writing by Chesnutt's immensely popular contemporary, Mark Twain. Our primary focus will be on Twain's *Adventures of Huckleberry Finn* (1885). Published only two years before "The Goophered Grapevine," and today regarded as one of American literature's greatest works, *Huckleberry Finn* shares with Chesnutt's conjure tales the use of a pre-Civil War setting to engage with racial controversies in the post-Reconstruction South. As we will see, however, the question of what point of view Twain's novel most strongly supports in the era's conflicts about race remains a matter of intense argument for readers.

Twain, Huck, and realism

Mark Twain's relationship to literary realism has always been ambiguous. In his own day Twain was not generally associated with realism in the public mind, despite the close friendship and mutual admiration he shared with William Dean Howells. Moreover, Twain himself avoided using the term realism in his own critical writing (Bell, *Problem of American Literary Realism* 44). Instead, Twain was popularly viewed as a humorist, especially during the first half of his career, which culminated in the writing of *Huckleberry Finn* (see Wuster, "'*Most Popular Humorist*'"). A prominent strand running through Twain's writing derived from the oral tradition of the southwestern tall tale, which creates humor from extravagant, inventive exaggerations delivered in a deadpan tone, as if the speaker himself recognizes nothing out of the ordinary in the increasingly ridiculous events he narrates. For instance, "The Notorious Jumping Frog of Calaveras County" (1865), Twain's first nation-wide success, tells of a frog-jumping contest with heavy bets riding on it, in which a California mining town's local champion proves unable to jump: the local frog "hysted up his shoulders – so – like a Frenchman," the tale's narrator says, "but it warn't no use – he couldn't budge." It later turns out that the stranger whose frog beats the champion had filled the latter with "five pound" of quail-shot, which belatedly explains why the latter frog "'pears to look mighty baggy" to its owner (18).

Despite Twain's attachment to this sort of literary "burlesque," numerous critics over the past one hundred years have found convincing reasons to link him to realist principles and practices (see Messent, "Mark Twain"). Twain indirectly conveyed his commitment to realist principles through relentless parodies and critiques of the style of writing he castigated as "sentimentality and sloppy romantics" – the same writing, in other words, against which leading realists such as Howells and James defined their own literary projects (quoted in Bell, *Problem* 42). Like Howells, Twain believed that the use of "sloppy romantics" in literature not only made for bad art, but actually caused harm to readers and to society at large. In Chapter 1, we saw that Twain only half-jokingly blamed the Civil War on novelist Sir Walter Scott, whose glorifications of chivalry, battle, and lost causes infiltrated white Southern culture. (In *Huckleberry Finn*, Twain names a wrecked steamship housing a gang of thieves the "Walter Scott.") In the same vein, Twain's 1889 novel *A Connecticut Yankee in King Arthur's Court* sets the entire "chivalry and nobility" of sixth-century Arthurian England (503) against the book's protagonist, a nineteenth-century New England engineer named Hank Morgan, who describes himself as a "champion of hard unsentimental common-sense and reason" and "nearly barren of sentiment … and poetry" (495, 222). The plot of *Connecticut Yankee* depends on an unexplained form of time travel, which in one obvious sense would seem to exclude the book from the category of literary realism. Yet critic Michael Davitt Bell persuasively argues that Hank Morgan's identification with hard-headed rationality makes Morgan "a fictional embodiment of the 'realist'" (Bell, *Problem* 58).

The strongest case for Mark Twain as a realist writer, however, rests on his acknowledged masterpiece, *Adventures of Huckleberry Finn* (1885). It rests especially on Twain's creation of Huck himself – and above all on Huck's voice. Generations of readers have testified to the effect Huck produces on them of being a real boy. His character mixes naïveté with knowingness; kindness and compassion with occasional acts of thoughtless cruelty; conscience with casual lies and small thefts; and skeptical self-protectiveness with a powerful desire to be accepted and loved. Twain's most powerful technical innovation in *Adventures of Huckleberry Finn* is his use of Huck as a first-person narrator, a narrator who is not only a child but also speaks and narrates in a non-standard dialect of English. Chapter 5's discussion of regionalist writing (a category that describes *Huckleberry Finn* in several important ways) noted that late-nineteenth-century realist writers took artistic pride in reproducing on the page accurate-sounding regional, ethnic and/or class-based American dialects. However, in virtually all realist works prior to *Adventures of Huckleberry Finn*, dialect appears within quotation marks and is surrounded by the standard English of a narrator.[3] Even in Joel Chandler Harris's Uncle Remus tales, which come very close to 100 percent dialect writing, Remus's narration always appears within quotation marks, which Harris refreshes at the start of each paragraph. Harris also inserts at least a few phrases of third-person standard English at the beginning of each tale to re-establish the ongoing fictional frame in which Uncle Remus tells his folk tales to entertain and instruct a young white boy whose parents now own the plantation. In this manner, Harris's readers are continually reminded that Remus's rural African-American dialect deviates from the "correct" English regarded as the nation's normative language.

Twain's novel, by contrast, begins not with a narrator using standard English but with Huck himself, speaking directly to readers with nary a quotation mark to mark his speech as in any way deviant from a more authoritative norm: "You don't know about me, without you have read a book by the name of 'The Adventures of Tom Sawyer,' but that ain't no matter. That book was made by Mr. Mark Twain, and he told the truth, mainly. There was things which he stretched, but mainly he told the truth" (13). With this opening statement, Huck lets readers know he, not "Mr. Mark Twain," will be narrating the entire novel to follow, and that he will do so entirely in his own vernacular voice. The standard-English narration used by "Mr. Mark Twain," when he "made" the book *Tom Sawyer* (which was published in 1876, and in which the character of Huck first appears) plays no role in *Adventures of Huckleberry Finn*. With no representation of "correct" English present in the later novel, Huck's language itself starts to assume the status of normal in the reader's ear. If Howells called for an American realist fiction that would "speak the dialect, the language, that most Americans know – the language of unaffected people everywhere," the language in which *Huckleberry Finn* is narrated represents the period's most successful and convincing response ("Editor's Study," 1887 [74.444] 987).

Huckleberry Finn and the Jim question

Especially over the past several decades, critics have been virtually unanimous in admiring the success of Twain's realism as evinced in both Huck's character and Huck's voice. By contrast, Twain's depiction of Jim, the runaway slave who becomes Huck's traveling partner, has been debated more hotly than any other facet of the novel. The question of how Twain represents Jim in his most realist novel had important political meaning in 1885, when *Adventures of Huckleberry Finn* was first published, and it continues to be politically and racially charged today. Parents and others disturbed by the frequency with which *Adventures of Huckleberry Finn* is assigned to high school students have argued that Twain's portrayal of Jim is marred by minstrel-show racism, and that the incessant use of the degrading word "nigger" in reference to Jim and other African Americans in the book may simultaneously offend black students forced to read it and implicitly make the word seem more acceptable to white students (see, e.g., John Wallace, "Huckleberry Finn"). When Twain's novel was first published, initial reviews did not comment on the representation of Jim, per se, but the political issues involved in that representation were, if anything, even more significant then than they are now. As a twenty-first-century reader, it can be easy to get caught up in Huck and Jim's dramatic river journey and forget the specific historical context in which the work was written. Twain set *Adventures of Huckleberry Finn* sometime in the 1840s, the era of his own boyhood, at a time when slavery was in full force in the South and the Civil War was barely looming on the horizon. He wrote it, however, during the late 1870s and early 1880s, years during which Reconstruction was being dismantled in states across the South. The novel becomes both richer and more complex when one considers its resonances with the fraught racial politics of these years.

As we have seen, during the latter decades of the nineteenth century most white people in the North acquiesced as Southern states systematically reversed gains achieved by freed slaves during Reconstruction. During this period some whites found supposedly "scientific" support for racist claims that African Americans did not, and by definition *could* not, possess sufficient mental capacity to be fit for civic, political, or social equality with whites. Today it may be easy to dismiss as both malevolent and ridiculous such nineteenth-century "sciences" as racial craniometry, which ranked the inherent capacities of different racial groups by measuring the size and shape of cadaver skulls. But in late-nineteenth- and early-twentieth-century America such pseudoscientific "data" were often regarded as authoritative by both popular and academic audiences, including at the nation's leading research institutions (see Gould,

Mismeasure of Man 105–41). For instance, a 1907 editorial in the academic journal *American Medicine* praised the work of Dr. Robert B. Bean, a laboratory scientist at the Johns Hopkins University in Baltimore. Bean's "discoveries" about "the negro brain" not only confirmed the "well known fact that the negro brain is considerably smaller than the European and particularly the northern types grouped together as Anglo-Saxon," but also revealed as another "fact" that "the negro ... has fewer brain cells [and] fewer of those connecting fibers, which by their number distinguish the human from all other brains. It is therefore more animal in type and incapable of producing those thoughts which have built up civilization" (Anon., "Editorial Comment" 197). The editorial argues that such biological "discoveries" scientifically prove that to allow African Americans the franchise is to jeopardize the fate of the entire nation by "placing it in the power of types so lacking in brain that they never can be educated to the point of being trusted with Republican institutions" (197). According to the same editorial in *American Medicine*, racial craniometry has further uncovered "the anatomical basis for the complete failure of negro schools to impart the higher studies – the brain cannot comprehend them any more than a horse can understand the rule of three" (197).

Robert B. Bean himself presented his "research" in an article called "The Negro Brain." I mention this fact because the article appeared in 1906 in the prestigious *Century Magazine* – the same high-culture periodical that some twenty years earlier had offered its readers pre-publication excerpts from Twain's *Adventures of Huckleberry Finn*. The coincidence of the shared publication venue aptly conveys some of the underlying racist beliefs about black people that even well-educated white Northern readers of Twain's work held. In other words, in the early decades of *Huckleberry Finn*'s existence, the question not merely of an escaped slave's basic humanity, but still more of his intelligence, his maturity, and his ability to grasp complex issues carried extremely high stakes for African Americans throughout the nation, especially when the escaped slave appeared in a text by an author as broadly popular as Mark Twain.

There are several scenes in Twain's writing that one might turn to in an effort to evaluate its racial politics, including Huck and Jim's debate about "king Sollermun," which is followed by another scene in which Jim refuses to believe that the French speak a different language from Americans. The latter discussion culminates with Huck declaring in frustration, "You can't learn a nigger to argue" (86–90). However, a more nuanced and significant exchange between Huck and Jim occurs during a night of "solid white fog" on the river, when a rushing current tears the roots from a sapling to which Huck is attempting to fasten the raft (91). Huck immediately finds himself alone in a small canoe as Jim and the raft, with all the travelers' supplies, disappear into the fog. Frightened and barely able to see, Huck spends the rest of the night shouting for Jim and desperately paddling toward where he thinks he hears Jim's answering calls. He does not spot the raft again until the next day when the fog has lifted. Paddling over to the raft, Huck finds Jim asleep, "with his head down between his knees." One of the raft's steering oars is broken, and the raft itself is "littered up with leaves and branches and dirt," so Huck knows that Jim has also had a difficult time in the fog. Yet when Jim awakens, deeply grateful to find Huck alive, Huck decides to play a trick by pretending not to have been gone at all. By repeatedly denying even the existence of the fog, Huck renders Jim comically confused (not unlike the stereotypical "darky" on the minstrel stage): "Well, looky here, boss, dey's sumf'n wrong, dey is. Is I *me*, or who is I? Is I heah, or whah *is* I? Now, dat's what I wants to know" (94). Huck tells Jim that he must have dreamt it all – the fog, the separation, the shouting in the night – and he leads Jim on to develop an elaborate allegorical interpretation of the "dream" as prophesying the future. Only after Huck feels that the joke has played out does he triumphantly point to the detritus on the edge of the raft and ask Jim, "what does *these* things stand for?" (95).

Jim stares at the dirt and smashed wood and then turns and looks again at Huck without smiling. "What do dey stan' for?" he repeats. "I's gwyne to tell you." He relates to Huck his own fear for Huck's safety during the fog, his exhausted despair when he thought Huck was gone, and his joy when he woke up and saw Huck safely back on the raft. "En all you wuz thinking 'bout," Jim continues, "wuz how you could make a fool uv ole Jim wid a lie. Dat truck is *trash*; en trash is what people is dat puts dirt on de head er dey fren's en makes 'em ashamed" (95). Jim walks slowly away. Huck tells us, "it was fifteen minutes before I could work myself up to go and humble myself to a nigger – but I done it, and I warn't ever sorry for it afterwards, neither" (95). The rhetorical force (the pathos) of Jim's speech and behavior in this scene elevate his moral stature, and Huck learns an important lesson about the dignity due to another human being, no matter the color of his skin. But the lesson has required Jim to appear comically gullible, easily tricked even by a child. Although the scene powerfully confirms Jim's basic humanity, does the ease with which Huck seems to have tricked Jim also imply something demeaning about what racist late-nineteenth-century scientists called "the Negro brain"?

The most obvious way of reading this scene is to assume, with Huck, that Jim was indeed fooled into believing the entire episode of the fog and separation had been a dream, whose individual elements he must immediately set out to "'terpret." Only after Huck draws his attention to the trash does Jim realize he has been duped. An alternative reading of this scene is also possible, however, one which casts Jim as something of a trickster figure. As an escaped slave with a reward on his head, the adult Jim must depend on the sometimes capricious good will of the white boy to protect him from re-capture as they make their way toward the North. Anxious not to offend Huck by calling him a liar, Jim simply pretends to fall into Huck's childish trap to create an opportunity by which he can teach the orphaned boy a key lesson about respect, even love. A screenplay adaptation of Twain's novel commissioned by contemporary film director Spike Lee in 1999 pushes this interpretation still further. The script remains true to Twain's text by employing only dialogue actually found in the book's version of the scene, but it parenthetically directs that the facial expressions and body language of the actor playing Jim should convey that his character realizes with disappointment that Huck craves the pleasure of making Jim look ludicrous for believing a patent falsehood. Jim reluctantly performs the role of dupe that Huck desires of him, but subsequently seizes the chance to deepen Huck's moral understanding of what is due to another human being (Fishkin, "In Praise"; see also Smith's discussion of this same scene ["Huck, Jim, and American Racial Discourse"]).

Readers continue to debate about the *Adventures of Huckleberry Finn*'s perspective on the raging racial conflicts of its time because evidence within the text points in different directions, suggesting that Twain's beliefs and attitudes about race were themselves conflicted, even contradictory. It cannot be denied that Twain often makes Jim appear comically ignorant and naïve, and sometimes has Jim engage in patter that sounds as if it could have come directly from a minstrel show (in fact, Twain was a big fan of such shows). Yet at times Jim also appears capable of sophisticated strategic thinking and, many have argued, displays more emotional maturity than any of the book's other characters, child or adult. The escaped slave crosses racial boundaries to serve as a surrogate father for Huck, teaching and caring for the white boy more than Huck's biological father ever did (Morrison, "Amazing"). Finally, even when Jim appears most to fall into demeaning racist stereotypes of the very sort being deployed after Reconstruction to deny African Americans the vote, Twain's text at least leaves room for an interpretation that Jim consciously *uses* those stereotypes for his own purposes.

Challenging Judge Lynch: *The Marrow of Tradition*

As we saw above, the conjure stories that Charles Chesnutt wrote in the 1880s and 1890s – in which Julius's tales, like Twain's narrative about Huck and Jim, were set "befo' the wah" – critiqued the noxious state of race relations in the contemporary South only indirectly. Chesnutt's 1901 full-length novel *The Marrow of Tradition* was based on an event that made national headlines only three years prior to its publication: the Wilmington massacre of November 10, 1898. The novel constitutes a direct attack on white racist violence, on Jim Crow segregation, and on Northern readers and newspapers alike for their willingness to accept white Southerners' perspective on the region's so-called Negro Problem.

Initially misrepresented in the white press (and many subsequent history books) as a spontaneous "race riot," the massacre actually resulted from a pre-planned political insurrection, or coup, by which an armed mob of local white supremacists, led by some of Wilmington's most publicly prominent citizens, launched a violent assault against the city's black residents. Though firm numbers have never been agreed upon, the attack killed up to one hundred African Americans, caused thousands more to leave the city permanently, and terrified those who stayed. The violence successfully achieved the secret intention of its leaders: to topple a legally elected "fusion" government, which had won recent city elections by managing to attract support both from white Populists and from black members of the state's Republican party (Wilmington Race Riot Commission, "1898 Wilmington Race Riot Report" 34–54). Planners of the coup (for which no one was ever punished) had already whipped up violent racist sentiment against the town's African-American citizens by giving wide distribution and publicity to an editorial published three months earlier in Wilmington's black newspaper the *Daily Record*; the editorial had the temerity to suggest that relationships between white women and black men might be consensual. Such relationships could "go on for some time, until the woman's infatuation or the man's boldness bring attention to them and the man is lynched for rape" ("1898 Report" 96, 99). The November 10 "riot" began with an angry march to the *Daily Record* office by 2,000 armed men, again led by prominent white citizens. Although the newspaper's editor escaped lynching by leaving town the night before, the mob set fire to the newspaper's office and destroyed its printing press ("1898 Report" 124–29).

Chesnutt's fictionalized retelling of the Wilmington massacre and the cir-cumstances leading up to it drew from press accounts and personal interviews he had conducted in the massacre's aftermath, as well as from accounts of similar "race riots" that had occurred in other Southern cities since the end of the Civil War. Chesnutt made clear that *The Marrow of Tradition* was a novel, not a history book, by altering the city of Wilmington's name to "Wellington." He also took the liberty of tinkering with certain historical details to bring the primary elements of his narrative more clearly into focus. But Chesnutt's retelling preserves the logic identified by African-American journalist Ida

B. Wells-Barnett, who described how white sexual anxieties about black men often functioned as a cover for violence that was at bottom politically and economically motivated (*Southern Horrors* 18–20). (Wells-Barnett herself narrowly escaped being lynched by a white mob in Memphis.)[4] Chesnutt includes a scene in *Marrow* in which the "Big Three" white leaders planning the coup (reduced from a real-life group of conspirators called the Secret Nine) discuss the inflammatory effect the black newspaper's editorial about interracial liaisons will have when they disseminate it to the town's white inhabitants. They then go on to list some of the black citizens they intend the resulting violence to "remove" from town, including a real-estate agent whom African-American clients patronize (instead of patronizing white agents) and a black lawyer who also gets "too much business" from the African-American community. The black lawyer's success means that certain of the town's "white lawyers, with families to support and social positions to keep up, are deprived of their legitimate source of income" (*Marrow* 198).

Chesnutt's novel features African-American characters whose socioeconomic positions range from highly educated upper-middle-class professionals to dialect-speaking manual laborers and house servants. The political and personal responses these varied characters have to white oppression are also diverse; they include an attempt to organize African Americans for armed resistance, a belief that hard work and racial uplift will make blacks more acceptable to whites, and a commitment to servility in hopes of earning white favor. Although Chesnutt is careful to indicate that none of these strategies succeed in preventing either the coup or the accompanying violence against black citizens – the character who advocates violent resistance *and* the character who consciously embraces servility are murdered during the massacre – the novel's success in capturing what one critical essay aptly describes as the "complex heterogeneity" of both the city's African-American and its white populations (Bentley and Gunning, "Introduction" 15) is without precedent in American fiction.

One additional feature of Chesnutt's complex realism in *The Marrow of Tradition* deserves mention before we move to our next chapter. Theorist of realism Henry James held that "relations stop nowhere" (*Essays* 1041). At key moments of *The Marrow of Tradition*, Chesnutt encourages his readers to recognize connections between the United States' treatment of African Americans at home and the nation's imperialist exploits in Latin America and the Pacific. General Belmont, who develops the specific strategy by which white supremacists will overthrow Wellington's democratically elected "fusion" government and seize power for themselves, bases part of his plan on the US-supported military coups he has observed "down in the American tropics" (197). Still

more pointedly, when the cultivated black professional Dr. Miller is kicked out
of a whites-only train car, he settles down to read with quiet irony a newspaper
"editorial which set forth in glowing language the inestimable advantages
which would follow to certain recently acquired islands by the introduction
of American liberty" (79). The islands the newspaper refers to are probably
the Philippines, Guam, and Puerto Rico, whose residents found themselves
living under the US flag after the Spanish–American War of 1898, but they
might also include Hawaii, annexed by the United States during the year of
the Wilmington Massacre as well. Inhabitants of those "recently acquired
islands" were hardly the only people to abruptly become American during
the late nineteenth century. Our next chapter explores realist writing both by
people who came voluntarily to the United States during the largest wave of
immigration the nation had ever experienced, and by Native Americans and
Mexicans who officially entered America when it conquered the land on which
they already lived.

Chapter 10

New Americans write realism

In 1895 Thomas Bailey Aldrich, who had served as editor of the *Atlantic Monthly* from 1881 to 1890 (the same position previously held by Howells), published a new collection of poetry. The collection's lead poem was also the book's title: "Unguarded Gates." The poem takes the form of a warning and plea to the Statue of Liberty. The statue had been dedicated in New York's harbor only nine years earlier in 1886 and did not yet bear its famous inscription ("Give me your tired, your poor, your huddled masses yearning to breathe free…").[1] But it had already come to serve as a symbol of the United States' historic policy of welcoming immigrants as they completed their long journeys across the ocean.

"Unguarded Gates" begins by praising America for no longer tolerating slavery on "an inch of earth within its bound" and for offering democratic liberties and freedom of opportunity to all its inhabitants. Aldrich also confirms for the Statue of Liberty that an important part of her mission is to "lift the down-trodden." But the main thrust of the poem is an admonition to the "white Goddess" about immigration:

> Wide open and unguarded stand our gates,
> And through them presses a wild motley throng –
> Men from the Volga and the Tartar steppes,
> Featureless figures of the Hoang-Ho,
> Malayan, Scythian, Teuton, Kelt, and Slav,
> Flying the Old World's poverty and scorn;
> These bringing with them unknown gods and rites,
> Those, tiger passions, here to stretch their claws.
> In street and alley what strange tongues are loud,
> Accents of menace alien to our air,

> Voices that once the Tower of Babel knew!
> O Liberty, white Goddess! Is it well
> To leave the gates unguarded?...

The poem expresses the combination of hostility, fear, and disgust that Aldrich and many other upper-class Anglo-Americans felt toward the unprecedented – and unprecedentedly diverse – millions of immigrants who arrived in the United States during the late nineteenth and early twentieth centuries.

The first major wave of voluntary European immigration to the territory that in 1776 would declare itself the United States had occurred during the Colonial period; it was primarily made up of people from Britain and, to a lesser extent, other Western European nations. These seventeenth- and eighteenth-century European immigrants were the people who, by the nineteenth century, had come to think of themselves as "real" or "native" Americans. (At the time, few seemed troubled by the irony of white Europeans regarding *themselves* as native Americans even as they actively displaced indigenous peoples whose ancestors had lived on the land for thousands of years.) Most of these self-designated "native" Americans of European descent soon began further to identify themselves as "Anglo-Saxon." The latter term entered public discourse in the United States in the 1840s, largely in reaction to the early stages of what would become an immense wave of new Americans entering the United States from the 1840s through the 1920s (Jacobson, *Whiteness* 206). Much larger than the total of all voluntary immigration to the future United States during the Colonial period, this "second wave" (as it is sometimes called) of immigration began in the middle of the nineteenth century with the arrival of millions of Irish fleeing famine and persecution by the English and a similarly large number of Germans seeking space and opportunity in a territory much larger than that available in their homeland. On the West coast, tens of thousands of Chinese traveled across the Pacific to participate in the Gold Rush of 1849 and to help build the Transcontinental Railroad. This second wave of immigration to the United States reached its numerical height in the years between 1880 and 1920, when over twenty million people arrived. The majority of these new arrivals came from places that had previously accounted for a negligible fraction of the US population, especially Southern and Eastern European nations such as Italy, Greece, Poland and Russia. Immigration from such regions tapered off only with Congress's passage in 1924 of the restrictive Johnson–Reed Immigration Act, modeled in part on the Chinese Exclusion Act of 1882, which had been the nation's first law restricting immigration by ethnicity or national origin.

In addition to immigrants from overseas, concerted late-nineteenth-century efforts first to conquer and then to "assimilate" remaining Indians into the United States pushed many Native peoples to surrender tribal allegiances and their collectively owned land in exchange for citizenship and the promise of individual farms, thus creating another sizable group of ostensibly "new" Americans. Finally, following the 1848 conclusion of the Mexico–United States War, the ongoing incorporation of formerly Mexican territory meant that approximately 80,000 Mexicans found themselves, according to the terms of the Treaty of Guadalupe Hidalgo, new citizens of the United States.

As Aldrich's poem makes clear, the "new" Americans of the late nineteenth and early twentieth centuries brought with them unfamiliar customs and religious beliefs ("unknown gods and rites"), strikingly different dialects and accents ("strange tongues ... accents of menace"), and, at least in the imaginations of Aldrich and his intended audience, a fearsome tendency toward savagery and lasciviousness ("tiger passions, here to stretch their claws"). All of these factors made their presence deeply unsettling to many longer-established white citizens. Although Aldrich's "Unguarded Gates" takes immigrants clustering in Northeastern cities as the primary target of its ethnic hostilities and anxieties, similar – and in many cases yet more virulent – responses were displayed by white Americans toward Mexicans, Asians, and Native Americans in other parts of the country. For that matter, as scholars studying the unstable history of racial designations and identities in the United States have shown, certain European immigrant groups arriving during this period who would later come to be regarded as "Caucasian" in the popular imagination were initially viewed as not white, or at best ambiguously white, and hence were subjected to explicitly racial discrimination. Such groups included Eastern European Jews, Southern Italians, and the Irish (see Ignatiev, *How the Irish Became White*; Brodkin, *How Jews Became White*; Jacobson, *Whiteness*; and Roediger, *Working Toward Whiteness*). Aldrich's book *Unguarded Gates and Other Poems* was issued by the elite publishing house of Houghton, Mifflin (which also published the *Atlantic Monthly*). Negative portrayals of new immigrants and other ethnic groups were spread still more widely by popular media, including newspapers, other periodicals, and dime novels. As we saw in Chapter 6's discussion of Jacob Riis's *How the Other Half Lives* (1890), even ostensibly sympathetic depictions of newer Americans often perpetuated harmful stereotypes. But the denigrated "new" Americans wrote back. The current chapter explores literary representations of marginalized or oppressed ethnic groups, written by members of those groups, that contest biased and harmful portrayals by established "Anglo-Saxon" writers. We will explore work by four writers: Abraham Cahan, who immigrated from Russia to the United States in 1882; Sui Sin Far (Edith Eaton), whose Anglo-Chinese family immigrated from England to North America in 1872; Zitkala-Ša (Gertrude Bonnin), who in 1884 at age nine left her mother and the Yankton Sioux Reservation in South Dakota to attend an Indiana Quaker school designed to "Americanize" Native children; and scholar and writer Américo Paredes. Paredes's South Texas family became United States residents in 1848 by the loss of a war and the stroke of a pen, when the Treaty of Guadalupe Hidalgo affirmed that the southern boundary of Texas, newly incorporated as an American state, would extend all the way downward to the Rio Grande river.

Paredes and Zitkala-Ša construct narratives around characters who become "Americans" by virtue of their territory having been incorporated into the United States by military force, while the fiction we will discuss by Abraham Cahan and Sui Sin Far articulates the experiences of voluntary immigrants from distant nations who, in many cases, discover that the United States is different, and far less welcoming, than they had expected. As we will see, all four of these writers draw heavily on literary realist forms and techniques. But at certain moments they also push the boundaries of realism, invoking themes and strategies of representation usually more associated with literary modernism – the aesthetic practice literary historians would come to view as having displaced realism, sometime around the First World War, as the cutting edge of US literary innovation. Narrative discontinuity, linguistic and cultural fragmentation, and extreme individual alienation make appearances in writings by and about new Americans as their authors strive to convey the effects of a number of disorienting transitions. In particular, the sometimes acute forms of self-division characters in these works experience result from radical dislocations in their lives that are not only geographic but also social, religious, and linguistic, all further exacerbated by the need to adjust to new forms of economic production and even to new ways of experiencing temporality.[2] Modernist representational strategies become most pronounced in Paredes's *George Washington Gómez*, chronologically the latest of the works we will discuss, but they appear as well in Abraham Cahan's 1896 novel *Yekl*.

Abraham Cahan: immigrant realism

Cahan was the first representative of the new European immigration to gain significant attention from English-language readers in the United States. A teacher, journalist, and labor activist born in Lithuania (then part of the Russian Empire), Cahan immigrated to the United States to escape persecution based on both his radical political beliefs and his Jewish identity. Arriving in 1882 at twenty-two years old, penniless and with virtually no knowledge of English, Cahan found work in a cigar factory and proceeded to immerse himself in the Lower East Side's vibrant community of Yiddish speakers. He would later describe New York's Jewish "Ghetto" oxymoronically as a "vast and compact city within a city" (*Yekl* 24). The Ghetto was "one of the most densely populated spots on the face of the earth – a seething human sea fed by streams, streamlets, and rills of immigration flowing from all the Yiddish-speaking centers of Europe" (*Yekl* 13). Cahan learned English quickly, and was soon reading widely in American and English literature as well as writing regularly for both the Yiddish and the English-language press, including the well-regarded *Commercial Advertiser* (Harap, *Image of the Jew* 486). In 1895 a short story Cahan had published in English in a New York periodical attracted the interest of William Dean Howells, whose novels as well as theories of realism Cahan admired and whom Cahan had personally assisted three years earlier when Howells wanted to learn more about labor unions and socialism (Taubenfeld 145). With Howells's enthusiastic encouragement to continue writing English-language fiction Cahan produced his first novel, *Yekl: A Tale of the New York Ghetto*. Even with Howells's active support, however, *Yekl* was rejected by several editors on the grounds, in the telling words of one, that "the life of an East Side Jew wouldn't interest the American reader." Frustrated, Cahan translated the novel into Yiddish so that it could be serialized in a Lower East Side newspaper (Taubenfeld 147). When *Yekl* was finally issued by an English-language publishing house associated with social reform (D. Appleton and Co.), Howells reviewed it together with Stephen Crane's *Maggie, a Girl of the Streets* (also published by Appleton) on the front page of the *New York World* (July 26, 1896). A headline hailed Cahan as a "new star of realism."

Emphasizing that *Yekl* was "intensely realistic," Howells's review contends that it is Cahan's double vision – "Hebraic" and "American" – that gives his writing such force and warrants the confident assertion that "we have in him a writer of foreign birth who will do honor to American letters" ("New York Low Life" 278). Writing in the *Atlantic Monthly* a year later, sociologist W. E. B. Du Bois would describe what he called "double consciousness" as fundamental to African-American experience: "One ever feels his twoness, – an American, a Negro; two souls, two thoughts, two unreconciled strivings; two warring ideals in one dark body" ("Strivings of the Negro People" 194). The concept of doubleness that Du Bois articulates here – a "twoness" of consciousness, of vision, of cultural allegiance and identity – is a defining theme in many works by minority authors of the late nineteenth and early twentieth centuries. Motifs of doubled or divided cultural identities, and the unique forms both of understanding and of sometimes unbearable internal conflicts that may arise from such divisions, manifest with particular exigency in the work of authors who broke new ground by producing English-language narratives offering depictions of minority American experiences from the cultural "inside," as it were.

Such authors often positioned themselves, or found themselves positioned, as cultural translators. Much of Cahan's writing in Yiddish, especially for the *Jewish Daily Forward* (in Yiddish, *Der Forverts*: an immensely successful newspaper Cahan helped found in 1897 and edited for most of the next fifty-three years), was aimed at easing the transition of Eastern European Jewish immigrants into their new lives in modern America. In a widely read personal advice column called *Bintel Briefs*, as well as other sections of the paper, Cahan employed simple everyday Yiddish to offer his readers insights into the customs, assumptions, and values of what was for them a new world. Conversely, Cahan's English-language fiction attempts to convey to white American audiences the experiences of recent immigrants. Among other goals, Cahan wished to correct what he saw as simplistic and ill-informed portrayals by "amateur slumologist[s]," a category in which he included Jacob Riis ("Not One Honest Shudder"). Cahan himself acted as a personal guide for Anglo-American writers (including Howells) who desired a first-hand view of immigrant life on the Lower East Side, and occasional footnotes in *Yekl* fulfill an analogous role by succinctly explaining foods, religious customs, and even jokes that require an insider's knowledge to grasp.

The cross-cultural translations performed by *Yekl*'s authorial persona become most evident in its treatment of the multiple forms of language employed or alluded to in the text, including several "subdialects" of Yiddish, urban American slang, standard English, and speech that mixes these in varying degrees (14). Cahan manipulates the different languages his text uses in a manner that effectively counters a pattern found in many popular literary depictions of the slums, including realist works such as Crane's *Maggie*, in which the dialect spoken by slum characters is represented as not merely different from but also markedly inferior to standard English's ability to express complex thoughts or nuanced emotions (see Chapter 6). Cahan's characters speak mostly in Yiddish, which he translates for them into standard English that in many cases retains the flavor of Yiddish syntax and poetic Yiddish idioms ("A weeping to me!") (56). As a result, what the narrator himself refers to as the immigrant characters' "broken and mispronounced" English, always printed in italics to distinguish it from his English translations of their native Yiddish, carries no negative implications regarding their cognitive abilities, as it does in *Maggie* (17). By translating the Yiddish in which his characters mostly speak (and exclusively think) into non-accented, correctly spelled English, Cahan is able to convey his characters' full humanity to middle-class American readers while still retaining the aura of linguistic authenticity so important to realist fiction. Yet at times, as Sara Blair has observed, the miscellaneous Yiddish dialects, italicized "broken" English, bilingual slang, poetic translations of Yiddish idioms, standard English narration, and explanatory footnotes that all "jostle and contend" on Cahan's pages approach the effect of a modernist collage (Blair, "Whose Modernism is it?" 261, 264). These collage-like moments draw Cahan's standard-English readers, however briefly, into a destabilizing but also exhilarating "place of estrangement" from rule-bound, clearly referential language: a space that is "definitively modern" (261).

As the only figure able to move fluently in and among the various linguistic cultures *Yekl* includes, Cahan's authorial persona lays claim to a privileged position of cosmopolitan distinction, a special version of the cultural and psychological expertise realist writers often implicitly claimed for themselves.[3] Thus for *Yekl*'s narrative voice, as well as for Cahan himself, the "double consciousness" that Du Bois theorizes as characteristic of minority experience in the United States, and for which Howells's review praises Cahan, serves as a literary advantage, a unique form of cultural capital. The book's eponymous protagonist, however, does not share his author's and narrator's ability to move fluidly through disjunctive cultures and languages. Instead, the character Yekl vividly and poignantly dramatizes the sometimes agonizing internal conflicts described by Du Bois as accompanying the sense of "twoness" that a minority American may experience. For Yekl, the twoness Du Bois describes is personal, cultural, and also geographical, as he attempts to adjust or evolve an identity constructed for life in one world to life in a new world.

Cahan's protagonist struggles even at the level of his first name, as he strives with only partial success to shed the Russian-Yiddish sounding "Yekl" in favor of the Jewish-American name "Jake." Although the Russian village blacksmith turned New York sweatshop worker succeeds in getting the majority of his acquaintances to call him Jake, the very title of the novel indicates that in the end he remains just as much the newly arrived immigrant as the acclimated "Yankee" he wishes to be (2). The novel closes with a self-doubting Yekl/Jake riding on the brand-new Third Avenue cable-car line. Having just divorced his orthodox wife Gitl, whom he had married while still in Russia and who has done her best to resist assimilation to American ways, Jake is on his way to New York's City Hall for a secular wedding to Mamie, a Polish-Jewish immigrant who is more Americanized and speaks better English even than her soon-to-be-husband. With the divorce having decisively cut a major tie to his old-world identity as Yekl, the cable-car journey toward his new "American" marriage becomes for Jake a small-scale repetition of his initial voyage from Russian village to American city. Convinced that he should be delighted at leaving a non-American aspect of his life behind – hoping to escape, as it were, the twoness of identity that has bound him ever since arriving in the United States – Jake cannot help but also feel panicked at the "impenetrable" future that now looms before him. The novel's final line suggests that in a sense the voyage from old to new world will never be complete for him: "Each time the car came to a halt he wished the pause could be prolonged indefinitely; and when it resumed its progress, the violent lurch it gave was accompanied by a corresponding sensation in his heart" (89).

The sense Cahan captures here of the alternating violent lurches and paralyzing pauses experienced by a character straddling two cultural identities integrally informs the work of the other writers we will discuss next in this chapter.

Sui Sin Far: combating exclusion and exoticization

Edith Eaton, born in 1865 in England to a Chinese mother and a white British father, published fiction, journalism, and essays in the United States and Canada under the name Sui Sin Far, which translates as "Water Lily." Edith Eaton did not start life with an ethnically marked name that she sought to exchange for a more Anglo-sounding one upon arriving in America. Only after she became an adult did she publicly claim the Chinese name "Sui Sin Far." Unlike the three other writers discussed in this chapter, Sui Sin Far did not grow up within a non-Anglo community about which she would later write. From birth to her 1914 death in Montreal, Sui Sin Far's "mother tongue" remained the language of her white British father. Until she was eighteen she knew virtually no one of Chinese descent other than her mother and her siblings (Sui Sin Far, *Mrs. Spring Fragrance* 292). Later, when she began to visit San Francisco's Chinatown (the oldest and biggest in North America), she found that her inability to speak Chinese and the Anglo facial features she had inherited from her father marked her as an outsider to the area's primarily first-generation immigrants: "The Americanized Chinamen actually laugh in my face when I tell them that I am of their race" (227). Only after she persistently claims Chinese heritage do some of the local women "discover that I have Chinese hair, color of eyes, and complexion, also that I love rice and tea. This settles the matter for them – and for their husbands" (227).

Sui Sin Far's commitment to exploring the Chinese side of her heritage, a commitment that seems only to have been strengthened by personal experiences of anti-Chinese racism (224–25), drove her to become the first writer of Asian descent known to have published English-language fiction about Asians living in North America. Many Asian-American writers today view Sui Sin Far as a forerunner – and foremother – of their own work. Eventually making friends and acquaintances in several "Chinatowns" around the country, Sui Sin Far published numerous short journalistic sketches for English-language newspapers and other periodicals about everyday life among those she called Chinese Americans; in fact, she was the first person ever to use the term "Chinese American" in print. Her research for these journalistic pieces deepened and broadened her knowledge of Chinese immigrants' experiences, and helped her to write fiction persuasively narrated from first-generation immigrants' point of view.

Throughout her career as a writer both of journalism and of short stories, Sui Sin Far strove to combat two seemingly different, but in fact closely related, forms of white racism against the Chinese: first, a feeling openly expressed by many white Americans at the time that the Chinese were not "humans like ourselves" (224). She once heard a white colleague who did not yet know of her mixed-race identity remark at dinner that, to him, "a Chinaman is … more repulsive than a nigger," a statement that expresses two vicious prejudices at once (224). Sinophobia (fear and hatred of the Chinese) was in part fed by white fears of immigrant competition for jobs, and it underlay numerous episodes of personal and mob violence perpetuated against Chinese immigrants during the nineteenth century (Daniels, *Not Like Us* 8–9). Sui Sin Far also used her writing to combat a second, subtler form of racism active at the time: an exaggerated, romanticized form of exoticization which insisted on Chinese people's essential difference from other Americans.

By 1898, the year Sui Sin Far arrived in San Francisco, Chinatown was considered one of the city's major tourist attractions. Numerous "guides" solicited white tourists by promising to show them such exotic sights as sword fights, opium dens, and Chinese temples full of colorful "pagan" idols (Vogel, *Rewriting Race* 110). A travel writer described Chinatown to potential visitors as "unique and outlandish, a foreign country of ten city squares … living its own customs, rites and practices" (quoted in Vogel, *Rewriting Race* 110). Although a white American fascination with Chinatown and its inhabitants as "unique and outlandish" may not appear as harmful as opinions that the Chinese were "repulsive" (Sui Sin Far, *Mrs. Spring Fragrance* 224) or not "humans like ourselves," such exoticization shared with more explicit forms of sinophobia the refusal of *individual* humanity or self-definition. Exoticization also denied any possibility that Chinese immigrants could ever be regarded as genuine members of modern American society. (Since 1882 the Chinese

Exclusion Acts had sought to keep most Chinese literally "outlandish" by keeping them outside of US borders.)

When Sui Sin Far first began to write fiction and to move in California literary circles, she encountered people who advised her to take professional advantage of the exotic fascination many white Americans felt toward the Chinese:

> They tell me that if I wish to succeed in literature in America I should dress in Chinese costume, carry a fan in my hand, wear a pair of scarlet beaded slippers, live in New York, and come of high birth. Instead of making myself familiar with the Chinese Americans around me, I should discourse on my spirit acquaintance with Chinese ancestors and … quote 'Confucius, Confucius, how great is Confucius … etc., etc., etc.,' or something like that, both illuminating and obscuring, don't you know. (230)

Rejecting this advice to attract attention by embracing an exotically foreign identity, Sui Sin Far chose instead to look for literary material in the lives of Chinese Americans around her. In making this choice, she aligned herself and her fiction with literary realist principles. Howells, the so-called "Dean" of American letters, had concluded his realist manifesto *Criticism and Fiction* (1891) by urging fellow writers to convey to their readers that, "Men are more like than unlike one another: let us make them know one another better, that they may be all humbled and strengthened with a sense of their fraternity" (188). In her own fiction, Sui Sin Far took on the double challenge of attempting to show both that the "customs, manners, and characteristics" of Chinese immigrants were often different from those familiar to most white Americans, but also that, "in a broad sense they are one with the other people of the earth. They think and act just as the white man … They love those who love them; they hate those who hate; are kind, affectionate, cruel or selfish, as the case may be … Indeed, there is no type of white person who cannot find his or her counterpart in some Chinese" (234–35).

Sui Sin Far's fiction employs several different strategies to undercut exotic fantasies of Chinese otherness as well as more crudely racist forms of dehumanization. For example, just as in the work of realist novelists of manners such as Howells, Henry James, and Edith Wharton, the main characters in Sui Sin Far's stories tend to be financially comfortable. Her fiction focuses more often on married and social life among the era's relatively small group of merchant-class Chinese Americans than on the numerically much more prevalent laundry, restaurant, agricultural, or sweatshop laborers. Reasons for this emphasis include Sui Sin Far's own class background (although she was brought up in genteel poverty her British father belonged to a prominent family of merchants), as well as the fact that successful businessmen were among the few Chinese immigrants still allowed to enter the United States after the Chinese Exclusion Act was passed in 1882. Even prior to the 1882 Act, legal and other barriers rendered it almost impossible for Chinese laborers to bring their wives with them when they immigrated (and anti-miscegenation laws blocked intermarriages), meaning that few first-generation Chinese-American laborers lived within nuclear families (Chan, "Exclusion of Chinese Women" 94–113).

The relative lack of attention in Sui Sin Far's fiction to manual laborers, who constituted the majority of Chinese people living in the United States at the time she wrote, risked excluding them from whatever forms of empathy or identification her portrayals of Chinese-American middle-class marriage and family life might succeed in encouraging. Yet during a period of intense race-based prejudice against Chinese Americans, when an early employer of Sui Sin Far could remark in her hearing that the Chinese people he'd seen possessed "faces so utterly devoid of emotion" that he doubted they had souls (Sui Sin Far, *Mrs. Spring Fragrance* 224), any effort seemed worthwhile that might push white readers toward recognizing shared values and feelings and thus toward seeing Chinese Americans as, again in Howells's words, "more like than unlike" themselves.

Mixing realism with devices associated with domestic and sentimental literature enabled Sui Sin Far to illustrate with intimate vividness the painful alienating effects of immigration. "Land of the Free," for instance, draws on domestic sentimentality's emphasis on the intensity of maternal feelings to illuminate the real-world pain of families separated by anti-Chinese immigration laws. The successful Chinese merchant Hom Hing and his wife Lae Choo are already settled in San Francisco's Chinatown when Lae Choo becomes pregnant. With the couple eager for their child to be born under ancestral skies, Lae Choo returns temporarily to China. Upon the birth of the son she affectionately refers to as Little One, Lae Choo remains in China for almost two additional years to care for her husband's dying parents. When Hom Hing finally meets their return ship at the San Francisco port, he innocently replies to a customs officer's question that the little boy – whom he himself is encountering for the first time – has never yet set foot in America. He does not realize that the Exclusion laws forbid entry, in an especially cruel twist, to Chinese-born children without papers even if a child's parents can both prove legal residency for themselves. The couple is forced to leave their child in the hands of the Customs Agency overnight, while local officers contact Washington for instructions. The boy ends up detained in legal limbo for months as his mother grows sick and weak with grief. Hom Hing is sympathetic but resigned to helplessness, even as Lae Choo insists to him that she cannot close her eyes at night with her "arms empty of the little body that has filled them every night for more than twenty moons! You do not know – man – what it is to miss the feel of the little fingers and the little toes and the soft round limbs of your little one. Even in the darkness his darling eyes used to shine up to mine" (95).

Sui Sin Far's evocation here of a mother's intimate, tactile bond with her child, verging on bodily oneness, seeks to establish a direct, cross-racial connection with white female readers who are, or might someday be, mothers ("You do not know – man"). As we saw in Chapter 1, sentimental writers such as Harriet Beecher Stowe had employed the same tactic a half-century earlier to gain Northern white women's support for the abolition of slavery (see discussion of *Uncle Tom's Cabin* on pp. 13–14). The desperate Lae Choo finally uses her own treasured jewelry to bribe a corrupt white lawyer into procuring "the precious paper" that will allow her to retrieve her Little One from detention (101). But the story ends on a painful note. When Lae Choo goes to the mission care center where he has been held, "the Little One shrunk from her and tried to hide himself in the folds of the white woman's skirt. 'Go 'way, go 'way!' he bade his mother" (101). American laws, which have prevented mother and child from seeing each other for ten crucial months, have led the little boy to forget his own mother. "The Land of the Free" demonstrates how US immigration policies that might have seemed rational, even natural to a white American with a xenophobic or racist perspective lead to results that are profoundly unnatural from a sentimental perspective centered on the primacy of emotional bonds.

Another powerful tactic Sui Sin Far employed to undercut a view of Chinese Americans as irredeemably other, or "outlandish," involved turning the touristic or ethnographic gaze that some white Americans brought to Chinese individuals and culture back on that gaze's owners. In a story called "The Inferior Woman," Mrs. Spring Fragrance, a memorable character who appears in two short stories (and whose English-language name Sui Sin Far borrowed to title the only complete book she published), considers writing a book about Americans for the benefit of her Chinese women friends: "The American people were so interesting and mysterious. Something of pride and pleasure crept into Mrs. Spring Fragrance's heart as she pictured Fei and Sie and Mai Gwi Far listening to [her] illuminating paragraphs" (28). In a newspaper sketch, Mrs. Spring Fragrance's idea is given a slightly threatening undertone when Sui Sin Far tells of interviewing a Chinese man named Go Ek Ju (the character may or may not be fictional), who also plans to write a book about Americans. Go Ek Ju emphasizes to his interviewer, "We Chinese people in America have fine facilities for learning all about the Americans. *We go into the*

American houses as servants; we enter the American schools and colleges as students; we ask questions and we think about what we hear and see" (emphasis in original; 236). Both Mrs. Spring Fragrance's vision of herself authoring a book about the "mysterious" manners and lives of white Americans and Go Ek Ju's reminder that Chinese Americans have "fine facilities" for observing not only the public, but also the private lives of middle- and upper-class white Americans undercut white Americans' usually unquestioned assumption that only Westerners can occupy the position of critically observing others, as well as white Americans' assumption that they and their culture embody simple normalcy by contrast to the exotically deviant Chinese. With a slight shift in perspective, white Americans' own manners, habits, and values might be depicted as alien, even bizarre.[4] The Yankton Sioux writer Zitkala-Ša, to whom we now turn, went still further in this direction. She sought to reverse both popular and anthropological views of her people as savages by instead designating white Americans as "specimens" whose manners are "worse than barbarian" (Zitkala-Ša, *American Indian Stories* 112, 103).

Zitkala-Ša: resisting the "civilizing machine"

Zitkala-Ša used these subversive phrases to describe white Americans in the course of three memoir-style essays she wrote for the *Atlantic Monthly*'s first three issues of the twentieth century: "Impressions of an Indian Childhood" (January 1900), "School Days of an Indian Girl" (February 1900), and "An Indian Teacher among Indians" (March 1900). The writer and future activist's first publications for a national audience describe her childhood on the Yankton Sioux reservation, South Dakota; her experiences as a student from ages eight to eighteen at a white-run boarding school for Indian children and subsequently at Earlham College (both institutions were in Indiana); the new sense of alienation she feels toward her mother and the reservation during visits home; and finally her brief, bitter time behind the scenes as a teacher working at another white-run boarding school for Indian children, this time in Pennsylvania. To grasp the significance of Zitkala-Ša's autobiographical essays it is important to realize that hundreds of white-run schools similar to those she attended and briefly taught at were created as part of a larger shift in private and public organizations' policies toward Native Americans in the decades after the Civil War, even as the so-called Indian Wars continued. Spurred by a combination of self-designated reformers and "friends" of Native Americans, many of them Christian missionaries, as well as by white settlers and ranchers eager to procure land the government had set aside for Indian reservations, these new policies were ostensibly designed to prevent the complete decimation of Native peoples by assimilating as many of them as possible to white American ways of life. To white proponents of Indian assimilation, however, "saving" Native Americans meant destroying their links to tribal cultures – and, ultimately, destroying those cultures as well.

So-called reform efforts accelerated as the Indian Wars wound down with the killing or capture of important Native leaders such as Crazy Horse and Sitting Bull. Large-scale armed resistance on the part of Indians to the loss of their traditional lands and freedom would effectively end in 1890 with the US army's brutal massacre, only a few miles from Zitkala-Ša's reservation, of 350 unarmed Sioux women and children at Wounded Knee. Even before Wounded Knee, however, reformers succeeded in getting Congress to pass the 1887 Dawes Severalty Act, whose announced intent was to spread "the habits of civilized life" among a people still widely seen as mired in savagery and, in doing so, to ready them for full US citizenship (United States Congress, "Dawes Act"). The Act, which stayed in force until 1934, attempted to undercut tribal sovereignty and shift Native Americans away from their long-standing tradition of possessing land communally by dividing reservation lands into discrete 160-acre parcels for individual farming and ownership. The parcels were then supposed to be allotted to individual Indians, with preference given to men who headed Anglo-American-style nuclear families. For numerous reasons, this plan to permanently change Indians' traditional ways of relating to land failed: its most lasting result was the transfer of millions of acres from Native American tribal possession to white settlers, ranchers, and mining interests, with much of the money Indian tribes and individuals were promised in exchange still not forthcoming to this day (Winter, *American Narratives* 57).

The Indian School movement was a key component of efforts by white reformers to "civilize" American Indians. The movement sought to "save" Native children from savagery by lifting them out of their families and home environments and placing them in English-only boarding schools (Spack, *America's Second Tongue* 13–38). The underlying philosophy of the educational movement's "reforms" is aptly summed up by a government agent stationed on the Yankton Sioux reservation where Zitkala-Ša lived until she was eight (at which age Zitkala-Ša's mother reluctantly permitted her daughter to accompany a missionary to a white-run boarding school 700 miles away in Indiana): "Education cuts the cord which binds them to a pagan life, places the Bible in their hands, and substitutes the true God for the false one, Christianity in place of idolatry, civilization in place of superstition, morality in place of vice, cleanliness in place of filth, industry in place of idleness, self-respect in place of servility and, in a word, humanity in place of abject degradation" (quoted in

Winter, *American Narratives* 77). In addition to religious training and enforced immersion in English, the actual education provided in such schools tended to be vocational, emphasizing the same sort of craft and farm skills that Booker T. Washington provided African Americans at his famed Tuskegee Institute in Alabama.

Zitkala-Ša's three *Atlantic Monthly* essays of 1900 center on the experiences of a young Dakota Sioux woman who spends several years navigating her way through the "civilizing machine" of two such institutions (Zitkala-Ša, *American Indian Stories* 96). The essays employ a first-person autobiographical frame and draw largely from Zitkala-Ša's personal experiences, though scholars believe that she also used literary license to claim as her own certain incidents that had in fact happened to other Indian students (Spack, *America's Second Tongue* 153). Although the young author did publish a few clearly fictional tales around the same time (including two in *Harper's Monthly*), as well as a book-length collection called *Old Indian Legends* in 1901, the memoir-style essays in the *Atlantic* constitute her strongest contribution to literary realism. In them, she uses and adapts realist techniques toward quintessentially literary realist ends: to represent major, ongoing historical change as it is experienced in the intimate details of an individual life, and thereby both to interrogate and to intervene in how the public represents such change to itself. In this respect, Zitkala-Ša's placement of her essays in the *Atlantic Monthly* was crucial, not only because of the *Atlantic's* ongoing prestige among influential Americans and its long association with major realist writers, but also because at the time the *Atlantic* itself was contributing to dangerous popular stereotypes of American Indians.

In the first year of the new century, Zitkala-Ša's autobiographical essays ran concurrently in the *Atlantic* with serial installments of Mary Johnston's wildly popular novel *To Have and to Hold*, a historical romance whose plot involves, among many other sensationalistic episodes, Indians kidnapping and holding for ransom its swashbuckling protagonist, Captain Ralph Percy (Okker, "Native American Literatures" 89). Subsequently adapted for the silver screen in 1916 and again in 1922, Johnston's romance was so popular while it ran in the *Atlantic* that it nearly doubled the magazine's usual circulation (Okker, "Native American Literatures" 90). As Patricia Okker notes, the installments of *To Have and to Hold* that appear in the same three *Atlantic* issues as Zitkala-Ša's essays repeatedly describe Indian characters as "violent 'heathens' and deceitful 'savages,' capable of 'hellish' torture" (89). A contemporary reviewer of the novel singled out for praise the "rare descriptive power" Johnston brings to her portrayal of Indians, above all the "picture" she gives readers "of the wily Opechancanough, his body sleek with oil, glistening all over in the sunshine

188 New Americans write realism

with powdered antimony, speaking fair words with a smiling face, while the inner devil looks through his cold snake eyes, – this is very fine" (quoted in Okker, "Native American Literatures" 90).

In contrast with the serial installments of *To Have and to Hold* that ran alongside them in the *Atlantic Monthly*, Zitkala-Ša's personal narratives involve no bloody battles between Indians and whites, no "cries of savage triumph" as Indians attack whites "with hatchet and knife" (Johnston, *To Have and to Hold*, Installment 1 56; Installment 3 344). Yet the essays describe smaller-scale conflicts, especially in her first years confronting the "iron routine" imposed at the boarding school (in real life named White's Technical Institute) that are just as sharp, visceral, and, in their own way, dramatic as any incident of bloody violence related by Mary Johnston's purple prose (Zitkala-Ša, *American Indian Stories* 95). Shortly after arriving with the other children from her reservation, for example, the narrator learns that an initial act of the school's "civilizing machine" (96) will be to cut off the children's "long, heavy hair" (96, 90). To the Indian children, their long hair is an important part of their identities. Further, their mothers have taught them that short hair is worn only by captured enemies and by mourners (90). Zitkala-Ša describes how, when her friend Judewin announces to the others, "we have to submit, because they are strong," she herself "rebelled": "No, I will not submit! I will struggle first!" (90). Determined to avoid what feels to her like an immense personal violation, she hides under a bed in a deserted room. Found after a search, she is "dragged out … kicking and scratching wildly" and "tied fast to a chair" (91). With "the cold blade of the scissors against my neck," she continues, "I heard them gnaw off one of my thick braids. Then I lost my spirit" (91). Henry James insisted that a realist writer could make the interior dramas of everyday life as "'interesting' as the surprise of a caravan or the identification of a pirate" (*Essays* 1084). No blood is shed when the 8-year-old Zitkala-Ša has her hair cut; nobody's throat is slit or "scalp" taken. But the violence in this everyday scene of scissors and hair – no doubt repeated again and again at the several hundred schools for Indians opened during the period – is more disturbing than anything that occurs in the sensationalistic *To Have and to Hold*.

Losing her long hair does not destroy Zitkala-Ša's spirit for long. The hair-cutting episode teaches her that direct physical resistance ("kicking and scratching wildly") will not avail against the more powerful adults who run the school. As she begins to comprehend how the school functions and develops some "broken English" with which to communicate, she finds more effective outlets for what she calls the "rebellion within me" (93, 94). Her rebellions transpire at the level of the everyday, and her internal experience of an act of resistance can be as significant as any effect it may have on others. In punishment for violating a "needlessly binding" rule, for example, she is "sent into the kitchen to mash the turnips for dinner." She hates turnips and finds the odor that comes from their brown jar "offensive": "With fire in my heart, I took the wooden tool that the paleface woman held out to me" (93).

Having mashed the turnips to a pulp, and aware that "further beating could not improve them," she nevertheless resolves, "the order was, 'Mash these turnips,' and mash them I would!" She mashes harder and harder until, when "a paleface woman" places "her red hands upon the rim of the jar" and lifts, "lo! The pulpy contents fell through the crumbled bottom to the floor!" (93–94). Though severely scolded for breaking the jar, Zitkala-Ša announces to readers, "I felt triumphant in my revenge." And when no turnips are served at dinner, "I whooped in my heart" (94). The narrator's internal "whoop" is significant here: whites viewed the "whoop" as a stereotypical Indian war yell (such as the "cries of savage triumph" featured in the racist *To Have and to Hold*).[5] Rather than a violent daybreak charge on the school, however, Zitkala-Ša's whoop registers her gratification at having turned a commonplace tool of so-called civilization – literally the turnip-masher, but, more broadly, the fact of her punishment for violating a "needlessly binding" rule – to her own rebellious purposes. One might take the turnip-mashing episode as representative of a larger strategy of resistance. The English-language education and knowledge of white American values and customs foisted upon Zitkala-Ša at White Technical Institute ultimately enable her not only to write these *Atlantic Monthly* essays critical of the Indian Boarding School system but, as her career developed, to become a well-known – and often quite effective – activist for Native American rights and welfare.[6] After a flurry of publications from 1900–1902, Zitkala-Ša stopped publishing in prestigious white-dominated periodicals. She continued to write in various other genres, however, publishing her work in venues more likely to be encountered by Indians, including the *American Indian Magazine* for which she also served as editor.

So far in this chapter we have discussed authors and literary protagonists, whether autobiographical or fictional, who find themselves grappling with two contrasting sets of manners and values, one set associated with the United States and its dominant (often hostile) white culture, the other with a minority or foreign culture. Because the fiction of Sui Sin Far and Abraham Cahan focuses on first-generation immigrants, the cultural divisions its characters navigate are aligned, at least in their most acute forms, with distinct geographical spaces – an "old country" and "new world" – that are separated by physical oceans. Cahan's Yekl has traveled across the Atlantic in immigrating from a Russian village to urban America, while the first-generation Chinese Americans in Sui Sin Far's fiction have crossed the Pacific (and the author herself was born in England). Even Native American writer Zitkala-Ša's *Atlantic Monthly* essays include a 700-mile train journey between the South Dakota reservation where the autobiographical protagonist spends her "Indian Childhood" and the Indiana boarding school where she strategically both resists and adopts elements of white American culture.

We turn now to the Mexican-American writer Américo Paredes's *George Washington Gómez: A Mexicotexan Novel*, which is set on the embattled border between South Texas and Mexico. The protagonist of Paredes's novel (George, more usually called Guálinto) does not physically move from one distinct geographic and cultural space to another. Rather, the borderland territory in which he grows up is aggressively claimed by two cultures in often-explosive conflict with one another across multiple fronts. Internally fractured by this conflict, George/Guálinto finds himself unable to construct a coherent mode of selfhood either through resistance to white American domination or through assimilation, or even by some combination of these two. Instead, violently antagonistic views of who he is – and of who he *should* be – struggle against each other in an ongoing fight whose location is not only the border-lands territory that surrounds the character but also his own consciousness.

Américo Paredes composed his novel during the years just prior to the Second World War, which places the work chronologically subsequent to the period we have so far covered. *George Washington Gómez* nonetheless makes for a fitting text with which to close both the current chapter and our larger discussion of American literary realism. Even as Paredes's work indisputably remains an "ethnographically keyed ... realist novel" (Limón, "Border Literary Histories" 164), the harsh border antagonisms that exert a fragmenting force on its protagonist are at moments rendered by Paredes with compellingly modernist representational techniques. In that sense, *George Washington Gómez* makes it easier for us to recognize that modernism, as I will briefly suggest in the conclusion following this chapter, did not so much supplant realism in American literature as extend it in new directions.

Américo Paredes: border realism/border modernism

Américo Paredes was born in 1915 in Brownsville, the southernmost city of Texas, which he fictionalized as "Jonesville" in *George Washington Gómez*. Paredes began his higher education at Brownsville Junior College when a high school principal who had been impressed with his potential saw him standing on a street corner looking for work and helped him get a scholarship (Morín,

Legacy 43). After some time spent in Asia as a soldier and journalist during and after the Second World War, he returned to earn his Ph.D. at the University of Texas, where he then became a professor of English, Folklore, and Anthropology. His 1958 study *With His Pistol in His Hand: A Border Ballad and its Hero* about militant folk songs (*corridos*) that circulated on the Texas–Mexico border became a founding text – and made Paredes a founding figure – of both Chicano Studies and Border Studies. Paredes wrote *George Washington Gómez* between 1935 and 1940 but did not have a chance to submit the novel to publishers before becoming engulfed in the US war effort. He assumed the novel was lost until 1986, when a yellowing, partially disintegrated typescript turned up in a carton at his family home in Brownsville (Saldívar, *Borderlands of Culture* 23). Published in 1990 without revisions to its original typescript in order to preserve the book's historical integrity, *George Washington Gómez* can be regarded as a recovered text in an unusually literal sense of the word.

To understand the weight of the conflicting pressures the book's main character experiences and the complexity of what Paredes calls "Mexicotexan" identity at the border, one must recognize that the Lower Rio Grande Valley was historically part of Mexico. The 1848 Treaty of Guadalupe Hidalgo, which ended the United States–Mexico War (launched under America's expansionist Manifest Destiny doctrine), forced Mexico to surrender nearly one-half of its territory, including all or part of current-day Texas, California, New Mexico, Nevada, Utah, Colorado, Arizona, and Wyoming, and affirmed South Texas's Rio Grande River as an official boundary between the nations. Although after 1848 they technically became American citizens, the vast majority of people living on the now-US side of the river remained Spanish speakers whose primary cultural identification was with their compatriots on the Mexican side. Over the following several decades, but especially from 1900–20, an influx of white business people and capital from the north, with their interests defended by US law and power (including the paramilitary Texas Rangers), transformed South Texas's traditional ranching economy into a profitable center of industrial-scale agriculture controlled mostly by Anglos (Morín, *Legacy* 18–20).

The protagonist of *George Washington Gómez* is born in the midst of a failed 1915 rebellion by border militants against US rule (the same year in which Paredes himself was born). The abortive revolution was followed by widespread bloody reprisals on the part of the Texas Rangers against the area's entire Mexican-descended population – the Rangers may have killed as many as 5,000 people without trials, many of whom had had no involvement in the uprising (Morín, *Legacy* 19). As a boy, Guálinto/George passionately fantasizes scenarios in which he himself exacts violent revenge against the Rangers and white Texans more generally. The boy's visions of violent resistance are alternately encouraged and discouraged by his ambivalent Uncle Feliciano. At the time of George's birth, Feliciano was an armed fighter for the revolutionary *Sediciosos*, scheming to overthrow US authority throughout the Southwest. But when Feliciano's militant activities caused a brutal attack by the Rangers on his uninvolved brother-in-law Gumersindo Gómez, who believed in peace and assimilation, Feliciano was overcome with guilt. He promised the dying Gumersindo to fulfill his vision for his infant son and raise him as a peaceful "Leader of His People." This same vision of the boy growing up to lead Texas Mexicans toward shared peace and progress with the more recently arrived Anglotexans had initially motivated Gumersindo to name George after the first US president. Feliciano's ambivalence about his promise to Gumersindo shows at key moments, however: for instance, although the nickname of Guálinto derives from the Spanish-speaking Goméz family's pronunciation of "Washington," Feliciano registers the boy as Guálinto at school, purposely misidentifying the name as deriving from an indigenous Mexican language to a curious official.

In school, the academically gifted Guálinto discovers that if he wishes to earn good grades, he must at least pretend to accept an Anglotexan worldview. The subject of Texas history, for example, "is a cross that he must bear. In written tests, if he expects to pass the course, he must put down in writing what he violently misbelieves" concerning such topics as the Battle of the Alamo (*George Washington Gómez* 149). As he continues in school, however, especially under the tutelage of a sympathetic white Northern female teacher, Guálinto finds that he cannot help but begin to develop "an Angloamerican self," one nurtured by his immersion in such books as Mark Twain's *Tom Sawyer* (147). He comes to feel a "pleasant warmth" when listening to "The Star-Spangled Banner" (148). At the same time, "a rousing Mexican song would make him feel like yelling" in "patriotic" excitement and he speaks only Spanish at home (147). Moreover, he continues to have "fancies" of battling against "Gringos" (148). Under these circumstances, even the question of what counts as "foreign" about Guálinto and what counts as "American" – the latter itself a contested term among Latin Americans and others who question the equation of the United States with "America" – becomes an irresolvable paradox. As Paredes notes, the twentieth-century *Tejano* lives with the irony of being born "a foreigner in his native land" (15).

From his early childhood through his high school graduation, Guálinto/ George experiences intense and conflicting pressures from family members and friends, from his teachers, from folk narratives and songs, from miscellaneous social institutions, from English- and Spanish-language literature and mass media, as well as from his own shifting dreams and ambitions. The "radically different and antagonistic" forces that converge on Paredes's protagonist have complex effects not only on the character but on the textual strategies Paredes utilizes to represent him (Paredes, *George Washington Gómez* 147): even as *George Washington Gómez*'s emphasis on everyday life within a densely specified social context continues and extends the realist tradition, at a few important moments disjunctive imagery and, in one case, a jarring narrative fracture work *against* the illusion, or "air," of reality that other writers in this study took as their defining aesthetic goal (James, *Essays* 53). The narrative fracture in Paredes's novel occurs near the end of the book when a temporal jump across seven unrepresented years yields a "George C. Gómez" inexplicably changed from the protagonist with whom we have become familiar (Paredes, *George Washington Gómez* 147). Raised by his uncle and mother as a committed "Leader of his People" who would use his education to advance the interests of the border Mexican community, and having privately fantasized for most of his life about violent rebellions against Anglo power, the character who now calls himself George C. Gómez informs on politically active Texas Mexicans for US army intelligence. Married to the blonde daughter of a former Texas Ranger, he desires nothing more than to finish "getting the Mexican out of himself" (283). Paredes does not offer reasons for the radical shift in his main character's allegiances and attitudes, nor does he help orient readers to it with any sort of narrative bridge. Instead, readers finish the book confronted with the typically modernist task of trying to construct meaning across a textual gap – or, alternatively, forced to concede that the knowledge that would make one person fully intelligible to another (or, given Guálinto's own puzzlements, even to himself) can only ever be deferred, elusive.

Even prior to this final, disorienting elision, Paredes's novel calls on recognizably modernist devices at moments when it makes its most concerted efforts to convey the fragmenting effects on Guálinto/George's subjectivity of the border area's multiply antagonistic pressures. In perhaps the most notable example, Paredes develops what Ramón Saldívar aptly identifies as a "cubistic image" (*Borderlands* 161) to visualize the infinite regress of "American" and "Mexican" selves in the character: "In fact, there were many Guálinto Gomézes, each of them double like the images reflected on the two glass surfaces of a shop window. The eternal conflict … produced a divided personality, made up of tight little cells independent and almost entirely ignorant of each other, spread out all over his consciousness, mixed with one another like squares on a checkerboard" (Paredes, *George Washington Gómez* 147). Here, like the subject of a cubist painting, Guálinto's personality breaks down into a series of discrete but mutually reflective "cells" laid out on a two-dimensional surface and "mixed" in what seems an arbitrary order. As with the jarring narrative break discussed above, this abstract two-dimensional design sits uneasily with any fictional "air" of tangible, three-dimensional reality. Paredes uses the image, however, not from any desire to obscure or turn away from the violently contradictory actualities of Guálinto's experience, but instead as part of his attempt to represent, as precisely as he can, the effect of those actualities on Guálinto's consciousness. As we will see below, the same can be said for much of the formal experimentation associated with literary modernism.

Conclusion: realisms after realism

This book has focused on the period during which realism rose to eminence as the cutting edge of literary innovation in the United States and enjoyed arguably its high point of critical prestige and creative productivity: from about 1865, when the American Civil War ended, to about 1914, when the First World War began. Realism has continued to play a major role in American fiction since then as well. Even in recent decades, several of the United States' most successful writers of literary fiction have chosen to work primarily in the modes of realism, regionalism, and naturalism (including intersections and overlaps among these) first developed in America by writers this book has discussed. A short list – which might easily be expanded – of recent and contemporary fiction authors who write mostly in such modes would include (in no particular order): John Updike, Eudora Welty, Barbara Kingsolver, Tom Wolfe, Joyce Carol Oates, Jonathan Franzen, Amy Tan, Russell Banks, Junot Diaz, and, especially in her early novels, Nobel-prize winner Toni Morrison.

In the years following the First World War, however, realism as a genre began to lose the high-culture luster that it had earlier accrued through, for instance, its association with such prestigious nineteenth-century publishing institutions as the *Atlantic Monthly*. Realism's status as a prominent object of controversy in the pages of elite magazines, especially during the 1880s, the decade of the "war" fought between realism's advocates and critics who rejected it as vulgar and mundane, had significantly contributed to its public recognition as an "advanced" form of literature even by those who disliked it. The years during and after the First World War, however, brought forth new fiction by young American and European writers – much of it first published in avant-garde "little magazines" devoted to Art with a capital A (including the *Chap-Book*, *Poetry*, and the *Dial*) – that struck reviewers and critics, many of them associated with universities, not only as more daring in content but also as far more radically innovative in form than earlier styles of realism that, by the 1920s, seemed commonplace (Glazener, *Reading for Realism* 237). Indeed, for many writers of this period whom we now classify as "modernist," the realism that had emerged into visibility on the American literary scene during the latter decades of the nineteenth century signified a worn-out tradition, one they lumped with other middle-class bourgeois conventions it was past time to jettison – including, for instance, traditional religious observances, hypocritical attitudes toward sexuality, and a naïve belief in the progress of Western civilization. All of these, to literary modernists, papered over what was actually most primal and authentic about human experience. This new generation rejected what they saw as artificial systems of meaning, including both the false sense of order that traditional realism seemed to impose on the flux and chaos of individual experience, especially in a fragmented modern world, and the legitimacy that such realism, in their view, too often accorded to hollow social conventions. Modernists wished to re-conceive art – in the words of poet Ezra Pound to "make it new!" – and in so doing to revitalize both individuals and society.

In their quest to move beyond conventional realism's illusions of coherence, modernist fiction writers experimented with alternatives and supplements to realism's by-then familiar representational techniques. For instance Ernest Hemingway's first book published in the United States, *In Our Time* (1925), featured short stories composed largely of dialogue that made only the most minimal of gestures toward the kinds of exposition and description readers had come to expect in prose fiction. Hemingway radically reduced narrative descriptions not only of characters' backgrounds and physical appearances, but also of their thoughts and emotions. In a text where what was unsaid was just as important as anything actually written, readers were left to grasp important emotional dynamics by reading, as it were, between the lines. The perhaps paradoxical effect in a story such as "Out of Season," where a young American couple on vacation tries unsuccessfully to go trout fishing in a small Italian town, is to make the never directly explained tension between husband and wife – which emerges as the unspoken but real topic of the story – feel more emotionally immediate, intense, and palpable to a reader than it might if the reason for the discord were described by, for instance, a highly articulate Howellsian narrator. *In Our Time*'s most striking challenge to conventional realist form, however, lies in its alternation between stories and apparently unrelated italicized, extremely brief "interchapters." Each interchapter consists of an isolated scene of war-related violence or death, in most cases set in Europe and involving Europeans. With no framing or explanation, the interchapters initially feel disjunctive and out of place next to the book's mostly American-focused short stories, few of which feature actual violence or death. The interchapters never lose their disjunctive feeling, but as the reader continues he or she may start to sense unexpected resonances between them and the stories. If nothing else, the juxtaposition of violent European episodes with stories in which Americans engage in normal-seeming activities such as fishing, skiing, and getting drunk forces the reader to experience in the act of reading the unsettling disjunctures, incongruities, and oft-times harsh ironies of a globalizing world.

Other experiments in form by modernist fiction writers included John Dos Passos's development in *Manhattan Transfer* (1925) and then further in his *USA* trilogy (1930–36) of a collage technique which mixes traditional realist narration and the new "stream of consciousness" technique (see below) with news clippings, biographies, speeches, popular songs, even advertisements. Dos Passos's modernist collages attempt to capture the felt experience of a rushed modern age in which Americans are bombarded with fragments of information and images. Meanwhile, William Faulkner devoted his 1929 novel *The Sound and the Fury* to stream-of-consciousness writing, in which he sought to present the unprocessed mixture of perceptions, sensations, and thoughts that flow through a character's mind over a given stretch of time. The combination of stimuli from the outside, including the sounds of other people's voices, with thoughts and flashes of memory; the often unmarked shifts in focus; and the paucity of conventional punctuation and capitalization can make *The Sound and the Fury* challenging to read. But Faulkner's stream-of-consciousness style attempts to give readers access to a more primal and immediate level of individual experience – experience in that evanescent, present-tense moment before it has been edited, ordered, and interpreted by an individual's own mind, let alone by an author.

Equally if not more challenging to readers were the experimental narratives of Gertrude Stein, who had studied "automatic writing" at Harvard with psychologist William James. (William, the older brother of novelist Henry James, also originated the term "stream of consciousness.") In works such as *The Making of Americans*, published in 1925 but written earlier, Stein developed a style notable for its heavy use of verbal repetition and idiosyncratic syntax in which language, she believed, found its own patterns of sound, sense, and rhythm. A typical sentence begins, for example, "The beauty in her then to any one who came to know all of them was, as beauty came to be in each one of them, a thing that when it was in any one of them then, was to any one who knew them then, something that was always in them always to be in them, always had been in them, in the others of them then there was not any sign of any such a change ever to be in them..." (102–103). Stein might here seem to have taken narrative prose about as far in the opposite direction as it was possible to go from the realist ideal, articulated by Howells, of a "colorless medium through which the reader clearly sees" ("Editor's Study," 1890 804). Narrative language, Howells insisted, is most effective when it does not remind us of its existence as words on a page but instead allows us temporarily to feel as if we are gaining direct access to real people in a real place (see Chapter 3). By contrast, Stein's language is anything but transparent – we cannot look past its dense materiality even for a moment. As with Faulkner's challenging style, however, it is important to note that Stein does not write as she does in order to evade or romanticize reality. Rather, her style continuously reminds us of a reality that, it could be argued, is more elemental than anything experienced by the fictional Hersland family in *The Making of Americans*. The sometimes virtually impenetrable repetitiveness of Stein's style makes it impossible to ignore that what we encounter first and foremost in *The Making of Americans*, as in all books, is the material fact of writing itself – language inscribed on paper – before it becomes, or represents, anything else.

Modernist fiction writers such as Stein, Faulkner, Dos Passos, and Hemingway experimented with form because they wished to access in their work dimensions of the modern world, of individual experience, of language itself that a reliance on traditional realist methods, in their view, overlooked, even obscured. Rather than art that aimed at producing the effect of reality, modernists desired to achieve a more radical level of authenticity. Certainly, as is indicated by our discussion in Chapter 10 of Américo Paredes's novel *George Washington Gómez*, texts may intermingle customary modes of realism with other, more experimental methods of representation. Each of the four modernist authors we have considered here incorporated recognizably realist elements and techniques into his or her fiction. Indeed, critics of the time frequently invoked the words "realist" and "naturalist" when discussing their work, including fiction by Stein less avant-garde than *The Making of Americans*. As with many categories used by literary historians, any boundary-line between "realism" and "modernism" must remain blurry at best. This is not to deny that important differences exist between the aims, methods, and results of modernist fiction and the literary realism on which this book has focused, as will be evident to any reader who compares a page from *The Sound and the Fury* to a page from Howells. Even at their most radically experimental, however, modernist fiction writers of the 1920s shared with the earlier realists covered in this book a conviction that the written fiction of their time had become overly conventional, overly artificial. Both strove to bring to that fiction a level of reality they felt was missing from it. In other words, modernist fiction – and, I would argue, much of the postmodern fiction that followed it in the second half of the twentieth century – should be seen not as an abandonment of the realist impulse that reshaped American literature after the Civil War, but as an extension, re-direction, and multiplication of that impulse: as realisms after realism.

Notes

1 Literary precursors, literary contexts

1 For a nuanced exploration of Hawthorne's and Melville's attempts to find a "neutral ground" between romance and realism, see Link and Thompson, *Neutral Ground* 53–156.

2 Such debates continued for decades at every level of literary culture. In an 1896 high-school textbook co-authored with a small-town Texas school superintendent, Nathaniel Hawthorne's son Julian implicitly defended the literary beliefs of his father's generation by insisting that the realists' emphasis on the surface details of everyday life ignores the fact that "appearances are deceptive." Hence, the novelist who records appearances only "is misleading in direct proportion to his success" (Hawthorne and Lemmon, *American Literature* 258).

3 In an 1893 defense of literary realism, the famous lawyer Clarence Darrow cleverly turned the tables on those who charged realism with vulgarity for not portraying ideal beauty: "It is only now that the world is growing so delicate and refined that it can see the beauty of a fact" ("Realism" 134).

4 In point of fact, Mark Twain did spend some weeks marching around in the Missouri woods with a group of Confederate sympathizers who called themselves the Ralls County Rangers. The group dissolved without ever encountering the enemy, and Twain spent the rest of the war as a neutral in the silver camps of Nevada (Powers, *Mark Twain* 97–99).

5 Sample historical romances include Lew Wallace's *Ben Hur* (1880), Charles Major's *When Knighthood Was in Flower* (1898), and Maurice Thompson's *Alice of Old Vincennes* (1900).

6 Twain complained that Scott's novels had undone the beneficent social effects of Cervante's satiric anti-romance *Don Quixote* (1605), which had "swept the world's admiration for the medieval chivalry-silliness out of existence" in the seventeenth century, only for Scott's 1819 publication of *Ivanhoe* to "restore" that same admiration, now even sillier, in the nineteenth century (*Mississippi* 502).

3 Creating the "odour" of the real

1 In 1854, domestic writer Fanny Fern (pseudonym of Sara Willis Parton) introduced her first novel, *Ruth Hall*, along similar lines, yet another example that

late-nineteenth-century literary realists sometimes followed more closely in the footsteps of mid-century women's domestic fiction than they cared to acknowledge (see Chapter 1, above). Fern's preface to *Ruth Hall* asserts, "There is no intricate plot; there are no startling developments, no hair-breadth escapes" (3).

2 Crane based "The Open Boat" on his own actual experience in a lifeboat after a ship-wreck. He narrated the real-life event in a non-fictional article for a newspaper, with the headline article titled "Stephen Crane's Own Story." Notably, Crane presents the non-fiction newspaper version of the story more sensationalistically than he does the fictional version in "The Open Boat." In his view, literary realism as an aesthetic mode meant eschewing sensationalism even when describing legitimately sensational events.

4 Conflicting manners

1 Exceptions include the final portion of Howells's *A Hazard of New Fortunes* (1890), discussed in Chapter 6, and James's *The Princess Casamassima* (1886), several of whose main characters are working-class revolutionaries in London.
2 I am indebted here and in the next two paragraphs to Dimock's "Debasing Exchange."

5 "Democracy in literature"?

1 Recent research into publication histories has suggested that the genre also had at least some readers in smaller towns and rural areas around the country, where regionalist stories would appear in syndicated newspapers (see Johanningsmeier, "Sarah Orne Jewett"). Nonetheless, rural readers were not those to whom regionalist or local-color authors typically addressed themselves.
2 This entire paragraph is indebted to Philip Leigh's illuminating study of the complexities involved, both in the nineteenth century and today, in evaluating literary representations of dialect ("Game of Confidence").

6 "The blab of the pave"

1 Beyond those discussed here, other novels by American realists in which the urban poor have a tangible presence include, for just a few examples, Frank Norris's *McTeague* (1899), Robert Herrick's *The Web of Life* (1900), Mary Wilkins Freeman's *The Portion of Labor* (1901), Paul Laurence Dunbar's, *The Sport of the Gods* (1902), Jack London's *Martin Eden* (1909), and Henry James's *The Princess Casamassima* (1886).
2 Even reviewers who disapproved of the book's subject matter and especially its lack of conventional moral judgments regarding sexual seduction (not to mention prostitution), implicitly accepted its treatment of slum life as realistic.

3 In contrast to Crane's entire lack of personal contact with battle when he wrote *Red Badge* in 1895, in 1892 when he wrote *Maggie* he had at least visited the Bowery several times. But not until later in his career, when he was researching some journalistic pieces to be published in newspapers, would he spend any extensive amount of time in the Bowery interacting with people who lived there (see Robertson, *Stephen Crane* 77–78).

7 Crisis of agency

1 See the collection of primary documents relating to *Sister Carrie*'s first publication assembled by editor Donald Pizer for the Norton Critical edition of the text (Dreiser, *Sister Carrie*).
2 Jack London himself "was never very successful at placing his critical prose with the *Atlantic Monthly*" (Auerbach, *Male Call* 191).
3 Michel Foucault offers what is still the most influential development of this argument (*History of Sexuality*).

8 "Certain facts of life"

1 Hjalmar Hjorth Boyesen, a Norwegian immigrant, a distinguished professor of languages at both Cornell and Columbia Universities, and a fierce partisan of realism, had a darker take than his friend Howells regarding female readers' baleful influence on American literature. In an 1887 magazine article that sought to explain "Why We Have No Great Novelists," Boyesen blamed the young American girl whose perceived needs and tastes, he contended, controlled editing and publishing decisions throughout the land: "Arrayed in stern and bewildering loveliness," the American girl is an "Iron Madonna who strangles in her fond embrace the American novelist" (618).
2 Howells himself much admired "The Yellow Wallpaper." After first trying unsuccessfully to have it published in *The Atlantic Monthly* (whose then-editor Horace Scudder told Gilman after reading the manuscript, "I could not forgive myself if I made others as miserable as I have made myself"), Howells helped arrange for it to be published in *The New England Magazine* (Gilman, *Yellow Wallpaper* 91, 15). He later included it in a prominent collection he edited called *The Great American Short Stories* (1920).
3 Novelist Jane Austen, whom Howells would later single out as an important early model of realist writing, wrote a parody of gothic fiction in 1798, *Northanger Abbey*, which was published in 1817 after her death.
4 In describing Edna's corporeal experience of sexual desire, *The Awakening* pushes further beyond conventional mores even than Dreiser's *Sister Carrie*, which Doubleday published amid controversy the following year (see Chapter 7).
5 The phrase derives from novelist and critic Toni Morrison's *Playing in the Dark* (13).
6 In *The Rise of Silas Lapham*, Penelope Lapham and her fiancé Tom Corey develop an affectionate meta-linguistic appreciation of the older Laphams' old-fashioned, often ungrammatical rural speech (Barrish, *American Literary Realism* 23–24).

9   "The unjust spirit of caste"

1 Foner's *Reconstruction* provides a superb overview both of African-American achievements and of white resistance to those achievements during the period 1863–77.
2 Chesnutt's grandmothers on both his mother's and father's side were of mixed race; his grandfathers were both white landowners.
3 Twain also drew, however, from a pre-Civil War tradition of American humor-writing that featured first-person dialect speakers, including, for example, Seba Smith's *Life and Writing of Major Jack Downing...Written by Himself* (1833).
4 Wells-Barnett was threatened with lynching and forced to move away from her home city of Memphis, Tennessee seven years prior to the Wilmington riot because she wrote a column for Memphis's black newspaper, *Free Speech*, implying that white women sometimes initiated sexual liaisons with black men. Wells-Barnett subsequently developed her claims in two pamphlets, *Southern Horrors: Lynch Law in All Its Phases* (1892) and *A Red Record* (1895), which used both personal and newspaper accounts (most of them from white sources), as well as concrete statistics, to demonstrate how few of the murders and horrifying mutilations performed by "Judge Lynch" had any connection with a genuine crime on the part of their victims (6).

10   New Americans write realism

1 Emma Lazarus wrote "The New Colossus" in 1883 for an exhibit raising money to support the statue's erection; the poem's famous lines were not actually inscribed on the pedestal until 1903 (Schor, *Emma Lazarus* 304–06).
2 Among scholars who have recently begun to view turn-of-the-twentieth-century ethnic US literatures as a crucial bridge between realism and modernism are Blair, Sollors, Saldívar, and González.
3 Also see Barrish, *American Literary Realism* 9–11.
4 I thank Julia H. Lee for the knowledge and insights she contributed to my discussion of Sui Sin Far.
5 The first definition of "whoop" in the Oxford English Dictionary notes that it is used "by N. American Indians, etc. as a signal or war-cry" and adds "see also 'war-whoop.'"
6 As Molly Crumpton Winter observes, "the children who attended the Dawes-era boarding schools and who learned to read and write in English became the generation to fight for the rights of their tribes, both locally and on a national level" (*American Narratives* 59).

Works cited

Anon. "Editorial Comment." *American Medicine* 13.4 (1907): 195–99.

Alcott, Louisa May. *Little Women. Louisa May Alcott: Little Women; Little Men; Jo's Boys.* Ed. Elaine Showalter. 1868. New York: Library of America, 2005.

Allen, James Lane. "Local Color." *Critic* 9 Jan. 1886: 13–14.

Allen, Judith A. *The Feminism of Charlotte Perkins Gilman: Sexualities, Histories, Progressivism.* University of Chicago Press, 2009.

Ammons, Elizabeth. *Conflicting Stories: American Women Writers at the Turn into the Twentieth Century.* New York: Oxford University Press, 1991.

    "Material Culture, Empire, and Jewett's *Country of the Pointed Firs.*" *New Essays on The Country of the Pointed Firs.* Cambridge University Press, 1994. 81–100.

Anesko, Michael. *Letters, Fictions, Lives: Henry James and William Dean Howells.* Oxford University Press, 1997.

Arthur, Timothy Shay. *Ten Nights in a Bar-Room and What I Saw There.* 1854. Philadelphia: Bradley, 1856. Rpt. in *Popular American Literature of the 19th Century.* Ed. Paul C. Guttjahr. New York: Oxford University Press, 2001. 652–750.

Auerbach, Jonathan. *Male Call: Becoming Jack London.* Durham, NC: Duke University Press, 1996.

Avirett, James Battle. *The Old Plantation: How We Lived in Great House and Cabin Before the War.* New York: F. Tennyson Neely, 1901. *Documenting the American South.* Available online: http://docsouth.unc.edu/fpn/avirett/avirett.html (last accessed January 11, 2010).

Barrish, Phillip. *American Literary Realism, Critical Theory, and Intellectual Prestige, 1880–1995.* New York: Cambridge University Press, 2001.

    White Liberal Identity, Literary Pedagogy, and Classic American Realism. Columbus: Ohio State University Press, 2005.

Barthes, Roland. *The Rustle of Language.* Trans. Richard Howard. Berkeley: University of California Press, 1989.

Becker, George J. "Modern Realism as a Literary Movement." Introduction. *Documents of Modern Literary Realism.* Ed. George J. Becker. Princeton University Press, 1963. 3–38.

Bederman, Gail. *Manliness and Civilization: A Cultural History of Gender and Race in the United States, 1880–1917.* University of Chicago Press, 1995.

Bell, Michael Davitt. *The Problem of American Literary Realism: Studies in the Cultural History of a Literary Idea*. Chicago and London: University of Chicago Press, 1993.

Bentley, Nancy, and Sandra Gunning. "Introduction: Cultural and Historical Background." *The Marrow of Tradition: Bedford Cultural Edition*. By Charles W. Chesnutt.. 3–26.

Birnbaum, Michele A. "'Alien Hands': Kate Chopin and the Colonization of Race." *American Literature* 66.2 (1994): 301–23.

Blair, Sara. "Whose Modernism Is It? Abraham Cahan, Fictions of Yiddish, and the Contest of Modernity." *Modern Fiction Studies* 51.2 (2005): 258–78. *Project MUSE Premium Collection*. Available online: http://muse.jhu. edu.ezproxy.lib.utexas.edu/journals/modern_fiction_studies/ (last accessed June 5, 2010).

Bourdieu, Pierre. *Distinction: A Social Critique of the Judgement of Taste*. Trans. Richard Nice. 1979. Cambridge: Harvard University Press, 1984.

"The Forms of Capital." 1983. Trans. Richard Nice. *The Sociology of Economic Life*. Ed. Mark Granovetter and Richard Swedberg. 2nd edn. Boulder, CO: Westview, 2001. 96–111.

Boyesen, Hjalmar Hjorth. "Why We Have No Great Novelists." *Forum* II (Feb. 1887): 615–22.

Brodhead, Richard H. *The School of Hawthorne*. Oxford University Press, 1986.

Cultures of Letters: Scenes of Reading and Writing in Nineteenth-Century America. University of Chicago Press, 1993.

Brodkin, Karen. *How Jews Became White Folks and What that Says about Race in America*. New Brunswick, NJ: Rutgers University Press, 1998.

Burgess, Douglas H. , and Joseph R. McElrath. *The Apprenticeship Writings of Frank Norris: 1896–1898*. Philadelphia, PA: The American Philosophical Society, 1996.

Cahan, Abraham. *Yekl and the Imported Bridegroom and Other Stories of Yiddish New York*. Orig. Publ. 1896. New York: Dover, 1970.

Grandma Never Lived in America: the New Journalism of Abraham Cahan. Ed. Moses Rischin. Bloomington: Indiana University Press, 1985.

The Rise of David Levinsky. 1917. New York: Penguin, 1993.

Camfield, Gregg. *Sentimental Twain: Samuel Clemens in the Maze of Moral Philosophy*. Philadelphia: University of Pennsylvania Press, 1994.

Chan, Sucheng. "The Exclusion of Chinese Women, 1870–1943." *Entry Denied: Exclusion and the Chinese Community in America, 1882–1943*. Comp. Sucheng Chan. Philadelphia, PA: Temple University Press, 1991. 94–146.

Chauncey, George. *Gay New York: Gender, Urban Culture, and the Making of the Gay Male World, 1890–1940*. New York: Basic Books, 1994.

Chesnutt, Charles W. *The Conjure Woman and Other Conjure Tales*. Ed. Richard Brodhead. 1899. Durham, NC: Duke University Press, 1993.

The Journals of Charles W. Chesnutt. Ed. Richard H. Brodhead. Durham, NC: Duke University Press, 1993.

The Marrow of Tradition: Bedford Cultural Edition. Ed. Nancy Bentley and
    Sandra Gunning. 1901. Boston: Bedford/St. Martins, 2002. Bedford
    Cultural Editions.

Chopin, Kate. *The Awakening: An Authoritative Text; Backgrounds and Historical
    Contexts; Criticism*. Ed. Margo Culley. 2nd edn. 1899. New York:
    W. W. Norton, 1994.

Cooke, Rose Terry. "Sally Parson's Duty." *Atlantic Monthly* 1.1 (1857): 24–33.
    Cornell University Library Making of America Collection. Available
    online: http://ebooks.library.cornell.edu/a/atla/atla.1857.html (last
    accessed August 4, 2009).

Corkin, Stanley. *Realism and the Birth of the Modern United States: Cinema,
    Literature, and Culture*. Athens: University of Georgia Press, 1996.

Cox, James M. "The Rise of Silas Lapham: The Business of Morals and Manners."
    New Essays on The Rise of Silas Lapham. Cambridge University Press,
    1991. 107–28.

Crane, Gregg David. *The Cambridge Introduction to the Nineteenth-Century
    American Novel*. Cambridge University Press, 2007.

Crane, Stephen. "Fears Realists Must Wait; An Interesting Talk with William
    Dean Howells." *New York Times* 28 Oct. 1894: 20. Available online:
    www.nytimes.com/ref/membercenter/nytarchive.html (last accessed
    August, 2009).

*Maggie, A Girl of the Streets (A Story of New York) (1893): An Authoritative
    Text; Backgrounds and Sources; The Author and the Novel; Reviews and
    Criticism*. Ed. Thomas A. Gullason. 1893. New York: W. W. Norton,
    1979.

*The Red Badge of Courage: An Authoritative Text; Backgrounds and Sources;
    Criticism*. Ed. Donald Pizer. 3rd edn. 1895. New York: W. W. Norton,
    1999.

Cruz, Denise. "Reconsidering McTeague's 'Mark' and 'Mac': Intersections of
    US Naturalism, Imperial Masculinities, and Desire Between Men."
    American Literature 78.3 (2006): 487–517.

Culler, Jonathan. *Structuralist Poetics: Structuralism, Linguistics, and the Study of
    Literature*. Ithaca, NY: Cornell University Press, 1975.

Cutler, Edward S. "Literary Modernity and the Problem of a National Literature:
    Understanding William Dean Howells' Critique of Walt Whitman."
    American Literary Realism, 38.2 (2006): 132–44.

Daniels, Roger. *Not like Us: Immigrants and Minorities in America, 1890–1924*.
    Chicago, IL: Ivan R. Dee, 1997.

Darrow, Clarence. "Realism in Literature and Art." *Arena* Dec. 1893: 98–113. Rpt.
    in *Documents of American Realism and Naturalism*. Ed. Donald Pizer.
    Southern Illinois University Press: Carbondale, 1998. 132–43.

Davis, Rebecca Harding. *Life in the Iron Mills*. Ed. Cecelia Tichi. 1861. Boston,
    MA: Bedford, 1998.

De Forest, John W. *Miss Ravenel's Conversion from Secession to Loyalty*. Ed. Gary
    Scharnhorst. 1867. New York: Penguin, 2000.

Derrick, Scott. "Making a Heterosexual Man: Gender, Sexuality, and Narrative in the Fiction of Jack London." *Rereading Jack London.* Ed. Leonard Cassuto and Jeanne Campbell Reesman. Stanford University Press, 1996. 110–29.

Monumental Anxieties: Homoerotic Desire and Feminine Influence in 19th-Century US Literature. New Brunswick, NJ: Rutgers University Press, 1997.

Dimock, Wai-chee. "Debasing Exchange: Edith Wharton's *The House of Mirth.*" *PMLA: Publications of the Modern Language Association of America* 100.5 (1985): 783–92.

Dos Passos, John. *Manhattan Transfer. Novels 1920–1925.* Ed. Townsend Ludington. 1925. New York: Library of America, 2003.

Dreiser, Theodore. *Sister Carrie: An Authoritative Text; Backgrounds and Sources; Criticism.* Ed. Donald Pizer. 1900. New York: W.W. Norton, 1970.

Du Bois, W. E. B. "Strivings of the Negro People." *The Atlantic Monthly* 80.478 (1897): 194–98. *Making of America.* Available online: http://ebooks. library.cornell.edu/a/atla/ (last accessed June 5, 2010).

Edwards, Rebecca. *New Spirits: Americans in the Gilded Age, 1865–1905.* New York: Oxford University Press, 2006.

Emerson, Ralph Waldo. *Essays and Lectures.* Ed. Joel Porte. New York: Library of America, 1983.

Evans, Brad. *Before Cultures: The Ethnographic Imagination in American Literature, 1865–1920.* University of Chicago Press, 2005.

Faulkner, William. *The Sound and the Fury. Novels 1926–1929.* Ed. Joseph Blotner and Noel Polk. 1929. New York: Library of America, 2006.

Faust, Drew Gilpin. *This Republic of Suffering: Death and the American Civil War.* New York: Alfred A. Knopf, 2008.

Fern, Fanny. *Ruth Hall and Other Writings.* Ed. Joyce W. Warren. New Brunswick: Rutgers University Press, 1986.

Fetterley, Judith, and Marjorie Pryse. *Writing Out of Place: Regionalism, Women, and American Literary Culture.* Urbana: University of Illinois Press, 2003.

eds. *American Women Regionalists 1850–1919: A Norton Anthology.* New York: W.W. Norton, 1992.

Fishkin, Shelley Fisher. "Dreiser and the Discourse of Gender." *Theodore Dreiser: Beyond Naturalism.* Ed. Miriam Gogol. New York University Press, 1995. 1–30.

"In Praise of 'Spike Lee's Huckleberry Finn' by Ralph Wiley." *Mark Twain Circular.* The Citadel, Oct. 1999. Available online http://faculty.citadel. edu/leonard/od99wiley.htm (last accessed June 2, 2010).

Fleissner, Jennifer L. *Women, Compulsion, Modernity: The Moment of American Naturalism.* University of Chicago Press, 2004.

Fluck, Winfried. "Morality, Modernity, and 'Malarial Restlessness': American Realism in its Anglo-European Contexts." *A Companion to American Fiction, 1865–1914.* Ed. Robert Paul Lamb and Gary Richard Thompson. Malden, MA: Blackwell Publishing, 2005. 77–95.

Foner, Eric. *Reconstruction: America's Unfinished Revolution 1863–1877*. New York: Harper & Row, 1988.

Foucault, Michel. *The History of Sexuality*. Trans. Robert Hurley. New York: Pantheon, 1978.

Fox, Richard Wightman, and T. J. Jackson Lears. *The Culture of Consumption: Critical Essays in American History, 1880–1980*. New York: Pantheon, 1983.

Freeman, Mary Wilkins. "A Mistaken Charity." *Harper's Bazaar* 26 May 1883: 328–30. *American Periodicals Series Online*.

Fuller, Henry Blake. *The Cliff-Dwellers*. New York: Harper, 1893.

Gandal, Keith. *The Virtues of the Vicious: Jacob Riis, Stephen Crane and the Spectacle of the Slum*. New York: Oxford University Press, 1997.

Gardner, Todd K., and Michael R. Haines (eds.)."Metropolitan Areas – Population: 1880–1990 [Part 1]." Chart.. *Historical Statistics of the United States*. Cambridge University Press. 2006

Garland, Hamlin. *Main-Travelled Roads*. 1891. Lincoln: University of Nebraska Press, 1995.

"Productive Conditions of American Literature." *Forum* Aug. 1894: 690–98. Rpt. in *Documents of American Realism and Naturalism*. Ed. Donald Pizer. Carbondale: Southern Illinois University Press, 1998. 151–58.

Gilman, Charlotte Perkins. *Charlotte Perkins Gilman's "The Yellow Wallpaper" and the History of Its Publication and Reception*. Comp. and ed. Julie Bates Dock. 1892. University Park, PA: Pennsylvania State University Press, 1998.

Glazener, Nancy. *Reading for Realism: The History of a US Literary Institution, 1850–1910*. Durham, NY: Duke University Press, 1997.

González, John Morán. *Border Renaissance: The Texas Centennial and the Emergence of Mexican American Literature*. Austin: University of Texas Press., 2009.

Goodman, Susan, and Carl Dawson. *William Dean Howells: A Writer's Life*. Berkeley: University of California Press, 2005.

Gould, Stephen Jay. *The Mismeasure of Man*. Revised edn. 1981. New York: W.W. Norton, 1996.

Harap, Louis. *The Image of the Jew in American Literature: From Early Republic to Mass Immigration*. Philadelphia, PA: Jewish Publication Society of America, 1978.

Harris, Joel Chandler. *Uncle Remus: His Songs and His Sayings; the Folk-lore of the Old Plantation*. New York: D. Appleton and Co., 1886.

Hawthorne, Julian, and Leonard Lemmon. *American Literature: A Textbook for Use by Schools and Colleges*. Boston, MA: D.C. Heath, 1896. *Google Books*. Available online: http://books.google.com/books?id=dFWtueM4EBcC&dq (last accessed Sept. 26, 2010).

Hawthorne, Nathaniel. *Collected Novels*. Ed. Millicent Bell. New York: Library of America, 1983.

Hemingway, Ernest. *In Our Time*. 1925. New York: Scribner, 2003.

Hofstadter, Richard. *Social Darwinism in American Thought:*. 1944. Boston, MA: Beacon Press, 1992.

Hopkins, Pauline E. *Contending Forces: A Romance Illustrative of Negro Life North and South.* 1900. New York: Oxford University Press, 1988.

Howard, June. *Form and History in American Literary Naturalism.* Chapel Hill: University of North Carolina Press, 1985.

Howells, William Dean. *Criticism and Fiction.* New York: Harper, 1891.

"Editor's Study." *Harper's New Monthly Magazine* 72.432 (1886): 972–76. *Making of America.* Available online: http://ebooks.library.cornell.edu/h/harp/ (last accessed August 4, 2009).

"Editor's Study." *Harper's New Monthly Magazine* 74.441 (1887): 482–86. *Making of America.* Available online: http://ebooks.library.cornell.edu/h/harp/ (last accessed August 8, 2009).

"Editor's Study." *Harper's New Monthly Magazine* 74.444 (1887): 983–87. *Making of America.* Available online: http://ebooks.library.cornell.edu/h/harp/ (last accessed June 2. 2010).

"Editor's Study." *Harper's New Monthly Magazine* 76.451 (1887): 153–56. *Making of America.* Available online: http://ebooks.library.cornell.edu/h/harp/ (last accessed August 4, 2009).

"Editor's Study." *Harper's New Monthly Magazine* 79.474 (1889): 962–67. *Making of America.* Available online: http://ebooks.library.cornell.edu/h/harp/ (last accessed May 29, 2010).

"Editor's Study." *Harper's New Monthly Magazine* 79.469 (1889): 151–55. *Making of America.* Available online: http://ebooks.library.cornell.edu/h/harp/ (last accessed May 30, 2010).

"Editor's Study." *Harper's New Monthly Magazine* 81.485 (1890): 800–806. *Making of America.* Available online: http://ebooks.library.cornell.edu/h/harp/ (last accessed August 4, 2009).

A Hazard of New Fortunes. Ed. Everett Carter. 1890. Bloomington: Indiana University Press, 1976. Vol. 16 of *A Selected Edition of W.D. Howells.*

Letter to Henry James. 10 Oct. 1888. *Selected Letters of W. D. Howells; Volume III: 1882–1891.* Ed. Robert C. Leitz, III, Richard H Ballinger, and Christoph K. Lohmann. Vol. 19. Bloomington: Indiana University Press, 1980. 231–32.

My Literary Passions. New York: Harper, 1895.

"The New Historical Romances." *North American Review* (Dec. 1890): 935–49.

"New York Low Life in Fiction." *New York World* 26 July 1896: 18.

"Review of *Miss Ravenel's Conversion from Secession to Loyalty*, by John W. De Forest." *Atlantic Monthly* 20.117 (1867): 120–22. *Making of America.* Available online: http://ebooks.library.cornell.edu/a/atla/ (last accessed August 8, 2009).

The Rise of Silas Lapham. Ed. Walter J. Meserve. 1885. Bloomington: Indiana University Press, 1971. Vol. 12 of *A Selected Edition of W.D. Howells.*

Selected Literary Criticism; Volume II: 1886–1897. Ed. Donald Pizer and Christoph K. Lohmann. Bloomington: Indiana University Press, 1993. Vol. 21 of *A Selected Edition of W. D. Howells.*

Selected Literary Criticism; Volume III: 1898–1920. Ed. Donald Pizer and
    Ulrich Halfmann. Bloomington: Indiana University Press, 1993. Vol. 30
    of A Selected Edition of W. D. Howells.

Their Wedding Journey. Ed. John K. Reeves. 1871. Bloomington: Indiana
    University Press, 1968. Vol. 5 of *A Selected Edition of W.D. Howells.*

Ignatiev, Noel. *How the Irish Became White.* New York: Routledge, 1995.

Jacobson, Matthew Frye. *Whiteness of a Different Color: European Immigrants
    and the Alchemy of Race.* Cambridge, MA: Harvard University Press,
    1999.

James, Henry. *The Bostonians.* 1886. Oxford University Press, 1984.

"Daisy Miller." *Henry James: Complete Stories 1874–1884.* Ed. William L.
    Vance. 1878. New York: Library of America, 1999, 238–95.

*Literary Criticism: Essays on Literature, American Writers and English
    Writers.* Ed. Mark Wilson and Leon Edel. Vol. I. New York: Library of
    America, 1984.

*Literary Criticism: French Writers, Other European Writers, Prefaces to the
    New York Edition.* Ed. Mark Wilson and Leon Edel. Vol. II. New York:
    Library of America, 1984.

The Portrait of a Lady. Henry James: Novels 1881–1886. Ed. William T.
    Stafford. 1881. New York: Library of America, 1984.

What Maisie Knew. Novels: 1896–1899. Ed. Myra Jehlen. 1897. New York:
    Library of America, 2003.

The Wings of the Dove. Henry James: Novels 1901–1902. Ed. Leo Bersani.
    1902. New York: Library of America, 2006.

Jewett, Sarah Orne. *Sarah Orne Jewett: Novels and Stories.* Ed. Michael Davitt
    Bell. 1877. New York: Library of America, 1996.

Johanningsmeier, Charles. "Sarah Orne Jewett and Mary E. Wilkins
    (Freeman): Two Shrewd Businesswomen in Search of New Markets."
    New England Quarterly 70.1 (1997): 57–82. JSTOR. Available online:
    www.jstor.org.ezproxy.lib.utexas.edu/stable/i215538 (last accessed
    March 9, 2009).

Johnson, Barbara. *The Feminist Difference: Literature, Psychoanalysis, Race, and
    Gender.* Cambridge, MA: Harvard University Press, 1998.

Johnston, Mary. *To Have and to Hold,* Installment 1. *The Atlantic Monthly* 85:507
    (January 1900): 54–66. Available online: http://ebooks.library.cornell.
    edu/a/atla/ (last accessed January 4, 2009).

To Have and to Hold, Installment 3. *The Atlantic Monthly* 85:509 (March
    1900): 335–54. Available online: http://ebooks.library.cornell.edu/a/atla/
    (last accessed January 4, 2009).

Kaplan, Amy. "Nation, Region, and Empire." *The Columbia History of the
    American Novel.* Ed. Emory Elliott *et al.* New York: Columbia University
    Press, 1991. 240–66.

"Romancing the Empire: The Embodiment of American Masculinity in the
    Popular Historical Novel of the 1890s." *American Literary History* 2.4
    (1990): 659–90.

The Social Construction of American Realism. University of Chicago Press, 1988.

Kelley, Mary. *Private Woman, Public State: Literary Domesticity in Nineteenth-Century America*. New York: Oxford University Press, 1984.

Lawson, Andrew. "Class Mimicry in Stephen Crane's City." *American Literary History* 16.4 (2004): 596–618.

Lee, Hermione. *Edith Wharton*. New York: Random House, 2007.

Leigh, Philip. "A Game of Confidence: Realism, Literary Dialect, and Linguistics." Diss. University of Texas at Austin, 2010.

Leverenz, David. *Paternalism Incorporated: Fables of American Fatherhood, 1865–1940*. Ithaca, NY: Cornell University Press, 2003.

Lewis, Sinclair. "The American Fear of Literature." Nobel Foundation. Stockholm. 12 June 1930. *NobelPrize.org*. Available online: http://nobelprize.org/nobel_prizes/literature/laureates/1930/lewis-lecture.html (last accessed July 10, 2009).

Limón, José E. "Border Literary Histories, Globalization, and Critical Regionalism." *American Literary History* 20.1–2 (2008): 160–82.

Link, Eric Carl. *The Vast and Terrible Drama: American Literary Naturalism in the Late Nineteenth Century*. Tuscaloosa: University of Alabama Press, 2004.

Link, Eric Carl, and Gary Richard Thompson. *Neutral Ground: New Traditionalism and the American Romance Controversy*. Baton Rouge: Louisiana State University Press, 1999.

London, Jack. *The Sea-Wolf. Jack London: Novels & Stories*. Ed. Donald Pizer. 1904. New York: Library of America, 1982.

Loving, Jerome. *The Last Titan: A Life of Theodore Dreiser*. Berkeley: University of California Press, 2005.

Lutz, Tom. *American Nervousness, 1903: An Anecdotal History*. Ithaca, NY: Cornell University Press, 1991.

Melville, Herman. *Moby-Dick, Or, The Whale*. 1851. New York: Penguin, 1992.

Messent, Peter. "Mark Twain, William Dean Howells, and Realism." *Companion to Mark Twain*. Ed. Peter Messent and Louis J. Budd. Oxford: Blackwell, 2005. 186–208.

Michaels, Walter Benn. *The Gold Standard and the Logic of Naturalism: American Literature at the Turn of the Century*. Berkeley: University of California Press, 1987.

Mizruchi, Susan L. *The Rise of Multicultural America: Economy and Print Culture 1865–1915*. Chapel Hill: University of North Carolina Press, 2008.

Morín, José R. López. *The Legacy of Américo Paredes*. College Station: Texas A&M University Press, 2006.

Morrison, Toni. *Playing in the Dark: Whiteness and the Literary Imagination*. Cambridge, MA: Harvard University Press, 1992.

"This Amazing, Troubling Book." In Mark Twain, *Adventures of Huckleberry Finn*. Ed. Thomas Cooley. New York: Norton, 1999. 385–92.

Murfree, Mary, and (pseud) Charles Egbert Craddock). "A-Playin' of Old Sledge at the Settlemint." *Atlantic Monthly* Oct. 1883: 544–57. Available online: http://ebooks.library.cornell.edu/a/atla/ (last accessed April 26, 2010).

Norris, Frank. *The Literary Criticism of Frank Norris*. Ed. Donald Pizer. Austin: University of Texas Press, 1964.

　McTeague. *Frank Norris: Novels and Essays*. Ed. Donald Pizer. 1914. New York: Library of America, 1986.

　The Octopus: A Story of California. 1901. New York: Penguin, 1986.

Okker, Patricia. "Native American Literatures and the Canon: The Case of Zitkala-Ša." *American Realism and the Canon*. Ed. Tom Quirk and Gary Scharnhorst. Newark: University of Delaware Press, 1994. 87–101.

Orvell, Miles. *The Real Thing: Imitation and Authenticity in American Culture, 1880–1940*. Chapel Hill: University of North Carolina Press, 1989.

Page, Thomas Nelson. "Marse Chan." *The Century* 27.6 (1884): 932–42. *Making of America*. Available online: http://ebooks.library.cornell.edu/c/cent/ (last accessed June 5, 2010).

Paredes, Américo. *George Washington Gómez*. Houston, TX: Arte Publico Press, 1990.

Phillips, Kevin. *Wealth and Democracy: A Political History of the American Rich*. New York: Broadway Books, 2002.

Powers, Ron. *Mark Twain: A Life*. New York: Free Press, 2005.

Reesman, Jeanne Campbell. *Jack London's Racial Lives: a Critical Biography*. Athens: University of Georgia Press, 2009.

Reeves, John K. "Introduction. *Their Wedding Journey*." By William Dean Howells. Bloomington: Indiana University Press, 1968.

Reynolds, Larry John. *A Historical Guide to Nathaniel Hawthorne*. Oxford University Press, 2001.

Riggio, Thomas P. "Biography of Theodore Dreiser." *Dreiser Web Source*. Penn Libraries, 2000. Available online: www.library.upenn.edu/collections/rbm/dreiser/tdbio.html (last accessed June 7, 2010).

Riis, Jacob. *How the Other Half Lives*. 1901. New York: Dover, 1971.

Robertson, Michael. *Steven Crane, Journalism, and the Making of Modern American Literature*. New York: Columbia University Press, 1997.

Roediger, David R. *Working toward Whiteness: How America's Immigrants Became White*. New York: Basic Books, 2005.

Roosevelt, Theodore. "The Strenuous Life." Hamilton Club. Chicago. 10 Apr. 1899. *Almanac of Theodore Roosevelt*. Available online: www.theodore-roosevelt.com/trstrenlife.html (last accessed August 24, 2009).

Saldívar, Ramón. *The Borderlands of Culture: Américo Paredes and the Transnational Imaginary*. Durham, NY: Duke University Press, 2006.

Scharnhorst, Gary. Introduction. *Miss Ravenel's Conversion from Secession to Loyalty*. By John W. De Forest. New York: Penguin, 2000.

Schmidt, Barbara. "Review of *The Works of Mark Twain. Volume 8. Adventures of Huckleberry Finn*, by Mark Twain." *Mark Twain Forum*. N.p., 8 Sept. 2003. www.twainweb.net/reviews/hf2003.html, last accessed August 8, 2009.

Schor, Esther. *Emma Lazarus*. New York: Schocken Books, 2006.

Sedgwick, Eve Kosofsky. *Between Men: English Literature and Male Homosocial Desire*. New York: Columbia University Press, 1985.

Seltzer, Mark. *Bodies and Machines*. New York: Routledge, 1992.

Shaw, Harry. *Narrating Reality: Austen, Scott, and Eliot*. Ithaca, NY: Cornell University Press, 1999.

Sinclair, Upton. *The Jungle: An Authoritative Text; Backgrounds and Contexts; Criticism*. Ed. Clare Virginia Eby. 1906. New York: W.W. Norton, 2003.

Smith, David L. "Huck, Jim, and American Racial Discourse." *Satire or Evasion?: Black Perspectives on Huckleberry Finn*. Ed. James S. Leonard, Thomas Asa Tenney, and Thadious M. Davis. Durham: Duke University Press, 1992. 103–120.

Sollors, Werner. *Ethnic Modernism*. Cambridge, MA: Harvard University Press, 2008.

Spack, Ruth. *America's Second Tongue: American Indian Education and the Ownership of English, 1860–1900*. Lincoln: University of Nebraska Press, 2002.

Stein, Gertrude. *The Making of Americans: Being a History of a Family's Progress*. 1925. Normal: Dalkey Archive, 1995.

Stowe, Harriet Beecher. *Uncle Tom's Cabin, or, Life Among the Lowly. Harriet Beecher Stowe: Three Novels*. Ed. Katherine Kish Sklar. 1852. New York: Library of America, 1982.

Sui Sin Far. *Mrs. Spring Fragrance and Other Writings*. Ed. Amy Ling and Annette White-Parks. Urbana: University of Illinois Press, 1995.

Sumner, William Graham. *Social Darwinism: Selected Essays of William Graham Sumner*. Englewood Cliffs, NJ: Prentice-Hall, 1963.

Tate, Claudia. *Domestic Allegories of Political Desire: The Black Heroine's Text at the Turn of the Century*. New York: Oxford University Press, 1992.

Taubenfeld, Aviva. "Only an 'L': Linguistic Borders and the Immigrant Author in Abraham Cahan's Yekl and Yankel der Yankee." *Multilingual America: Transnationalism, Ethnicity, and the Languages of American Literature*. Ed. Werner Sollors. New York: New York University Press, 1998. N. pag.

Tichi, Claudia. Introduction. *Life in the Iron-Mills*. By Rebecca Harding Davis. Boston: Bedford, 1998. 3–25.

Tocqueville, Alexis De. *Democracy in America*. Ed. J. P. Mayer. Trans. George Lawrence. 1840. Anchor City, NY: Doubleday, 1969.

Tompkins, Jane. *Sensational Designs: The Cultural Work of American Fiction, 1790–1860*. New York: Oxford University Press, 1985.

Trachtenberg, Alan. *The Incorporation of America: Culture and Society in the Gilded Age*. 25th anniversary edn. New York: Hill and Wang, 2007.

Trilling, Lionel. "Manners, Morals, and the Novel." *The Kenyon Review* 10.1 (1948): 11–27.

Twain, Mark. *Adventures of Huckleberry Finn*. Ed. Thomas Cooley. 3rd edn. 1885. New York: W. W. Norton, 1999.

A Connecticut Yankee at King Arthur's Court. 1889. London: Penguin, 1971.

A Connecticut Yankee in King Arthur's Court. Historical romances: The prince and the pauper, A Connecticut Yankee in King Arthur's court, Personal recollections of Joan of Arc. Ed. Susan K. Harris. 1889. New York: Library of America, 1994.

Life on the Mississippi. 1883. *Mississippi Writings.* Ed. Guy Cardwell. New York: Library of America, 1982. 217–616.

"The Notorious Jumping Frog of Calaveras County." 1865. *Selected Shorter Writings of Mark Twain.* Ed. Walter Blair. Boston, MA: Houghton Mifflin, 1962. 13–18.

United States Congress. "Dawes Act." *Native American Documents Project.* California State University, San Marcos, 8 Feb. 1887. Available online: http://www2.csusm.edu/nadp/a1887.htm (last accessed June 5, 2010).

Veblen, Thorstein. *The Theory of the Leisure Class.* 1899. Oxford University Press, 2007.

Vogel, Todd. *Rewriting Race: Race, Class, and Cultural Capital in Nineteenth-century America.* New Brunswick, NJ: Rutgers University Press, 2004.

Wallace, John. "'Huckleberry Finn Is Offensive.'" *Washington Post* 11 Apr. 1982: B8. *The Washington Post Historical Archive.*

Wallace, Lew. *Ben Hur: A Tale of the Christ.* 1880. New York: Modern Library, 2002.

Warner, Charles Dudley. "Editor's Study." *Harper's New Monthly Magazine* 86.511 (1892): 148–54. *Making of America.* Available online: http://ebooks.library.cornell.edu/h/harp/ (last accessed August 8, 2009).

Watt, Ian. *The Rise of the Novel.* 1957. Berkeley: University of California Press, 2001.

Weatherford, Richard M., ed. *Stephen Crane, the Critical Heritage.* Boston, MA: Routledge and Kegan Paul, 1973.

Wells-Barnett, Ida B. *On Lynchings: Southern Horrors, A Red Record, Mob Rule in New Orleans.* 1892, 1895, 1900. New York: Arno, 1969.

Welter, Barbara. "The Cult of True Womanhood: 1820–1860." *American Quarterly* 18.2 (1966): 151–74.

Wharton, Edith. *The Custom of the Country. Edith Wharton: Novels.* Ed. R. W. B. Lewis. 1913. New York: Library of America, 1985.

The House of Mirth. Ed. R. W. B. Lewis. 1905. New York: Library of America, 1985.

A Backword Glance. Orig. Published 1933. New York: Scribners, 1964.

Wiebe, Robert H. *The Search for Order 1870–1920.* New York: Hill and Wang, 1967.

Williams, John Alexander. *West Virginia, a History: Bicentennial and History Guide.* New York: W. W. Norton and Company, 1984.

Wilmington Race Riot Commission. "1898 Wilmington Race Riot Report." North Carolina Office of Archives and History, 31 May 2006. Available online: www.history.ncdcr.gov/1898-wrrc/report/report.htm (last accessed June 5, 2010).

Winter, Molly Crumpton. *American Narratives: Multiethnic Writing in the Age of Realism.* Baton Rouge: Louisiana State University Press, 2007.

Woodhull, Victoria Claflin. *The Victoria Woodhull Reader.* Ed. Madeline B. Stern. Weston, MA: M&S Press, 1974.

Woolson, Constance Fenimore. "In Search of the Picturesque." *Harper's New Monthly Magazine* 45.266 (1872): 161–68. *Cornell Making of America Collection.* Available online: http://ebooks.library.cornell.edu/h/harp/ (last accessed August 8, 2009.

Wuster, Tracy. "The Most Popular Humorist Who Ever Lived": *Mark Twain and the Transformation of Gilded Age America.* Diss. University of Texas at Austin, 2010.

Zeller, Bob. *The Blue and Gray in Black and White: A History of Civil War Photography.* Westport, CT: Praeger, 2005.

Zitkala-Ša. *American Indian Stories, Legends, and Other Writings.* Ed. Cathy N. Davidson and Ada Norris. New York: Penguin, 2003.

Index

Page numbers with '*b*' indicate information in text boxes; 'n' indicates a note.

Cambridge Introductions to...

AUTHORS

Margaret Atwood Heidi Macpherson

Jane Austen Janet Todd

Samuel Beckett Ronan McDonald

Walter Benjamin David Ferris

Chekhov James N. Loehlin

J. M. Coetzee Dominic Head

Samuel Taylor Coleridge John Worthen

Joseph Conrad John Peters

Jacques Derrida Leslie Hill

Charles Dickens Jon Mee

Emily Dickinson Wendy Martin

George Eliot Nancy Henry

T. S. Eliot John Xiros Cooper

William Faulkner Theresa M. Towner

F. Scott Fitzgerald Kirk Curnutt

Michel Foucault Lisa Downing

Robert Frost Robert Faggen

Nathaniel Hawthorne Leland S. Person

Zora Neale Hurston Lovalerie King

James Joyce Eric Bulson

Thomas Mann Todd Kontje

Herman Melville Kevin J. Hayes

Sylvia Plath Jo Gill

Edgar Allan Poe Benjamin F. Fisher

Ezra Pound Ira Nadel

Marcel Proust Adam Watt

Jean Rhys Elaine Savory

Edward Said Conor McCarthy

Shakespeare Emma Smith

Shakespeare's Comedies Penny Gay

Shakespeare's History Plays Warren Chernaik

Shakespeare's Poetry Michael Schoenfeldt

Shakespeare's Tragedies Janette Dillon

Harriet Beecher Stowe Sarah Robbins

Mark Twain Peter Messent

Edith Wharton Pamela Knights

Walt Whitman M. Jimmie Killingsworth

Virginia Woolf Jane Goldman

William Wordsworth Emma Mason

W. B. Yeats David Holdeman

TOPICS

American Literary Realism Phillip J. Barrish

The American Short Story Martin Scofield

Anglo-Saxon Literature Hugh Magennis

Comedy Eric Weitz

Creative Writing David Morley

Early English Theatre Janette Dillon

English Theatre, 1660–1900 Peter Thomson

Francophone Literature Patrick Corcoran

Printed in the United States
By Bookmasters